Culture and the Making
of Identity in
Contemporary India

Culture and the Making of Identity in Contemporary India

Edited by

Kamala Ganesh
Usha Thakkar

The Asiatic Society of Mumbai Bicentenary Volume

Sage Publications
New Delhi/Thousand Oaks/London

First published in 2005 by

Sage Publications India Pvt Ltd
B-42, Panchsheel Enclave
New Delhi 110 017
www.indiasage.com

Sage Publications Inc.   **Sage Publications Ltd**
2455 Teller Road   1 Oliver's Yard, 55 City Road
Thousand Oaks, California 91320   London EC1Y SP

Published by Tejeshwar Singh for Sage Publications India Pvt Ltd, photo-
typeset in 10 pt BruceOldStyle BT by Star Compugraphics Private Limited,
Delhi and printed at Chaman Enterprises, New Delhi.

Library of Congress Cataloging-in-Publication Data

Culture and the making of identity in contemporary India/edited by Kamala
Ganesh, Usha Thakkar.
      p. cm.
   "The Asiatic Society of Mumbai, Bicentenary Volume"
   Includes bibliographical references and index.
   1. India—Civilization—1947. 2. Feminism—India. 3. India—
Historiography. 4. Science—Study and teaching—India. I. Ganesh,
Kamala. II. Thakkar, Usha. III. Asiatic Society of Mumbai.
DS428.2.C87   306'.0954'09045—dc22   2005   2005003590

ISBN: 0–7619–3381–6 (HB)   81–7829–524–5 (India–HB)
         0–7619–3307–7 (PB)   81–7829–431–1 (India–PB)

Sage Production Team: Payal Dhar, Shweta Vachani, Radha Dev Raj and
                Santosh Rawat

To the staff and the honorary members of
the many committees of the Asiatic Society of Mumbai
who work to preserve its heritage

Contents

List of Illustrations

Foreword

A few years ago, the Asiatic Society had organised a series of lectures and panel discussions at the Durbar Hall on the theme 'Cultural Transformations in Post-colonial India'. The essays in this volume have been developed from those lectures and discussions. The theme is interdisciplinary. The contributors are distinguished experts and specialists, but here they have written for a general audience. The articles thus embody scholarship without losing out on accessibility. The volume covers a range of fields: art, music, theatre, literature, philosophy, science, history and feminism. The contributors map the developments in the respective fields in the last half of 20th century and evaluate the issues in the contemporary Indian context.

Asiatic Society publications are usually in the field of Indology. In this bicentenary year, the Society is for the first time venturing into a publication with topics of contemporary relevance. I welcome this volume and hope that the editors will set a trend for future publications.

B.G. Deshmukh   Mumbai
President   April 2004
Asiatic Society of Mumbai

Acknowledgements

As editors, it is our pleasure to acknowledge the many friends and colleagues who helped us organise the lectures and panel discussions at the Asiatic Society of Mumbai and prepare the volume for publication. We are indebted to Sadanand Menon for his insights in developing the theme. Discussions with A.R. Momin helped sharpen the anthropological thrust of the Introduction.

Our warm thanks to:
Prof. D.R. SarDesai, former President of the Asiatic Society, who arranged to underwrite the series, and to Vimal Shah, who tirelessly and enthusiastically helped in organising the events;

Gita Chadha, who helped in many ways during the stages of concep-tualising, organising and editing;

Mani Kamerkar, Nalini Pandit, Nalini Malani and Gita Kapur, who helped in identifying and contacting contributors;

Mehrengiz Acharia, Gita Chadha, M.T. Joseph, Aparna Kapadia, Manjusha Patwardhan, Shireen Shah and Vasavi for rapporteuring, and Denzil Pontes for unstinting secretarial help;

Mimi Choudhury for her exacting yet sympathetic editorial interventions.

We would also like to record our appreciation of the contributors who came to Mumbai and made their presentations. One unforgettable image during the series was that of U.R. Ananthamurthy, whose flight was held up and who, after waiting for a whole day at Bangalore airport, walked into the panel discussion like Phileas Fogg, just as his co-panelists had finished their presentations and the packed Durbar Hall was looking expectantly at the door. Thanks also to the contributors who later responded gamely to the relentless editorial chase, by updating and rewriting.

Kamala Ganesh   Mumbai
Usha Thakkar   April 2004

Introduction
Fields of Culture:
Conversations and Contestations

Kamala Ganesh

Backdrop

Culture as a specialist field of study was closely associated with the disciplines of anthropology and sociology over the last century and a half. In recent decades it has increasingly been claimed by a broad-based academic discourse spanning many disciplines. Simultaneously, it has pervaded the broader public domain with greater volubility than ever before. One signpost in this expansion is the emergence of the interdisciplinary area of cultural studies, drawing from theories and methods of anthropology, sociology, literature, linguistics, communication theory, critical theory, marxism, feminism and post-modernism. The overall direction in studies of culture—whether within disciplinary or interdisciplinary frameworks—is towards a loosening of conventional notions of fixity, eternality and holism. It is being re-visioned as a dynamic, dialogical and contested domain, inextricably intertwined with structures of power. At the other end of the academic spectrum, the topic of culture is also gaining currency in traditionally positivist disciplines like economics, political science, international relations and management, and is being famously analysed as a factor (see, for example, Sen 2002) or **the** factor (see, for example, Harrison and Huntington 2000) in the development and progress of nations.

But culture is also a common-sense concept, on which everyone has views. Recent changes worldwide that can be encompassed under the broad rubric of globalisation have brought about some osmosis between the specialist and popular concepts of culture. The unprecedented scale of international migrations in the last few decades has jettisoned diverse and often contrasting cultures into close proximity, creating the potential for pluralistic societies in Europe and North America. These juxtapositions and the active links—electronic and other—between the home countries in Asia, Africa, Latin America and the far-flung diaspora have precipitated a heightened consciousness of cultural and ethnic identity. An entire vocabulary of multiculturalism has evolved for grappling with a range of phenomena—cultural difference, confluence, domination and confrontation. Of course, compared to Europe and North America, these phenomena are part of a longer and deeper historical experience in countries like India. They also seem to have been dealt with here in a less self-conscious manner and with more enduring and syncretic patterns of shared cultural space than in the present globalised scenario. But that is a whole separate topic.

Culture today is firmly established as a subject of scrutiny and discussion in the public domain on a global scale: in media, policy debates, development plans and programmes, social and political movements. It is in imminent danger of being used as a catch-all for explaining a variety of trends. Yet the nascent and emerging theorisations have not completely replaced earlier notions. What we are often confronted with is a jostling of a number of competing ideas in the same space.

Within this vast territory, teeming with many voices, the contributions to the present volume cover a small, specific area. As part of the golden jubilee celebrations of Indian independence, the Asiatic Society of Mumbai had organised a series of lectures and panel discussions titled 'Cultural Transformations in Post-colonial India'. Most of the contributions to this volume have been developed from that nucleus. Temporally tied to the five and a half decades after independence, and concentrating on a handful of areas, the articles nevertheless capture the multiple approaches and meanings that are currently prevalent in the cultural disciplines. The brief to the contributors was to focus on areas where the dialogue of indigenous traditions with contemporary perspectives has had the most significant outcomes. While colonial rule created a rupture in mature indigenous traditions, it was also the medium for opening up to new ideas and, flowing from it, numerous shifts in economic and social configurations. But the passage to modernity was not of a simple or singular mode. The anti-colonial project of self-recovery through reinterpretation and reconstruction of tradition was integral to the consolidation of a pan-Indian cultural identity. Such identity building was a vital constituent of the national movement. The majority of cultural disciplines today continue to carry the representational burden of this interaction, despite new elements having entered their scope.

The debate on what constitutes 'Indian culture' and 'Indianness' is a hoary and rambling one, spread across many areas of life and art. This volume focuses on a handful of fields. Contributions range from long, detailed and academic articles, to critical reviews of literature and reflections on the state of the art in the field, to musings on experience and condensed comments. But the common temporal and spatial setting has led to a converging of issues around the theme of culture and identity. Even though a few articles are meticulous about deploying the historian's craft, mostly this conversation with the past avoids following a rigid chronology. Implicitly then, a 'civilisational perspective' is invoked. However, a demarcation is generally kept between three phases: colonial, nationalist and post-independence. The rapidly globalising present and the pre-colonial, pre-modern 'traditional' India are invoked but not analysed in detail.

The articles have been arranged in four sections. The first two sections together have eight articles, which deal with music, art, literature and translation, theatre, and the philosophy of the performing and visual arts: fields of knowledge and practice in which there are well-developed indigenous traditions. Of these, the four in section 1 are fully elaborated articles. The four in section 2, while covering related fields, are in the nature of musings and comments. The other eight articles, in sections 3 and 4, are from fields in which the very existence of indigenous traditions is a matter of controversy and debate—feminism, the writing of history, and science. Of these, the two articles on science have been put in a separate section because, conventionally, science is seen as culture-free. While both articles question this convention, the argumentation nevertheless is somewhat distinct from the other, more obviously cultural disciplines.

The articles are by distinguished scholars and practitioners, including academics, researchers, teachers, writers, poets, translators and activists. Yet they are aimed at a general readership.

Cumulatively, they acquaint the reader with a range of positions and thus map the developments in this arena.

Contributions

The opening piece by Kapila Vatsyayan takes on a difficult and loaded concept: tradition or *parampara*. Questioning the static quality attributed to it, she focuses on the dynamic relationship between continuity and change, and between multiplicity and unity in creative expression in the fields of literature, and visual and performing arts. She contrasts this with their erosion by thoughtless appropriation by the electronic media. Ashok Ranade maps current musical changes in India through the parameters of tone, tempo and meaning. He looks at fusion in contemporary music, not as a unique phenomenon, but as part of the tradition of *sankara* or 'mixing', which is a constant feature in the history of Indian music. Tapati Guha-Thakurta engages with the need to build a historical context for developments in art in the post-independence period. She focuses on the five decades prior to independence to map the emergence of modernism in art, implicated as it was in colonialism, nationalism and the project of modernity.

Three articles traverse the field of literature and translation, discussing the craft, skill, aesthetics, commerce and politics of trans-lating. Meenakshi Mukherjee situates herself in the new field of translation studies and concentrates on the Indian novel: in English, translated into English and translated between Indian languages. Dilip Chitre squarely places himself in the realm of practice and talks about the nitty-gritty of translation as a process of complex inter-cultural negotiation. U.R. Ananthamurthy talks about the pluri-lingual ambience of India, which not only does not come in the way of mutual communication but actually fosters it. Living within this web of languages, oral translation is happening all the time without people even being aware of it—a situation unique to India. The articles by Anuradha Kapur and Vijaya Mehta engage with inter-culturism and intra-culturism, concepts that together encompass questions of identity and nationhood in a range of cultural disciplines. Kapur illustrates the concepts with some well-known and some lesser-known examples from theatre productions.

Mehta reflects on her long engagement with Marathi theatre and argues that 'Indianness' is not incompatible with a regionally rooted theatre.

The question of whether it is possible to talk of an indigenous feminism is tackled by four contributions, but in slightly different ways. Activist Vimla Bahuguna narrates how she mobilised hill women on issues pertaining to their survival and well-being by drawing on the culture, and social and economic realities of the Uttarakhand region. Her struggles include the anti-liquor agitation, the Chipko movement and in recent years the movement against the Tehri dam. In the context of the decline of Gandhian ideology in contemporary times, Usha Thakkar draws attention to the fact that there are still several individuals who whose life and work are inspired by Gandhi, though they may not always carry the label. She presents a biographical sketch of Vimla Bahuguna, linking her personal and political selves. Beginning with a critical review of the modern scholarship on Marathi *varkari* movements, Vidyut Bhagwat goes on to reflect on the meaning and significance of the long line of women *sant*s of Maharashtra and their *bhakti* poetry. She offers a reading of their lives and writings, locating them not so much in a feminist but a universalist and humanist critique of hierarchy. Devaki Jain expresses her concern at the fragmentation of the contemporary women's movement. She stresses on the political need for unity that goes beyond 'difference' and specificities. She suggests that feminist practice, keeping poor women's perspectives in the forefront, could be a viable basis for unification. The two articles on new modes of writing history are by Uma Chakravarti and Mariam Dossal. Chakravarti critically reviews the major trends in history writing in India from a gendered perspective. The real impetus for a gendered history came from the women's movement. She suggests that in the craft of history writing, reading against the grain and in between the lines is a must for building the history of powerlesss groups. Dossal looks for the thread of humanism that weaves through both old and new history writing, and argues that history can perform a didactic role even while maintaining the highest traditions of scholarship.

In the panel on science, both the contributions emphasise the grounding of science in culture and challenge the view that scientific knowledge stands outside power structures. Claude Alvares is critical of the current search for indigenous science, anchored as it is in the desire to patent traditional knowledge and exploit it for commercial purposes without understanding or respecting the underlying world-view. He elaborates on the inherent violence and hegemony of science as a field of knowledge. Gita Chadha maps the spectrum of positions in the post-independence debate on science in India. She is critical of both unreflective scientism as well as radical critiques that appear to idealise traditional systems. She makes a plea for clearing a pluralistic space within mainstream science.

I have implicitly kept the debates and discussions in anthropology, the discipline I was trained in, as a reference point while commenting upon the contributions.[1] It is evident that the discourse around 'Indian culture' and in general the link between knowledge, culture and identity are recurring concerns in all the articles. These concerns have also been prominent in social and cultural anthropology in India, thus inflecting my personal choice of framework with a larger relevance. In the following section I have briefly sketched the main developments in anthropological discourses on culture both internationally and in India by way of providing a broad context to the issues raised by the articles.

Anthropology and the Debate on Indian Culture

The one distinguishing feature of the anthropological approach to culture has been its comprehensive sweep, encompassing all aspects of the world fashioned by human intervention. Long back, Tylor (1964: 18), in a still cited definition, declared that 'culture is that complex whole which includes knowledge, belief, art, morals, law, custom and any other capabilities and habits acquired by man as a member of society'.

In contrast, the most prevalent popular meaning of culture was, till fairly recently, that it includes the best achievements and products in art, literature and music, and in general constitutes refinement, grace and civilisation. This interpretation has an impressive lineage from the 19th century, which includes the likes of Mathew Arnold and T.S. Eliot. It arose from a wide spectrum of political positions, all attempting to theorise about the nature of transformations in western society in the wake of the Industrial Revolution. Loosely termed as 'mass society theories', they shared a common *angst* at what they saw as a loss of community and organicity in the face of unbridled industrialism. There also was a shared denigration of the emergent 'mass' or 'popular' culture. In contrast, the pre-existing 'high/classical' and 'folk' cultures were rated as superior, though each had its own distinctive features. This three-fold categorisation of culture also became the basis for classifying art forms and genres. (For a succinct account, see, Billington et al. 1991: 1–20.) Despite many criticisms and refinements, this categorisation continues to be influential in the realm of 'art and culture' in India as well.

Coming back to anthropology, its distinctive origins, in the context of the colonial discovery of the 'other' in Asia, Africa and Latin America, coloured its methodology. Participant observation by the individual researcher in small-scale societies over a long period became its hallmark. Under these conditions, it developed the concept of holism: looking at a culture in its totality, as an integrated unity, as experienced by those who lived within it. The work of Franz Boas and Clifford Geertz, representing two different generations, gives us an idea of the sweep of holism. This was certainly a contrast to the emphasis on high culture in literary and philosophical engagements.

But anthropology also had ingrained in it problematic notions about other cultures as simple, backward, homogenous and unchanging. The mobilising of anthropological data to justify and bolster colonial rule has been severely criticised both from within and without (see, for example, Asad 1975 and Hymes 1974). The obverse of holism was an invoking of culture as almost mystically pure, unaffected by political and economic processes. As Joseph (1998: 9) points out, in both the narrower and wider definitions of culture, its relationship with other material dimensions of social life continues to remain under-theorised.

Recent work, both within disciplinary and interdisciplinary frameworks, has tried to prise out culture from a rarefied and overspecialised cocoon and integrate it into a wider understanding of social processes. They have questioned its earlier characterisation as fixed and static. They have stressed its processual, unfolding character. Culture is seen not as pristine, but in constant interaction and exchange with other cultures. It is not a sealed or locally bound domain, but is shaped by and in turn influences macro political, economic and social domains. It codes power relations and is contested from within.

Such radical shifts have come about especially sharply within the framework of cultural studies (for a succinct account, see, Barker 2002 and Tudor 1999). But conventional social science disciplines like anthropology have not remained untouched. The decolonisation process and other political developments in the Euro-American world, developments in the philosophy of science challenging the notion of objective knowledge, and the growth of new social movements the world over have had an impact upon the self-definition of several social sciences. Specifically, in anthropology, the fundamental equation of the western researcher studying non-western cultures has been shaken up by the dismantling of colonial regimes, the rise of independent nation-states, the integration of small-scale cultures into macro-processes of development and the rise of 'native' anthropologists ready to contest others' versions of their culture, as also the insistent claims of subaltern voices from within the culture, challenging the dominant version of the chief informant. The growth of sub-disciplines like critical anthropology, action anthropology, feminist anthropology and post-modern ethnography, to mention a few, have contributed substantially to an internal critique within the discipline (for an overview, see, Barnard 2000, Layton 1997 and Ortner 1984).

Debates on Indian culture in the last 50 years reflect these worldwide trends although configurations and developments within the country have shaped them in specific ways imparting a distinctive flavour. Anthropological writing in India over more than 50 years has provided some of the key reference points for these debates (Ganesh 2002).

In recent times the domain of culture has been a prime source of self-conscious mobilisation for questions of identity in India. In the public perception, cultural fields are seen as the rightful location for a discussion on 'Indianness'.[2] The question of Indianness had already arisen in the 19th century during the social reform movement and then developed in a complex way during the nationalist movement. The dynamics of colonialism provided the impetus for the birth of a new discipline that came to be known as Indology. The vast knowledge on Indian society and culture generated under the aegis of Indology cumulatively recreated India as the 'other' of Europe. As forcefully argued by Nandy (1983) and others, the recovery of the Indian self from this orientalist framework and its problematic relationship with modernity was negotiated through the harnessing of the cultural resources of the past. The overriding political needs of the time pushed towards submerging of diversities and creation of a pan-Indian identity, inflected with ideas on what constituted authentic Indian culture.

Since independence the particularities previously rendered invisible have been reasserting themselves. Movements for regional, linguistic and tribal rights, and affirmative action for *dalit* and backward castes, minorities and women have been challenging the idea of homogenous Indianness and have highlighted the simultaneity of multiple identities. Initially these identities were dubbed with mild disapproval as 'sub-national'. In their eventual acceptance in the popular imagination, the work of Indian anthropologists has played a role.

Despite the power and influence of Indology, with its reliance on classical texts and high culture, the bulk of the work of sociologists and anthropologists after independence has been biased towards empirical documentation of the enormous diversities in society and culture in India.[3] Srinivas' (1997: 21) famous formulation of the relative merits of the 'book' view and 'field' view of Indian society has generated a fertile and productive discussion over the decades. It has informed the popular debate on Indian culture, inflecting it with anthropological insights. The notion of culture as pervading all strata and segments in an interconnected fashion and the importance of engaging with the empirical realm of practice and behaviour, rather than concentrating on norms, are both accepted ideas now.

Many social scientists of the post-independence era were, sometimes willy-nilly, engaged in the project of nationalism and nation building. They were committed to the idea of a united India, but not at the cost of downplaying its diversities. To the recurrent question of what constitutes Indian culture and identity, they emphasised its composite character and put forward a framework of pluralism.

The works of D.P. Mukherji (1979) and N.K. Bose (1975) are prime examples of theorisations on the character of traditional Indian society, its capacity to assimilate, absorb or accommodate cultural diversities drawn from a variety of sources, and to form a loosely integrated unity with considerable autonomy of the constituent elements. This underlying process has been named as syncretism—an accommodation of new elements without rejecting the old. Irawati Karve (1961: 7) has vividly described this process of accretion as leading to a coexistence of many disparate forms, old and new, in many aspects of social life, from worship of gods to marriage codes, dress and food.

The existence of multiple cultural and social layers and segments in India has given rise to several conceptualisations on their mutual interaction. Beginning from the controversial notion of the 'Great' and 'Little' Traditions, there has been analytical writing on the reciprocal communication between the segments and layers. Reacting against Redfieldian ideas of the superiority of the Great Tradition and the passivity of the Little Traditions, McKim Marriott (1955), for instance, has argued that the mutual linkages between the two, in a circular flow with no beginning or end, are connected to the fact of India being a 'primary' civilisation. It has grown out of its own folk culture and not by a superimposed, imported culture.[4] The power and pervasiveness of the 'folk' stream of Indian civilisation, its symbiotic relationship with the classical stream or 'high' culture, while at the same time retaining a certain level of autonomy, have been insightfully analysed by Ramanujan (1994) and Blackburn and Ramanujan (1986). What one may refer to as peasant culture in India, encompassing the lived realities of the mainstream majority, is in fact a useful site for grasping the continuities between folk and high culture. 'Examining the relationship of Indian civilisational centres to each other and to peasant culture is like studying a room whose walls are lined with mirrors great and small. In each, one sees reflected something of all the others' (Cohn and Marriott 1987: 85).

Thus, cumulatively, this body of knowledge throws light on the complex way in which different cultural segments, genres, forms and elements are related, sometimes in opposition and at other times in complementarity. They each have distinct characteristics, but are not unconnected to each other. Nor are they tightly integrated into a cohesive whole. Clearly separated categories like 'classical', 'folk' and 'popular', which inform theoretical discussions in the cultural disciplines in general, do not match the reality on the ground in India. Empirical documentation of popular religion, ritual, visual and performing arts, and literature reveal symbiotic interconnections, blurring categorical boundaries.

The more recent social science scholarship has been focusing attention on the overarching terms within which the process of syncretism and loose integration with cultural autonomy operated. Given the deeply hierarchical nature of caste society, the domination by mainstream and elite groups and the material and ideological subordination of the socially marginal groups was the structural concomitant of the process of integration. N.K. Bose (1975: 182–89) has pinpointed the two distinct features of traditional Indian society: pluralism and hierarchy—the equal tolerance of diverse modes of living, and their unequal ranking on a widely accepted scale. Still, the precise nature of the conjunction of hierarchy and pluralism, and its role on the character of cultural realms and forms remain a theoretical enigma.

There are two major axes along which issues of culture are currently manifesting in India. The first axis carries the tension between two notions. One is an idealised, homogenised notion of Indian culture (with its new domestic and global political ramifications). The other is a contrasting notion of composite culture that does not merely acknowledge diversity, but builds it into the very conceptualisation of Indian culture as plural and syncretic.

The second axis contains the dialectic of the above syncretism—seen as part of the traditional pluralist social order—with contemporary processes of 'mixings'. The former, that is, traditional syncretism, needs to be interrogated more sharply for its articulation within a framework of hierarchy. The latter, namely, the mixings, the fusion, hybridisation, abundantly found in many aspects of contemporary popular culture, need to be analysed more sharply for their linkages with global politics and commerce. These two axes and their ramifications are at the heart of debates on culture and identity in India today.

The realm of popular culture is dominant and pervasive in the contemporary Indian scenario.[5] Here, too, mixings in forms and genres are a prominent feature. Popular culture is mass mediated. With its dependence on advanced technology and its close response to market forces, it is different in its inspiration and dynamics from folk and high cultures, though it often uses their forms and recasts them. The content of mass-mediated culture is also coloured by questions of Indianness and identity, but its technological savvy and intimate connections with global culture gives it a special character. Diversity is the hallmark of contemporary popular culture as much as it is of traditional culture in India. But the framework of pluralism and hierarchy, characteristic of the traditional fabric, gets implicated in current times within the dynamics of international politics and economics. The existence of a pervasive and ubiquitous realm of popular culture has, interestingly enough, strengthened classical cultural forms. But they have become confined to a narrow and fiercely guarded territory. However, the performance and dissemination of these classical forms are still tied to current technology. 'Folk', with its mandatory face-to-face interaction, is retracting in the conventional sense. Ethnicisation of the folk and its link as a product with the market and with elite culture simulate a new 'folk' whose inner dynamics is different from the old 'folk'.

Any serious consideration of contemporary culture in India, therefore, would have to begin with its syncretic roots and their articulation within a hierarchical framework. The intermeshing of this base with global and globalised culture generates new dynamics with unprecedented consequences. The logic and power of this process are not always immediately apparent since contemporary cultural expressions often take recourse to nostalgic reclamations of old forms recast in the language of identity.

Beneath the fabric of syncretism lies this subtext of contemporary culture that the contributions to this volume try, in varying degrees, to recognise and read.

Issues Raised

The papers in this volume, in one way or another, coalesce around the issue of identity, located largely in the contested terrain of culture. Among the many meanings of culture, the most common one is its association with the arts. The papers in the first two sections are directly in this terrain. In the third and fourth sections, even though the themes seem to be more disparate, the second-order discussions return to issues of identity and culture.

Three sets of issues emerge with surprising consistency from across the variety of fields covered. The first has to do with the idea of authenticity. The second concerns the manner and politics of invoking of the pre-colonial, pre-modern past as the source for authenticity. The last joins issue with alien and superimposed categories that do not reflect the ground reality.

Search for Authenticity

In recent decades the search for 'authenticity' has been a dominating concern in many cultural disciplines. Authenticity has increasingly been defined as an Indianness that includes modernity. This is certainly a moving on from the earlier preoccupation with tradition–modernity polarities. Even in the field of science, which is considered to be removed from the arena of culture and identity, Chadha has noted the centrality of the issue of 'Indian science'. Bahuguna, involved in mobilising poor women on issues of survival, environment and development, feels the need to keep Indian tradition as a touchstone, though, as Thakkar notes, she gives it a fresh interpretation through the politics of her action.

What constitutes authenticity differs somewhat in different fields, as the articles by Ranade, Guha-Thakurta, Kapur, Mehta, Mukherjee and Ananthamurthy illustrate. In music and dance, the reigning 'high' cultural form, or what one might call the defining genre, is classical, in which authenticity is predicated on notions of purity. Modernity can enter into its scope only via technology for better performance, reproduction and dissemination, and not in the content. On the other hand, in art and in theatre, the defining genre is one that has already had some dialogue with western genres and fits into neither 'classical' nor 'folk' nor 'popular' categories in the usual sense. In both art and theatre, modernity blended with 'Indianness' is accepted. So while there is a search for authenticity, purity is not a cardinal value. Traditional form is used as a resource and take-off point rather than as a model for faithful imitation.

In all the above disciplines—music, art and theatre—authenticity is linked to the nationalist reinterpretation of the 'self'. But in the arena of literature and translation, specifically Indian writing in English and translation of Indian language writing into English, authenticity has become linked to the global market and its compulsions.

This could bear with a little elaboration. In the current scenario in music, as Ranade points out, many different forms and genres flourish. There is a large volume of mass-mediated popular music, which is commercially profitable. This includes film music, fusion music like Indipop, and devotional music, in all of which borrowings and mixings are accepted, even celebrated. But there is also a clear-cut space for classical or 'art music' where, despite a semi-commercial format, purity and fidelity to a presumed original are key values. Here, even innovations have to be clothed in the idiom of purity (see, for instance, Ganesh 2000: 9). Ranade demonstrates that borrowings, assimilations and mixings are quite common to music in India in the past and, therefore, that contemporary 'fusion' is not so new after all. He suggests that 'purity', as currently defined, has become a standard for judging music only recently. Research in the modern history of performing arts in south India (see, for instance, Gaston 1997) have documented how in the 1930s the opening out of '*sadir*' from its exclusive linkage to traditional performing arts families and its rechristening as '*bharatanatyam*' also got implicated in the nationalist project. Classical music and dance were harnessed to create a lineage of cultural purity and authenticity that would feed into a nationalist Indian identity. The trend continued after independence.

Not that popular music in the commercial format is devoid of concern with Indianness. Exclusively western genres are (like classical music) the kingdoms of a minority. All popular genres have some 'Indian' element in them, drawing from classical or folk or devotional, even while creatively plagiarising from western and lately from world music genres. Developments in the field of popular music in India in the last few decades have been overwhelming. They have established the validity of every genre, classical music being only the first among equals. Emblematic of this new reality is the fact that at the Government of India's official function to mark 50 years of independence, a rendition of 'Vande Mataram' by A.R. Rahman was given pride of place. The ultimate symbol of the nation, what had been the Song of India at a particular historical moment, gave itself up for fusion at the hands of an enormously popular film music director.

In art a clear break has been made with exclusively traditional genres, except where it is revived as craft or antiquarian art, as, for example, in the case of the Thanjavur paintings. As Guha-Thakurta has painstakingly pieced together, the emergence of modernism ran parallel to the emergence of modernity as negotiated by nationalism. The modern in Indian art was at every stage of its growth inextricably intertwined with a notion of Indianness. At every succeeding phase the precise contents of 'modern' and 'national' were inter-rogated and shifted around, but the search for identity was within these two axes. Modernity could enter art in a serious way only by making a link with tradition. This involved rejection of imitative European conventions as well as of Indian classical traditions, clearing the ground for exploration of alternative traditions as well as alternative modernity.

In theatre, as in art, the defining genre has assimilated modernity and, in fact, the search for Indianness is through the lens of western theory. Post independence, the self-conscious efforts, particularly state-sponsored, at making a national theatre have been flanked on the one hand by international directors taking up Indian play texts, and on the other by regionally rooted theatre directors. The former—inter-culturism/multiculturism—is seen by Kapur as a response to the homogenising notion of monoculturism. Inter-culturism valourises locality, difference and identity, challenging positivist notions of culture-free values and universal progress. But there are hidden dangers in its potential to be exclusionary as well as forcibly inclusionary. Theatre, which in the context of a plural society like India interrogates the totalising notion of a homogenous nation, is termed by Kapur as intra-cultural. Vijaya Mehta gives a slightly different interpretation to the terms inter-culturism and intra-culturism, underlining the fluidity of definitions and multivalence of terms in this field. The former for her denotes a coming together of different arts at the level of a region into a cogent culture and lifestyle. The latter comprises of structured attempts to calibrate a larger national identity for theatre. The debates on inter-culturism and intra-culturism have shaken up taken-for-granted equations between the nation and Indianness in a variety of ways.

The exercise of writing in English and translation into English brings to the surface issues of Indianness in complex ways. Mukherjee makes the point that while English has arguably become an Indian language, it has after all been the language of the colonial masters and its relationship of power with the vernaculars simply cannot be wished away. In the current scenario, where such writing has become successful, it cannot be separated from its consumers—the readers—mediated by an international market that demands a specific kind of authenticity. The criteria of selection of the piece, its presentation in formulaic capsules to achieve smoothness and acceptability have been perfected by third world cosmopolitans with their metropolitan metalanguage of narrative, as Williams (1997) trenchantly points out.

Trivedi (1994) vividly brings home this point by chronicling a translation workshop by Sahitya Akademi, a state-sponsored organisation in which the authors of the pieces participated and collaborated in the translating process. An American poet from the University of Iowa was present, and his job was to revise the translations into an internationally acceptable style, 'to sprinkle on top a seasoning of contemporary Anglo-American poetic idiom so that our dish would be ready to be served worldwide'. When the revised versions arrived eventually, many of the original participants felt that the whole feel of Hindi poetry had undergone a change, and the project just got quietly dropped.

The other sort of anxiety in writing and translation comes from the location of the writer outside India in the diaspora, wherein the pressure to identify one's Indianness in specific and obvious ways is intense. Yet another dimension in translation activity is the anxiety to remain faithful to the original, which Paniker (1994) sees as a response to western, specifically missionary, impact. He contrasts this with the traditional method of translating from one Indian language to another, adapting and modifying. Deviation from the original was liberally tolerated, and the translated epics became classics in the translated-into language and culture, too. Perhaps this had also to do with the fact that the translator usually belonged to the translated-into language, and could identify with the longings and aspirations of the readership.

The weight of English as the colonial language pressing on the Indian self has to be counterbalanced with the current scenario of English as the global language. According to Chitre, by opening up opportunities for literary translations into English, this can become the basis for a truly global literary tradition. At the everyday work level, English as the language of information technology is sought after all over the world. Indians are using their English advantage profitably. Bilingual fusions, with English as one element, are frequent in the Internet, television and to an extent the print media. In popular discourses within India the earlier concern with pure language is not salient any more, nor is there overwhelming pressure to distance oneself from English as part of establishing Indianness.

Reconstructing the Past

If authenticity—variously defined—is a guiding value, then underlying it is an implicit assumption of an original or earlier stage. The precise nature and structure of pre-colonial Indian society has been the subject of intense discussion and controversy in academic and public discourses. While the contributions to this volume do not attempt to develop a picture of pre-modern, pre-colonial India in historical detail, they do make insightful observations from the vantage point of their particular fields. In effect, they take a position that until the moment of colonial disjuncture, diversity and multiplicity prevailed at many levels in a society that was loosely integrated and in which syncretism was an organising principle. Some of our contributors also introduce a note of caution against romanticising the past, as we shall see later.

The totalising effect of colonialism has had an impact more on the elite of Indian society. In Vatsyayan's words, 'we started seeing ourselves through their eyes'. She, along with Ananthamurthy and Alvares, is critical of their imitativeness and their eager adoption of a linear view of progress and development. This is the reason for our second-hand scientific and social scientific research as well. In this view, the so-called backwards, the unlettered, are the source of hope, for their link with that syncretic past is not ruptured yet. They allow us to infer from the present and reconstruct what the past may have been. At another level, Bahuguna echoes this point when she talks about the hidden power of the illiterate women of the hills. The source for this, though, is the shared environment and life circumstances of the hill region, according to her.

As all the three articles on translation note, the pluri-lingual ambience, in which languages have a resonance with each other, is evident in the ease and spontaneity with which people switch between house language, street language and office language. Chitre illustrates this from his personal biography and his work, Indeed, Singh and Manoharan (1993: 20–24) have statistically documented the fact that most people in India—and not merely those who speak English—are freely bilingual. Speaking of Sanskrit vis-à-vis regional and local languages, Ananthamurthy has made the observation that the relationship was not hegemonic in the sense of the weaker being completely erased, but hierarchical in the sense that it was allowed to exist with a lower status. Thus, a script-less Tulu coexisted with a strong regional language like Kannada, and at a later historical moment, when Tulu speakers were in an influential position, they could revive the language. Mukherjee bemoans the decline of a vigorous tradition of translating from one Indian language to another. Vatsyayan locates the dynamism of tradition in the underlying philosophy of the one and the many that pervaded performing and visual arts in ancient and medieval India. Multiplicity was not perceived as a problem and creative genius lay in incorporating the temporal and ephemeral in the eternal. Alvares evokes ancient Indian traditions of debate and fair play with reference to contending ideologies in contrast to the totalising discourse of science.

It is not enough to construct the past as the 'other' of colonised India. It is necessary to subject it to the same kind of sharp analysis. 'Eternality' or 'essence' as categories for instance may be justified in specific modes like philosophy, but they also need to be historicised. Dossal, like several other social scientists, points out the dangers of resurrecting a past of retrograde values in the name of being authentically Indian. While Chakravarti grants that the Indian view of history may be cyclical in contrast to a linear world-view from which history as a discipline emerged, this does not exempt it from critical scrutiny. The past that emerges through such scrutiny is hierarchical and biased in favour of ruling groups and the male gender.

Battle for Categories

A powerful recent theme in the social sciences and humanities is the mismatch created by theoretical categories emanating from contexts other than that in which the subject of enquiry is located. To recognise syncretism as a motif of cultural forms in India is to recognise the permeability of boundaries of cultural categories. The folk–classical–popular interlinkages in the Indian context, both at the level of culture in general and performing arts in particular, are illustrated by a number of articles.[6] Ranade shows how folk and art music have a two-way relationship and how we can detect elements of one in the other. Devotional music, an entire genre by itself, flows in two streams, one close to art music and the other to folk music. The concert format of a classical music concert, both Hindustani and Carnatic, typically include in the second half of the concert some space for folk and devotional compositions. So, though given a lesser place, they are integrated within the format. Though each linguistic region of the country has its own folk music, he notes that certain features appear to be common to all regional traditions. Thus, folk is also in a way, as Ramanujan (1994) argues, a pan-Indian category. Talking of theatre, Mehta remarks that the efforts after independence to translate play texts into different Indian languages laid the ground for true pan-Indianism, and those directors who were distinguished for their Indian sensibilities were in fact those who were rooted in regional theatre. Regional and pan-Indian are not opposed categories.

The category of 'tradition' also comes up for interrogation. Vatsyayan, for example, shows the dynamism in a concept that is often attributed with static qualities. In a quite different context, Thakkar demonstrates how Gandhian praxis changes the meaning of tradition, even while ostensibly working within its parameters.

At another level, the lack of rigid compartmentalisation also means that one cannot presume that these categories will provide qualitatively different kinds or different order of data when used as source material. While applauding the new history writing that goes beyond official sources and taps a variety of oral sources, Chakravarti cautions against a simple assumption that they are necessarily folk or people oriented. They could equally be reinforcing an official view. Dube (2001), for example, has shown how proverbs and folk sayings in many Indian languages actually reinforce the patriarchal norms that are set up in classical texts. Indeed, as Ramanujan (1994: 98–99) has perceptively argued, orality and textuality are in close communion and could sometimes reflect the same set of material interests, though at other times oral sources do provide an alternate view of events and systems.

What we learn from the situation on the ground about cultural forms is that the categories currently in use do not quite fit the reality. The obvious question then is why they are still in use, which leads us to the contentious area of the power of different systems of knowledge and the theoretical categories derived from the dominant systems that become established as universal categories.

Alvares' article takes up this issue unambiguously. For him, sciences and social sciences are part of the hegemony of occidental knowledge systems. The question of whether there was an indigenous tradition of science in India, a question that has been part of the debate on science, is itself flawed, he argues. It reveals the hold of the world-view of science, which measures all other systems with reference to its own self. Chadha raises the issue of externalist versus internalist categories of criticism, and points out that the latter, too, is important and necessary.

The basic issue of cultural groundedness versus universality of categories is present in nuanced forms in other articles as well. Indeed, it is a much larger issue and a central discussion point in academic social sciences and humanities as they have developed in India after independence.

Women's studies is a relatively recent area of enquiry to enter the university system, and in the debate whose two sides are presented by Jain and Bhagwat, the battle is joined for categories and their definitions. Questions about whether feminist practice by itself generates feminist consciousness, or whether a particular theoretical perspective is needed, and whether practice without consciousness can be called feminism, and finally that recurring question, who is a feminist, are all reflections of the unease felt by a monolithic ironing out of differences into a pre-defined category, even while recognising the political need for unity among women. On the other hand, there have also been debates about *bhakti* poetry and its 'uses' for the women's movement, and whether in today's context, where we have secular modes of critiquing social hierarchies, the *bhakti* idiom of the individual's direct access to the divine can really be an adequate or relevant idiom of protest. Bhagwat joins issue with this category of evaluation itself, arguing that the women poets of the Bhakti movement saw gender, caste and other oppressions as a totality and their consciousness reveals a humanist and universalist base.

Discussions on gender as a category have been given a prominent place in many social sciences and humanities in the last few decades, and the piece by Chakravarti, even though primarily focusing on the discipline of history, condenses the issues on gender across disciplines. While scholars on gender have noted the invisibility of women/gender in the contents of disciplines like political science and economics, the situation is different in history, anthropology, biology, medicine and so on, where women are visible subjects.

But till recently, gender as a category was not problematised. Specifically, ancient India, as it was written about during the heydey of nationalism, was invoked as a 'golden age', and the status of women became the symbol of that golden age. Internal hierarchies and the status of lower-caste women were ignored in this construction.

The issue of categories and definitions is one that has been surfacing in social sciences periodically. In anthropology, for instance, the deployment of eurocentric categories for looking at Indian reality have been critiqued by those advocating a search for native/ indigenous categories (for example, Marriott 1990), but 'indigenous' itself is a problematic and contested arena in a pluralistic and hierarchical society. Are 'native' categories representative of the various segments of society, including tribal communities, lower castes and women?

In recent times the process of identity making has been the focus of a critical, analytical gaze from different vantage points. The multiplicity and simultaneity of identities is by now an accepted idea even at the popular level. That identities are products both of deliberate construction and happenstance, and that they are perennially recreated and reinvented is also a recurring theme, albeit in academic discourses of recent vintage. However, the specific situations and ways in which these processes are worked out need much greater explication and documentation. Identity making is, of course, more patently visible in arenas of everyday politics and religion in contemporary India. But the issues raised by the contributions to this volume testify that even in the more abstract, formal, academic, creative and symbolic realms—in what can be called fields of culture—the theme of identity continues to be a potent reference point.

Notes

1. In the Indian context, there has been a long-standing consensus among scholars that sociology and social and cultural anthropology need not be

demarcated rigidly. I, therefore, implicitly include sociology when talking about social and cultural anthropology.

2. Intellectuals from various fields engage themselves from time to time with this question in popular fora as well. The 20 August 2001 issue of *Outlook* magazine exclusively devoted to this topic by a galaxy of writers, journalists and social scientists is an example.

3. Between the 19th century district gazetteers and the recent encylopaedic multi-volume People of India project lies a huge body of documentation on diversities.

4. Though the terms high culture, classical, folk, popular, etc. are contested ones when used in the context of Indian arts and culture, I have used them here without the appellation so-called purely for convenience.

5. A concerted analysis of this realm has taken off relatively recently under the rubric of cultural studies (see, for example, Ghosh 1996). Increasingly, such analysis is also emerging from within sociology and social anthropology (Appadurai 2003).

6. As far back as 1937, Ananda Coomaraswamy had made the point for the performing arts in India, that the '*marga*' and '*desi*' classifications prevailing in the traditional arts did not correspond to the 'classical' and 'folk' categories that were being used.

References

Appadurai, Arjun (2003). 'Public Culture', in Veena Das (ed.), *The Oxford India Companion to Sociology and Social Anthropology*, pp. 654–74. New Delhi: Oxford University Press.

Asad, Talal (ed.) (1975). *Anthropology and the Colonial Encounter*. London: Ithaca Press.

Barker, Chris (2002). *Making Sense of Cultural Studies: Central Problems and Critical Debates*. London: Sage Publications.

Barnard, Alan (2000). *History and Theory in Anthropology*. Cambridge: Cambridge University Press.

Billington, Rosamund, Sheelagh Strawbridge, Lenore Greensides and Annette Fitzsimons (1991). *Culture and Society: A Sociology of Culture*. Hampshire and London: Macmillan.

Blackburn, Stuart H. and A.K. Ramanujan (1986). 'Introduction', in *Another Harmony: New Essays on the Folklore of India*, pp. 1–37. Delhi: Oxford University Press.

Bose, N.K. (1975). *The Structure of Hindu Society*, translated from Bengali with introduction and notes by Andre Beteille. New Delhi: Orient Longman.

Cohn, Bernard and McKim Marriott (1987). 'Networks and Centres in the Integration of Indian Civilization', in Bernard Cohn (ed.), *An Anthropologist Among Historians and Other Essays*, pp. 78–87. New Delhi: Oxford University Press.

Coomaraswamy, Ananda K. (1937). 'The Nature of "Folklore" and "Popular Art"', *Indian Art and Letters*, 11(2): 76–84.

Dube, Leela (2001). 'On the Construction of Gender: Socialization of Hindu Girls in Patrilineal India', in *Anthropological Explorations in Gender: Intersecting Fields*, pp. 87–118. New Delhi: Sage Publications.

Ganesh, Kamala (2000). 'Weaving a Syncretic Baaj: The Music of Ustad Abdul Halim Jaffer Khan', in Abdul Halim Jaffer Khan, *Jafferkhani Baaj: Innovation in Sitar Music*, pp. 1–24. Mumbai: H.J. Khan.

――― (2002). '"Indian Culture" through the Lens of Diversity'. *Public Lecture in the Practice Lecture Series on the Arts and Cultures of India* organised by the Practice Performing Arts School, Singapore Art Museum, Singapore, 7 September.

Gaston, Anne-Marie (1997). *Bharata Natyam: From Temple to Theatre*. New Delhi: Manohar.

Ghosh, Anjan (1996). 'The Problem', *Seminar*, October (special issue on cultural studies), 446: 12–15.

Hymes, Dell (ed.) (1974). *Reinventing Anthropology*. New York: Random House.

Harrison, L. and S. Huntington (2000). *Culture Matters: How Values Shape Human Progress*. New York: Basic Books.

Joseph, Sarah (1998). *Interrogating Culture: Critical Perspectives on Contemporary Social Theory*. New Delhi: Sage Publications.

Karve, Irawati (1961). *Hindu Society: An Interpretation*. Poona: Deccan College.

Layton, Robert (1997). *An Introduction to Theory in Anthropology*. Cambridge: Cambridge University Press.

Marriott, McKim (1955). 'Little Communities in an Indigenous Civilization', in *Village India: Studies in the Little Community*, pp. 171–222. Chicago: University of Chicago Press.

――― (1990). 'Constructing an Indian Ethnosociology', in M. Marriott (ed.), *India Through Hindu Categories*, pp. 1–40. New Delhi: Sage Publications.

Mukerji, Dhurjati Prasad (1979). *Sociology of Indian Culture*. Jaipur: Rawat Publications (first published in 1942).

Nandy, Ashish (1983). *The Intimate Enemy: Loss and Recovery of Self under Colonialism*. New Delhi: Oxford University Press.

Ortner, Sherry B. (1984). 'Theory in Anthropology Since the Sixties', *Journal of the Society for Comparative Study of Society and History*, 26(3): 126–66.

Paniker, Ayyappa K. (1994). 'The Anxiety of Authenticity: Reflections on Literary Translation', *Indian Literature*, 37(4): 128–38.

Ramanujan, A.K. (1994). 'Who Needs Folklore? The Relevance of Oral Traditions to South Asian Studies'. First Rama Watamull Lecture, University of Hawaii, March 1988, reprinted in *Indian Literature*, 37(4): 93–106.

Redfield, Margaret Park (1962). *Human Nature and the Study of Society*: The papers of Robert Redfield. Chicago and London: University of Chicago Press.

Sen, Amartya (2002). 'Culture and Development'. Public Lecture, University of Mumbai Convocation Hall, Mumbai, 26 February.

Singh, K.S. (ed.) (1992). *People of India: Introduction*, People of India National Series, Anthropological Survey of India, Vol. 1. Calcutta: Seagull Books.

Singh, K.S. and S. Manoharan (1993). *Languages and Scripts*, People of India National Series, Anthropological Survey of India, Vol. 9. New Delhi: Oxford University Press.

Srinivas, M.N. (1997). 'Practicing Social Anthropology in India', *Annual Review of Anthropology*, 26(1): 1–24.

Tylor, E. (1964). 'Culture Defined', in L.A. Coser and B. Rosenburg (eds.), *Sociological Theory: A Book of Readings*, pp. 18–21. West Drayton: Collier-Macmillan (first published in 1891).

Tudor, Andrew (1999). *Decoding Culture: Theory and Method in Cultural Studies*. London: Sage Publications.

Trivedi, Harish (1994). Translating Together for Home and Abroad: An Experiment and an Experience, *Indian Literature*, 162 (July–August): 109–27.

Williams, Adebayo (1997). 'The Post Colonial Flaneur and Other Fellow Travelers: Conceits for a Narrative of Redemption', *Third World Quarterly*, 18(5): 821–41.

Part 1

1

From Interior Landscapes into Cyberspace: Fluidity and Dynamics of Tradition

Kapila Vatsyayan

Implicit in the theme of this volume is the question of the flow of tradition and, in a larger and deeper sense, of a civilisation and culture, not only as linear, historical progression, but also in its dynamics of being multi-layered and multidimensional at any given moment of time. The conceptual framework of the volume anchors culture within historical and political processes. In posing the questions of pre-colonial, colonial and post-colonial India, perhaps there is a tacit assumption that all levels and dimensions of a culture are directly affected by political developments. The totality of life experience (and, therefore, its vital expressions) could be attributed exclusively to the effect of the polity only with much stretching. The situation in India is far more complex, especially when we look at the processes at work in civilisational and cultural terms. Political subjugation, oppression or patronage undoubtedly affect some aspects and dimensions of living, but not all. There were, and continue to be, areas, dimensions of the human psyche, individual and collective human endeavour, which show inward growth or decay despite the positive or negative political environment. These core values of a civilisation are like the leaves of a lotus plant, which float unsullied in clear or muddy waters. They exist in the waters of the pond, but are not of it. These core values and thought systems are deeply grounded, share the temporality of the muddy waters and yet transcend the turmoil. Ultimately, it is these values that sustain and outlive the ephemeral turbulence of socio-political history. In a manner of speaking, many crucial and creatively transforming events have taken place outside the pale of the ups and downs of political domination and

subjugation. Furthermore, any individual/group of people has concurrent, multiple identities. While one identity can be influenced,
threatened or extinguished, another layer can remain unaffected
or relatively untouched. Also, concurrency of many moments of
time is characteristic of Indian society and culture, the rule rather
than the exception.

The flow of a tradition may be compared to a double-reed flute.
One reed is a perennial strain, a tonic, immutable trans-space
and -time; the other reed plays the tune of immediate time and space.
The one is repetitive but stable; the other changing. The two
together create the music that sounds different at different times.

Tradition: The One and the Many

In any discussion of 'tradition' we have to identify the immutable
aspects that provide continuity and others that facilitate change.
The word 'tradition' itself has become problematic through overuse
and misuse. We often speak of tradition as a static quantity, denoting
a past at a particular period of history. It then becomes synonymous
with the words 'heritage', 'of the past', as opposed to the 'other':
'modern' or 'western' or 'contemporary'. Furthermore, when tradition is equated to indigenous, it then begins to connote 'local'
and 'native' as opposed to the other: 'foreign' or 'alien'. Often tradition connotes conventions and codes as opposed to freedom and
innovation. The jigsaw puzzle of varied interpretations reflects a
polarised understanding—either at the conceptual level of a body
of ideas and values and cognitive system, or at the historical,
temporal level of only outer form, content and conduct. Finally,
distinctions are made at the spatial levels where one tradition is
distinguished from another. Then indigenous is juxtaposed against
foreign, local against regional, regional against national, national
against international and global. In this maze of categories, largely
articulated in the English language, there is tacit acceptance of a
critical discourse that emerged in Europe at a particular historical
moment, first the Renaissance, then the Industrial Revolution
and finally the era of Enlightenment. In India it is not uncommon
to uncritically internalise the perceptions of the tradition by this

'other'. Resultantly the 'self' is evaluated by categories evolved for and by the 'other'.

While this is the intellectual level, there is life as it is actually felt, 'lived'. One is the realm of the intellect (*buddhi*), the other of the emotions. While formulating ideas we adopt one mode, while in actual living, another. One pushes us to deduce concepts, the other pulsates within us as feeling (*bhavana*) and experience (*anubhava*). When there is consistency between the two, there is equilibrium and harmony. When there is a hiatus, there is chaos. The inherited or transmitted experience and wisdom shapes the temporal existence of life. This is the inner core, the immutable; outer events demand adjustments, assimilation and rejection, but the transformative process, the alchemy between the receiver and the received, is unique and special.

It is against these general observations that we may once again look at the definitions of the terms 'tradition' in English and '*parampara*' in Sanskrit. Tradition or *parampara* at its best connotes a flow, a vertical transmission in time and a spatial spread hori-zontally. It does not constitute a frozen, static object or even a corpus of values and behavioural patterns. When the dynamics of the flow is sustained, we recognise it as world-view and lifestyle, distinctive but not static. It is only when the constant movement of inflow and outflow stops that there is the stagnation of a pool. India throughout its history has known the movements of transmission as also moments of rigidity and fixity.

To return to our metaphor of the double-reed flute, the one is immutable, continuing, repetitive and sustaining, the unchanging, *sasvata* and *sanatana*, while the other is changing, full of variants. Despite the changes in socio-economic and political structures and underlying the multiplicity of the regional traditions, there is no denying the fact that there was a commitment to what were defined as the perennial values of life at its most fundamental. This is evident from the pattern of evolution of regional Indian languages and literatures, musical forms, dance styles, architectural schools and philosophic systems of early and late medieval India. Amongst these was the primary one of considering the universe and all forms of life as one integrated, organic system in which the inanimate and animate—*jada* and *chetana*—were reversible categories. Equally seminal was the view that there was a primary level of undifferentiation, be it as the *anda* (the cosmic egg) or as nothingness. The manifested creativity and multiplicity was recognised as the peacock coming to life in variegated colours. *Mayura anda vada* was the medieval name for the phenomenon. Alternatively, there were the countless myths of the eternal waters of the ocean and the appearance of the coiled snake and ultimately the lotus. The *Rg Veda* had spoken of the one truth and the multiple ways to seek it, and medieval poets and thinkers explored and asserted the multiple paths to seek the truth. There was also continued the adherence to the *Rg Vedic* and Upanisadic dictum of no form, one form, multiple forms, primary forms, secondary forms, all leading to 'beyond form'. From *arupa* to *rupam rupam pratirupa bavuho* to *para rupa*. While life could be categorised in terms of the one and the many, there were the systems of tripartite and fours, whether of time or space, groups of people or stages of life (*trikala, triloka, chatur varna, chatur asrama*).

The movement of time was also conceived as multiple. There was, thus, an adherence to the notion of time, both in its rhythmic cyclicity of coiling and recoiling as also some linearity. Micro and macro levels were easily recognisable. From the blinking of an eye (*nimesa*) to the aeons (*yuga*) was the span of time. Life was not situated only in calendric, linear time, arbitrarily divided, it was situated in different orders of time, astronomical (celestial) and terrestrial. Each moment was both mundane and sacred. There was a notion of space in terms of place, locale, region and country, and the universe. There were different spatial orders (*loka*) as there were different temporal (*kala*). The two together provided the basis of multiple identities and local distinctiveness. The movement was from undifferentiation to differentiation, defined roles and distinctiveness, back to transcendence and to a unified field. This is the burden of most medieval poetry, be it Kabir or Dadu, the Alvars or Naynamars, Eknath or Tukaram. While their message of crossing boundaries at the socio-economic level was loud and clear, equally so was the message of the perennial and unified. This can be discerned in the multiple voices of medieval poetry, and is clear in the regional schools of medieval architecture throughout the subcontinent: Hindu, Buddhist and Jain alike, and even Islamic. The fundamentals as also an overarching unity permeated each single manifestation of distinctive identity and expression. To read these developments as caused and affected by political and economic factors only would be to take a partial and unidimensional view. Indeed, the creative genius lay in incorporating the temporal and the ephemeral in the eternal and the perennial. The case of the Brihadisvara temple in Tanjore is an outstanding example of the multiple dimensions of the play of the eternal, perennial and the temporal, the sacred and the political. Raja Raja Chola appropriated the form of the *Dakshinamurti*. The creative artist went further by making a structure and design that was polyvalent with layers of meaning.

This world-view of values and modes of expression continued in varying degrees up to the beginning of the colonial period. The Indian psyche found multiple ways to respond to external pressures: sometimes outright rejection, at other times partial acceptance, and at yet other times reinterpretation and reform of the indigenous. The second reed of the flute resonated with the perennial reed and its unchanging 'tonic'. Occasionally there was dissonance, but the double-reed flute was never broken or rejected so as to acquire another that could only play pre-cooked melodies of borrowed ideas, values, forms and systems. It had the inner resilience to sustain multiple identities in multiple orders of space and time. This is evident in the countless forms of traditional theatre that emerged in early and late medieval India up to the early 19th century. This is evident in the varied schools of music and dance, painting, oral literature and much else. Politically, no doubt, there was subjugation, disruption and turmoil, but deep inside there was a still undisturbed centre, a *bija*, a kernel.

Tradition was thus literally transmission, *parampara*, a vertical flow from undifferentiated, glacial levels of thought and know-ledge systems to a wide variety of expressions in distinctive modes: genres, forms and styles. The multiple streams, dual, tripartite or foursome, met at particular spatio-temporal moments and formed a confluence, a *prayaga*, and flowed again along their distinctive paths (*marga*). Today we recognise these processes as linear trans-mission and inter-cultural dialogue.

There continued to be space here for the local, regional and na-tional (pan-Indian but not pertaining to the political nation-state). Communication and interaction, not without some conflict, took place through the many strategies of fairs, festivals and community gatherings within a region. Pilgrimages and travels across regions were almost obligatory. Social, economic, political and even cultural historians have dwelt either on political developments or subaltern histories of localities or groups, but not on the process of transmission and interaction of the traditions.

The two currents—a directional path and a confluence of streams in defined time and space—were comprehended by the two indicative terms *marga* and *desa*. Both eschewed a monolithic, fixed, uniform structure and accommodated the notions of what we understand by the term multiplicity and plurality within a unified field. It was cultural diversity, much like biodiversity, neither heterogeneity nor homogenisation.

Colonial Rule: Cultural Assault and the Response of Tradition

Colonial rule and its concomitants—modern education, legal systems, administration, the era of Enlightenment and its twin, the orientalist discourse—brought in their wake, momentous changes at the upper levels, but not at all levels of society. Now there were responses: questioning, awakening, reformist zeal and, finally, alas, the internalisation of the perceptions of the 'other' about the 'self'. The first reed of the double-reed flute was for the first time discarded by the educated elite. The tonic of the perennial—*sasvata*—lost, the flute no longer played variations and change on a secure inner scale, but the borrowed tunes of duality, objectivity, rationality, the thought system of the positivist. We became the objects of our own viewing and not the subjects of our living. The Upanishadic view of the *bhokta* and the *drsta*—the experience and the watcher—was replaced by a decontextualising of our categories of thought and speech from the life we lived. A definite fissure had taken place in the minds of many who first utilised the intellectual baggage of the 'other' to understand the 'self' and then were left with the baggage and no or little 'self'. There were, of course, notable gigantic exceptions in the 19th and early 20th centuries.

This is not the occasion to delineate the complex history of how the intellectual paradigms of the 'other', generated by Descartes, Newton, later Freud and the positivists, penetrated our mindscape. The Indian response was either total assimilation and internalisation or a complete rejection. The possibilities of a healthy and equal dialogue were meagre. Intellectual discourses became insulated. At best, we took up defensive postures.

Though in actual life we were still living at the level of *anubhava* and *bhavana*, even if gasping for fresh air, we began to look at ourselves as the vestiges of a dead past, the precious evidence of archaeology. We felt that we had a glorious history, no present and an uncertain future. We did not view tradition as the flow of the river or as the lotus leaf or double-reed flute. Instead, now it was a illumined mirror whose fragments we had to gather to reconstruct or reassemble a lost antiquity into a virtual reality. Concurrently, we began to run along the path of progressive linear time and socio-economic material growth so as to keep pace with those 'others', our political masters who represented the movements of rationalism and scientific thought of Newton, the dualism of Descartes, and Freud's fragmentation of the psyche. If seers, visionaries and even political leaders such as Mahatma Gandhi advocated a path of renewal of the 'self' from the ground of the 'self' at different psychic levels and social structures, we paid little heed or were not fully convinced. Our articulations did not cohere with our resolve, nor our resolve with our actions. The nationalist enterprise and the response to it have perhaps to be assessed against the backdrop of the loss of this capacity to be attuned to the double-reed flute of the Indian psyche, the one stable, the other changing and transmuting. Little wonder that Ramakrishna, Aurobindo and Ramana focused on transformation from within and not external transformation. The implements of this transformation could only be the deep psyche and not the intellect.

It was this self awareness of loss and bewilderment that brought forth the many significant voices of questioning and reinterpretation in many artistic genres. Late 19th- and early 20th-century literature of all regional languages reverberates with reinterpretation of the age-old myths of India. The *Ramayana* and *Mahabharata* are not retold, they are renewed or reinterpreted. The characters are re-modelled. Minor characters, Urmila (Lakshman's wife) Karna, Bhishma, Yashodha are reshaped. Countless oral versions continue uninterruptedly under the surface while, in what we call the mainstream, the historical social novels of Walter Scott or later Voltaire and yet later Tolstoy and Turgenev make an impact. In theatre, too, there is a similar picture of the subterranean and subtler streams of indigenous forms, below the derived theatre of European and British realism.

After Independence: The Freezing of Tradition

Political independence attained, there was idealism and optimism not without the trauma and the continuing scars of partition and division. However, the left-behind baggage of the colonial ruler, especially the intellectual, critical apparatus and the structures it generated, were neither rejected nor questioned with any great sense of rigour or urgency. The educational, administrative, legal and political systems were all patterned on the design of the 'other', with suitable modifications and even distortions. After the first decade and a half, that is, after the first flush of the new-found enthusiasm and idealism had subsided, coinciding with Jawaharlal Nehru's demise in 1964, it was already becoming clear that many of the institutional frameworks and the institutions established on derived models were either anachronistic, had outlived their efficacy or were inappropriate. Worse, they were impediments and counterproductive for the articulated goals of the nation-state. While we were proud members of a global community, and achieved heroic and impressive goals in the matter of food production and economic growth, there was the vast, important and fundamental field of education and culture that dealt with the human development of millions of people. Some policies were articulated but not rigorously implemented. Ambiguity and ambivalence towards the core 'self' besieged us. While state resources were available, there was little or no priority given to this crucial dimension of fostering, nurturing sensitively, a multiple plural society and the multi-identities of the 'self'.

Tradition or *parampara* now was indeed a thing of the past, an exotic family heirloom fit to be displayed on ceremonial occasions in international forums. It had no longer any envisaged role in achieving the developmental goals of tribal, rural and urban India. Life was dissociated from intellect-ation. The life of function was dissociated from values, ideas and art. Education was dissonant from culture, and both from the goals of socio-economic growth, and policy and planning. Neither at the level of policy or programming nor at grassroots levels did the socio-economic, administrative, developmental schemes relate to education or culture, or what we may now call the constantly renewing tradition. In a few exceptional cases, non-formal education and community activities were integrated. Significant as these exceptions were, there was no all-India impact. And, of course, this left no space for sustaining the vitality of the inner spaces and sounds of the immutable. And yet every effort was made to patronise, disseminate, present and globalise the many wondrous and glittering gems of intrinsic pulsation and vitality of all that which resounds on ceremonial occasions as the thunderous drums: the dances and theatre forms of tribal and rural India. Undoubtedly, there was prolific activity in reviving forms and equally undoubtedly there was decontextualisation of these culture-specific manifestations integral to lifestyle and life functions.

It is time to reflect upon the reasons for this fragmentation and consequent decontextualisation. A closer look will convince us that in the absence of a cohesive, integral vision about India and 'Indian', and the adoption of largely uniform models of development understood only as socio-economic growth, little or no attention was given to integrate the functional with the creative, the creative with development. Our planning was aggregative.

Despite this, there was and is vitality with remarkable tenacity in traditional forms. In turn, they are utilised by the urban elite with a new, contemporary, unidimensional sensibility. However, what is the state of the living human repositories of these traditions and creativity? Occasional awards, national, even international, trips, some economic gains and yet no social status: Warlis, Madhubani painters, Pandavani, Tamasha, Yatra performers alike. Also their own sensibility is influenced by the contrived ceremonials as also the mass media and the plethora of images—aural, visual and kinetic—which are as distasteful as polluting.

At the sophisticated levels of intellectual discourse and within the precincts of academia, we analyse and measure our multi-traditions exactly as the 'other' does, little realising that what we are exhibiting and analysing is part of our 'self', the vital 'self' that flows largely in the non-sophisticated and the socio-economically deprived sections of Indian society. Harsh as this may sound, perhaps it is time to turn a serious inward gaze on what the internalisation of the perception of the 'self' by the 'other' has done to the 'self' of self-awareness.

The subject is vast and complex, being made more disorderly and chaotic with the increasing disenchantment with institutional systems of governance of one's own making. Nevertheless, there is still time to retune ourselves on the basis of establishing a relevant and more meaningful relationship with the tonic of the first reed of the perennial flow, which still exists and can be heard and can be re-legitimised if we so will.

Reconstruction of Tradition in the Electronic Media

So far I have attempted to outline the vast and deep landscape of the tradition(s), its glacial levels and multiple streams, its surface streams or dry river beds and its subterranean springs. All these exist; re-energising is possible, feasible and desirable.

A new and significant factor in the dynamics between tradition and lived life is its mediation by the electronic media. Suddenly, a multidimensional flow in constant flux—changing and yet not changing with each performance—becomes a fixed category. To take only one example, the countless interpretations of the myths and legends, the characters of the *Ramayana* and *Mahabharata* were and are still reinterpreted and recreated in innumerable ways, each valid and meaningful. The stereotyping of the myths into melodramatic black and white, into heroes and villains matching commercial cinema, leads to its disempowerment. The potency of the characters due to polyvalence of meaning and form is lost. It is not technology itself but the motivations, and the commerce and trade of the technology that must be held responsible. The ecological and social significance of these myths is all but lost in these presentations of the electronic media. Alongside is the marked preference for a type of verbal and kinetic language that is neither hybrid nor homogeneous: it is simply unaesthetic and discordant. The potential of the medium to reach out to vast audiences is the real danger. The power of the virtual to influence—even subvert— the real is indeed immense, at least judging from some of the presentations in the mass media.

But at best and at worst, technology is a tool in the minds and hands of men and women. There have been many brave and courageous attempts at using the electronic media for not only dissemination and entertainment, but also documentation and critical analysis. Some of these have been superbly visualised and sensitively crafted. Many forms that have become extinct have been conserved. Valuable documentation of languishing genres, forms and styles will enable posterity to peep into this vast storehouse. Nevertheless, even these attempts have restricted themselves to documenting the forms, the performance, the art. The documentation has not been extended to include the natural and cultural environment, the lifestyle, life function, the rites and rituals of life cycle, which are intrinsic to the performance, and the visual act of painting, narration, dance or drama. In many instances the ritual performance in its life context is a socio-economic, educational strategy of environmental conservation of earth and water resources, or an instrumentality of restoring balances and order in cohesive communities. The capturing of the totality could serve as an educative experience for policy makers and planning specialists who pour over files to evolve viable and appropriate models for development.

Finally, there is the significant role of CD-ROM and multimedia technologies. Here, also, the negative and positive potential of technology is immense. While as finished products they can be commercially marketed for profit, they can be used with great sensitivity and dexterity to establish a meaningful dialogue between science, technology and tradition. The evolution of the gist card by C-DAC for electronic and automatic transcription from one Indian script to another is one such success story. There are now a few examples available of skilful and productive harnessing of this new technology.[1] But is still a nascent area full of possibilities and perils. How successful and effective a medium it will prove to be in the reconstruction of a holistic vision of tradition in 'virtual form' is an open question.

Note

1. I have been involved in some of these projects at the Indira Gandhi National Centre for the Arts. They use cyber technology in decoding and understanding

manifestations of tradition. The films on Lai Haroba, Garos of Meghalaya and Todas of Nilgiris are examples. Experiments on multimedia presentations of the vedic *yajna*, the *Gita Govinda*, and the temples of Brihadisvara and Muktesvara have also been attempted. These and other such projects could enable the younger generation to establish a new contemporary dialogue with a precious heritage of which they are inheritors and transmitters.

2

From Sankara to Fusion: An Indian Musical Spectrum

Ashok Ranade

In India the term *sankara*, traditionally speaking, has negative connotations. Due of historical and cultural reasons, it has been regarded an undesirable mixture, dilution or hybridisation. On the other hand, fusion is today a prestige word. With fusion are associated positive developments and happy images such as 'a capacity to lead to newer unions' and 'a release of massive energy'. As far as the Indian musical scene is concerned, both *sankara* and fusion represent genuine responses to what is happening. There are some who decry the musical intermingling taking place as *sankara*, while others welcome the activity. Obviously, the time is ripe to consider the Indian musical situation through larger conceptual perspectives offered by musico-cultural studies, now validly and collectively described as ethnomusicology.

Apart from the abundance and variety of musical traditions and genres in India, the country also boasts of a long and alive historical 'past'. Performing arts have a tendency not to allow complete breaks in traditions. Often, a kind of subterranean existence of performing concepts and practices characterise traditions. This does not negate the constant and ongoing processes of musical change at multiple levels.

I have pointed out elsewhere (Ranade 1992: 9–10) that cultures can come together in at least four different, though connected, ways. I describe the modes as juxtaposition, confrontation, borrowing and conscious/unconscious assimilation. Of interest is the fact that music may also come together in equally varied modes— sometimes consequent to movements in non-musical areas of the parent culture or sometimes independent of them. In fact, one of the most provoking ethnomusicological insights is that in normal circumstances, music is the last life aspect to change, and when it does, it is symptomatic of deeper and fundamental cultural changes. When such changes become too obvious to miss, it is already too late for Jeremiads in music to sing their elegies! On the other hand, if and when cultural thinkers care to listen—with their inner ears as well—they are likely to find music actually useful in making a prognosis, rather than a diagnosis, of many socio-cultural ills. The coming together of various musics, taking place in India now due to globalisation, media explosion, new social re-alignments and so on, is hardly definable in simple terms and binary modes generated by either/or attitudes that appear to colour our efforts in construing cultural events.

Keeping in mind the chronological length, phenomenal breadth and the experiential depth of music in India, one can look at contemporary development with a set of questions: Is the coming together of musics new to India? Are the factors leading to this situation unique to the present moment? Are we justified in giving so much weightage to the '50-year-span' in the Indian context? What are the specific reasons that should prompt us to press panic buttons in considering cultural situations in general and musical situations in particular? In this article I propose to develop and illustrate the point that the current scenario of heavy inter-category mixing of music is not unique and that in the historical past we have many examples of mutual exchange, shifts in emphasis and radical transitions. The diverse and seemingly chaotic developments in the contemporary musical scene can be comprehended and evaluated through the three structural aspects of tone, tempo and language, which are applicable to all the categories of music, namely, primitive, folk, popular, religious and art music.

Categories of Music in India

One special feature of the increasing coming together of types of music in India is what I choose to call an inter-category circulation of musical material. It needs to be appreciated that in India primitive, folk, religious, popular and art music constitute experiential and structural categories that are not producer oriented. Before I proceed to develop my substantive argument, perhaps it would be useful to note the salient features of these five music categories.

Primitive Music or *Aadima Sangeet*

This is a kind of composite expression often combining singing with the playing of instruments and dancing. This is perhaps connected with the fact that it represents an attempt to respond to three natural cycles that largely determine the course of life—the cycles of day and night, birth and death, and the seasons. On account of this larger relationship, *aadima* music is not made for its own sake and appears to be directed at some higher power, including nature. The evocative function of music is reflected in the special regard displayed for rituals: they have a place in the conception, presentation as well as preservation of music.

It is not an exaggeration to say that *aadima* music means music for everyone, everything and for every occasion. General participation is encouraged to such an extent in the making of *aadima* music that there is a near absence of audience as a separate entity: no one is entirely engaged in listening. The role of the community as such is so vital that the cultural group or the community rather than the solitary composer is said to be responsible for creating music. Normally all activities stressing the collective aspect of human life depend on rhythm as a binding agent. It is, therefore, natural that this music gives more scope to rhythm than melody. Very often the former is also more attractive.

By and large, the category holds songs to be more important than music, and yet primitive song can hardly be fitted into the usually accepted definition of song! This is so chiefly because of the norms applied in the category.

To make, receive or appreciate *aadima* music, certain identifiable criteria are applied and sweetness is certainly not one of them! This point needs to be stressed because most people assume that all music has to be invariably sweet. This is as valid as expecting good food to always be sweet. The category holds sounds to be important *as sounds*. This is in contrast to the general tendency to prefer sound only if it is meaningful, as in language.

Very often primitive music stands for something else outside itself and a very pervasive symbolism can therefore be detected.

In some respects *aadima* music keeps very close to day-to-day life and its different aspects. One of the interesting consequences is that ordinary objects and procedures may be used in music making. It is logical to assume that the sense of hearing would rule supreme in any musical activity. However, in primitive music the sense of touch also strongly comes into play. For example, holding hands, stamping on the ground, body thumping and so on become notable contributors to the final result.

Folk Music

Broadly speaking, each of the well-defined linguistic regions of the country has its own folk music and, hence, many researchers now emphasise plurality while discussing folk music. Certain features, however, appear to be common to all regional traditions, a fact indicating the pan-Indian nature of the category as also the essential unity of Indian culture as such.

When compared with the primitive, the folk category is distinguished by a clear dominance of melodic songs. An elaborate and technically sound definition of 'song' is very complex and is not being attempted here. But two salient song features can easily be identified: first, it should consist of sustained, unbroken sounds; and, second, it should be 'hummable'.

Instrumental music enjoys a kind of ubiquity in the folk category of music. It is almost everywhere and yet it cannot be said to enjoy an independent position. Instruments are pressed into service mostly to accompany singers/dancers. Even when music is made solo, instruments try to follow or imitate music originally composed for or produced by human voices. The effectiveness and the musical value of musical instruments is judged according to their capacity to approximate vocal music.

Collectivity reigns supreme in creation, presentation, reception and also perhaps in preservation of folk music. Folk music is meant for the entire body of an organised human group bound by specific cultural ties, indicating commonality of language, geographical location, social convention and so on. Folk music emerges, circulates and lives as their expression.

A number of items in folk music are linked to certain non-musical activities, tasks or actions in a definite manner. For example, in many regions of India, harvesting and pounding of corn and other similar chores have songs associated with them. This is described as the functionality of folk music. Functionality means that the association between music and the tasks mentioned is not a vague psychological or accidental coexistence of the two, but a firmer mutual relationship that goes beyond mere suggestivity. Very often these non-musical activities provide purpose as well as structure to folk music and make the forms functional. The feature usually makes the concerned music more immediate and endows it with a direct appeal not easily paralleled.

It has often been said that folk music has no beginning and no perceivable end. The remark is obviously intended to emphasise the element of continuity it enjoys. Cultural groups can rarely be firmly and exactly placed on the time and space axis. Hence, their music, that is, folk music, is also expected to flow on and become one with the life of the community. This is why it is described as eternal.

Contrary to common perception, folk music does change, though selectively. It accepts changes in certain aspects, while in some others it is extremely reluctant to do so. For example, those facets and forms oriented towards entertaining are prone to change faster than the religious or ritualistic aspects. Referring to strictly musical contexts, for instance, rhythms change less readily than melodies or tunes.

Folk music tends to maintain a two-way relationship with the contemporary art music of the land. Some features of art music percolate to folk music, or folk musicians try to borrow, change or assimilate them. On the other hand, history is full of instances where art music seized select aspects of folk music, to polish or refine them for an easier accommodation in its own existing codified systems. This is why features of art and folk music are detected in one another. Thus, many *raga*s are 'found' in Indian folk music, while folk flourishes, rhythms and so on have been espied in the repertoires of art musicians.

A cultural group and its folk music are so intimately connected that the latter can legitimately claim to be the national expression of the concerned community. Normally, nations are understood to be homogeneous as political or cultural entities, and to that extent folk music can be described as a national expression. However, in a country like India, each region has its own folk music even though the regions taken together form a nation. Various folk musics are therefore to be understood as systems representing regional identities severally. If a nation is defined as a cohesive cultural unit irrespective of its place in the hierarchy of political set-ups, then folk music in India may be called a national expression.

Folk music, as expected, allocates meaningful roles to both language and literature. Stories and songs are brought together and a unique phenomenon of song-cycles or its variants assumes importance in the total corpus of folk music.

Popular Music

Popular music can be defined as a product of many subcultures that coexist and interact in a society. New waves of migrants, temporary fascination with cults or political movements, sudden exposure to new musical formulae are some of the more obvious factors conducive to the making of popular music. A growing middle class and acceleration of the processes of urbanisation also contribute to the making of popular music. Concepts of leisure time, desire and capacity for recreation, and a pressing demand for entertainment create an industry to make music.

The mass media functions as a major shaping influence. Media language, time restrictions/allocations, transmission facilities and such other operational features govern the form as well as content of popular music. An increase in population and demographic redistribution generally encourage generation and spread of popular musical products.

The music of this category is patently patron oriented. Consequently, every change in patronage is reflected more readily here than elsewhere. No other category is so inexorably ruled by market economy as is popular music. Demand and supply, distribution and profit margin forcefully come into play. Fashions, topical interests and prohibitions operate to determine almost every aspect of music. The target audience is less selective and the term 'mass' indicates a rather indiscriminating body of receivers of this music.

In the final analysis, it is sociocultural and not aesthetic criteria that become more relevant in popular music.

Religious Music

In India, religious music is largely synonymous with devotional music or *bhakti sangeet*. Devotional music as a category came into existence largely as a result of the work of saint poets and their followers in different regions of the country. To begin with, the saint poets were composers devoted to either Shiva or Vishnu, though in the later centuries deities as well as cult loyalties became more diverse. The saint poets composed, sang and passed on thousands of songs through oral tradition. Their songs became the common property of the land and the people. They continue to serve as models even for contemporary efforts in composing devotional songs. Compositions in this category are in different regional languages collectively known as the Prakrits (in contrast with Sanskrit). According to many experts, the Prakrit tongues are inherently more musical.

Devotional music exhibits some easily identifiable structural features. Compositions in the category invariably carry the name of the composer in the last line. Names of the guru as well as the worshipped deity also find a mention. Predictably, the metrical moulds employed by the saint poets are of Prakrit origin. One special metrical feature of the Prakrit tradition (apart from the notable variety) is the inherent flexibility, which renders the metres more conducive to making music. An uninhibited stretching of individual words, midline breaks, variable line lengths and other such features obviously allow more freedom to composers as well as performers.

Rhythms employed in this category are less expansive. For example, in most cases they have four beats (or multiples of four). Rhythmic cycles thus constructed are easy to grasp. Rhythms in this category are therefore aptly described as 'catchy'. Rhythms have always proved more effective than melodies in reaching out to the masses.

In terms of melody, too, the category gives priority to mass appeal. Devotional melodies often have structures describable as *dhun raga*s. These are *raga*s with identifiable and recurring tonal phrases, which are free from the constraints imposed by the rigid grammatical frameworks usually displayed by full-fledged *raga*s. Further, *dhun raga*s used are noticeably similar to melodies often classified as regional on account of their origin or due to the greater circulation they seem to enjoy in particular geographical areas. For example, melodies like *pahadi*, *kafi*, *des* and *mand* unambiguously declare their regional affiliations. In addition, devotional music also employs seasonal melodies that have a long and widespread tradition in the country. Names of *raga*s such as *malhar*, *hindol* and *des* remind us of this link.

A judicious mixture of solo and choral modes of rendering is evident in this category. Audiences participate in making music according to the norms (usually unwritten) prescribed in the tradition. For example, iteration of a deity's name and hailing the God or guru become points at which the entire congregation joins in lustily. Predictable, regular and noticeable audience participation makes the music intense.

A great majority of the musical instruments used in the category act as generators of rhythmic pulses. This is remarkably so even in the case of instruments ostensibly designed to function as melodic. For example, string instruments often supply rhythm beats in addition to the drone or melody they produce. It is also true that instruments in this category are easily given to grosser musical effects and are low on nuances, subtleties and sophistications. As many musicians have succinctly pointed out, 'devotional instruments require less maintenance'.

Indian devotional music surges in two streams, one of them flows nearer to art music while the other remains closer to folk music.

Art Music

Performers in this category intentionally strive to attain aesthetic or artistic goals. In return, they also expect aesthetic appreciation from the audience. It will not be incorrect to say that in a concert of Hindustani art music, the most crucial test a listener has to pass is to express his approval/disapproval of the musical proceedings at the right moment and in a proper manner.

One of the most distinctive features of art music is its flow in two concurrent streams: the scholastic and the performing. The former stream formulates, systematises and records rules expected to govern musical operations in the category, while the second is related to actual presentations. In the long run, the latter outpaces the former—a case that has a parallel in literature and grammar, too.

Art music deliberately concentrates on expressing itself entirely (or mostly) through the auditory channel. To that extent, it is more abstract, unlike folk or primitive music, both of which are more concrete on account of their appeal to many senses, in addition, of course, to the auditory.

Art music affords more scope to individuals than to groups. The predominance of the solo mode in the Hindustani system is to be placed in this context. An individual performer is consequently allowed more freedom. He can elaborate or improvise on the basic musical structures according to his own aesthetic intentions and ideas. Thus, unlike the collective quality of folk, primitive and devotional music, art music tends to emphasise the individuality of the artist.

This category displays an impressive array of forms or genres of music. In Hindustani music, for example, *dhrupad, dhamar, khayal, tarana, trivat, gat* and *peshkar* are among the different forms of music. Such variety also exists in other musical categories, but those in the art category result largely from aesthetic and musicological considerations.

It is in this category that styles, schools, guru–*shishya* lineages and other systems have been set up with more deliberation. Codification becomes mandatory, as also the conscious verbalisation of rules to be meticulously followed. Also notable is the fact that theoretical, grammatical and expository works in the category are written, as is to be expected, in a scholastic tradition.

It is, of course, obvious that an overall sweetness, appeal of evocative words and gestures, and other such factors will fascinate the listener, irrespective of his knowledge of music. And yet, being a product of human effort at its imaginative best, it helps to know the norms that channelise, govern and guide art music and musicians. To a certain degree, music making is like participating in a game you can play and enjoy if you know the rules. Otherwise, you have to rest content with the thrill, the physicality and the exhilaration you feel when blood circulates faster and limbs move smoothly.

Art music often joins hands with other artistic efforts realised in painting, drama, dance, etc. to devise new combinations for attaining new artistic goals. At the same time, it needs to assert its independence and achieve aesthetic excellence. Hence, it also attempts to sever its connection with the other arts or areas of life. This aspect of its functioning becomes clear when schools of art music, forms and styles are discussed.

Almost as a corollary to the features enumerated so far, art music claims a kind of autonomy. It, therefore, tries to move away from the incidents, events and processes that characterise our daily life. With equal alacrity, it also shies away from personal (as distinct from individual) joys and sorrows. In some measure this detachment from the mundane makes its appeal more enduring. Herein lies the secret of the longevity of *ragas*, *talas* and *bandishe*s in Hindustani art music.

Musical Exchanges, Shifts and Transitions

From this background, it would become obvious that never before in the past have we seen so heavy a musical exchange between the five categories of music as we are witnessing in recent decades. Ideas, instruments, idioms, imagery and the like are moving from one category to the other with remarkable ease and sometimes as a result of notable deliberation and craftsmanship. Admittedly, the results are not always as satisfying as intended, and sometimes the motivation itself may be suspect! However, use, abuse and mis-use must be distinguished and deviation ought to be understood as an inevitable step towards creativity. Only then would the scene cease to be painful and puzzling.

For obvious reasons, I choose not to go far back in ancient Indian music or look back with nostalgia to the middle ages, which were far from dark. However, even a cursory examination would reveal that what is happening today has close parallels in many early periods. Coming together of different musics and the consequent changes in music are not new to us. For example, *sama* music was shaped by musical moulds often alien to the composers of the *Rg vedic* hymns who then processed them for conversion into *sama*s for musical rendering. In other words, there were tunes, already existing, as if hovering in the air. They were so well entrenched in people's minds that the Aryan composers found it wise to use those tunes as communicating units rather than reject them as alien. For the sacred music of the Aryans, music of non-Aryan origin was no taboo.

Another interesting instance of the musical tradition's openness to the alien can be seen in Bharata's general injunction that music cannot be composed with four or less notes. And yet the perceptive sage refers to Shabaradi tribes as users of such music. With his wholehearted acceptance of the *lokadharmi* mode of theatric presentation, he had no hesitation in taking note of this music of minimal structure. I am sure that he would not have been averse to using it if the theatric occasion so demanded.

And what about the notable shift from *venu* culture to *veena* culture in ancient India, as also to the general upward musical contour, that is, *aroha*, instead of the downward, *avaroha*, of the ancient *sama gayan*? Why did it became necessary for the *Naradiya Shiksha*, the earliest work in India to examine music in a spirit of scientific inquiry, to describe positions of musical intervals in terms of correspondences between voice and *venu*? Organological symbolism indicates that *venu*-centred culture presents a more primitive, elemental and undifferentiated cultural state. On the other hand, *veena* bespeaks of a notably differentiated, sophisticated and stratified society as well as culture. Does this not point to a radical change in musical temper at a very early period, and that too as a result of greater exchange of cultures? Perhaps the argument can be elaborated a little more without delving deep into too many musicological details.

Vedic Phase: From *Venu* to *Veena*

The *Rg Veda* can be left aside, as it does not mention *veena*, though there was an identifiable chordophone called *vana* that accompanied singing and probably dancing. In the present context, it is, of course, the *Sama Veda* that needs looking into. There are clear references to the role of *veena* as an accompanying instrument for vocal music in the related literature.

However, I suggest that the most significant change in this connection happened when a radical departure was made from the descending order of *sama* music to orient it upwards. A rather speculative query is: was this due to a more purposeful and firm recourse to *veena* as an accompanying instrument—the change referred to being a switch-over from *venu* to *veena*?. Less speculatively, one notes that *Naradiya Shiksha*, which codified the singing of *sama* music, felt it essential to equate *sama* notes with their placements on *veena*, indicating thereby the increasing importance of *veena* and the receding role of *venu* in the kind of music made. As the pioneering organologist, the late Dr. B.C. Deva (1977: 10) pointed out, referring to the strategy of 'fixing' musical scales with the help of string lengths, 'It is perhaps doubtful if there could have been a stable musicology without instruments.' Other sources on vedic music, namely, the Brahmana, Aranyaka, Upanishad and Sutra literature confirm this 'upward' trend of music as also the increasing role of *veena* (which was mostly of the bowed-harp type). Classical organology speaks of four main types of chordophones, namely, zithers, lutes, harps and lyres. In simple terms, the early Indian preference was for the plucked, horizontal-stringed, bow-type *veena*.

   This, however is, not the place to go into the history of the *sama* music, which, during its evolution, allocated differing roles to the *veena*. It suffices to note that *sama* music obviously passed through phases, perhaps successively, in which music was based on forms identified as *richa*, *gatha* and *sama*. Rendering of the first kind (*archik*) employed one note, the second (*gathik*) consisted of two notes and the third (*samik*) was extended to three (and later more) notes. However, the decision to abandon *venu* and opt in favour of a greater role for the *veena* was obviously not related to availability of a greater number of notes, because there is no reason to assume that the gamut of *venu* was too restricted. By all accounts, the *veena* accompanying the *sama* music was not a bowed variety. The musico-cultural resolve to effect a changeover from a blown wind instrument to a plucked string instrument, therefore, meant an interesting change of strategy keen on a different timbre and dynamics (that is, variation in force or intensity). Inducting the softer tones of *veena* in music making to enrich the timbre spectrum under exploration was not an isolated act. It is instructive to note that in vocalisation also a similar concern for timbre and dynamics was apparent. For example, *sama*s audible at close quarters were known as *deva* or *sarvaparoksha samhita*. Those rendered in high pitch and audible from afar were described as *asur* or *sarvapratyaksha* *samhita*, while those exploring the middle ranges were called *rishi* or *paroksha-pratyaksha samhita*. Yet another classification of *sama*s impresses because of its direct reference to timbre. According to it, singing in bass voice was known as *devahu*, to do so in thin/ weak tone was called *vakvashahu*, while that which resembled crying aloud was described as *amitrahu*. To carry this line of thinking further, a question can be raised: why was the changeover made? What could have been the compulsions?

One could attempt a response on the following lines: First, *sama* music gradually came to connote vocalisation identified as singing, that is, an act of music making very elaborate in comparison with the *richa* chanting. The *richa* chanting was, in brief, a minimal movement away from an unadorned prose, a unilinear delivery of the sacred material or message. Chanting, as deviation from prose, has limited musical aspirations. It generates minimal music. Hence, when a desire to elaborate musical ideas arose (which *sama* music was trying to project), it became necessary to change the supporting musical agent. *Veena* obviously proved more amenable to the production of a greater variety of timbres, whether the intention was to correspond or contrast with the vocal tones used.

Second, unlike *venu*, *veena* made it possible for the *samagah*s (the singers of the *sama*s) to accompany themselves. This mode naturally indicates music making that demands closer and more purposeful coordination of the main and secondary channels engaged to express musical ideas. It also suggested a different kind of approach to the patterning of the available body of musical sounds. Simultaneity of different notes, phrases and tempos became possible. As *sama* music was not, it is speculated, accompanied by rhythm instruments, this observation assumes additional importance. Authorities have enumerated the kinds of *veena*s in use during the period of *sama* singing. They have also debated the exact nature of some of the instruments mentioned. Differences in instrumental holds, compositions played on them, processes of making them and other such features have been attended to. However, some significant points about the voice–music relationship need to be separately stated. In my opinion, the following are noteworthy.

The *veena*s employed were mostly plucked/strummed polychords (that is, instruments having separate strings for each different note). As such, they generated discontinuous sounds unlike the sustained and unbroken vocal lines projected by the *samagah*s. It could be said that the result must have been of running two adjacent, independent and simultaneous music streams adding notably to the tonal colour. Perhaps, there was an opportunity to produce supportive (that is, non-identical) melodies.

Singers often accompanied themselves on the *veena*—a felt need or desire obviously impossible to satisfy on *venu*. It is worth noting that even in a later period Nayak Bakshu was reportedly rated higher as a musician because he accompanied himself on the *pakhawaj!*

In view of the fact that a number of *veena*s had numerous strings, their employment obviously resulted in more complex music.

It is to be stressed that though the instrument was probably not allowed musical freedom, it appears to toe a different line regarding timbre and perhaps draws separate tonal contours, too. In the final analysis, this would hardly mean that it had a subsidiary role.

The foregoing discussion on *venu* and *veena* was an organological detour of an illustrative sort made to sensitise one to look at technical/musical/performing changes from a cultural perspective. It brings home to us the complexity of the situation and the need for careful analysis.

Recent Trends of Assimilation and Change

There are scores of historical examples in all musical categories recording how Indian musical culture has encountered, assimilated and changed itself under the impact of an alien culture—if and when the motivation was adequate. Musical changes are always, in the final analysis, voluntary. A society makes the music it chooses to. Music cannot be imposed from outside—like uniforms, languages, currencies or even political systems. To anticipate a little, once a culture has chosen what is to be its song, musical changes are inevitable.

Structure of Musical Changes

Some basic tenets of musical changes and the reasons prompting them are briefly discussed. In this context, three structural aspects can be identified as basic: tonal material, tempo and words

or language. Of course, presentation formats, distribution of performing sets, audience composition, patronage hierarchy and other
such features are also to be considered for a deeper analysis. However,
attention to the basic constructional trinity is adequate to make
the position clear. Further, the fundamental character of these
features may elicit observations that will successfully cross cultural
boundaries, historical divisions and geographical borders.

Tone

The first feature, the tonal material, consists of individual sounds
accepted by a culture as 'notes'. In the next phase, notes are brought
together according to organisational principles preferred by the
concerned culture. The question often asked (and the response to
which is being repeatedly refined—in other words, postponed!)
is: are there sounds that are inherently, and therefore universally,
musical? Is it possible to have a music of and for the whole of human-
kind? Is there a universal language of music, agreed to and understood by human cultures the world over irrespective of language,
religion, caste, race, etc.? A somewhat simplified answer in respect
of tonal material is as brief as a Sanskrit aphorism. It says: 'Con-
sonances are universal and scales are man-made.' In other words,
for various reasons, no music of any culture is satisfied with con-
sonances alone. The history of music the world over stands witness
to repeated acts of legitimising intervals once regarded dissonant,
that is, unfit for music. The moral is clear: there cannot be music that
is inherently musical and universally acceptable. Cultures obviously
prefer not to be consonant and thereby universal, because this
choice enables them to express themselves as themselves. It is as
if individual cultures are intent on persuading others to accord them
a status of distinct entities through notes, tunes and tones that are
not customarily accepted as consonant. Even at the cost of producing
music that is less than agreeable, all cultures strive to create, preserve and project their respective identities and persuade others
to regard them as such. It was certainly perceptive of Plato to note
that 'tones are persuasive'.

In other words, if a culture is heard to try out (or cry out for)
'new sounds' as components of new tunes and tones, it is a sign
of its intention to undergo a change of identity. Simultaneously,
it is also an expression of the desire that the culture should be

acknowledged as initiator of the transforming act. Further, and more importantly, the need to compose new songs (closely bound with the desire for new sounds) is symptomatic of the craving to point to changes—desired as also actual—in the prevailing social hierarchy. It is necessary to realise that songs are at once a parameter and a barometer of deeper cultural changes. To put it baldly, the phenomenon of song is actually located at the end of a long exploratory curve, which consists of processes designed and destined to find musical correlatives for cultural compulsions. A sociocultural group may, for example, complete its march towards a new song by passing through the generally successive phases of murmuring, humming, chanting, reciting, singing and song composing.

Does contemporary Indian culture, intensely desirous of a new song, feel that its melodic thinking is constrained by the dominating *raga* philosophy? Perhaps I should put the question temporarily aside, for later consideration, after covering some more ground.

Tempo

And what about the second component of the basic musical structure—tempo? It is necessary to avoid the temptation to rush to the universally appealing term 'rhythm'. Rhythm, in reality, represents a much more sophisticated, processed and culture-conditioned concept than tempo. Tempo is a result of manipulating durations, that is, distances between time divisions. We are obliged to divide time in order to comprehend and manipulate it. This is how, and why, the three basic tempos, namely, slow, medium and fast, are discussed and used. It is instructive to note that despite repeated and widespread attempts to find objective measurements for the three tempos, Indian musicology in general has settled on the principle of 'the relativity of tempo' (as also of pitch, it helps to remember). Therefore, for Indian music makers, and in traditional musical thinking, slow tempo is half the medium, which, in its turn, is double the slow and, finally, fast is double the medium. This position is almost an invitation to decide for oneself the value of any one phase—and the rest will take their places automatically.

One may well ask why there is apparent indecisiveness in fixing the value of something so fundamental in holding together every musical manifestation. In brief, the answer could be stated thus: in order to initiate a creative effort, the principle of individual freedom is brought into operation. However, the moment one moves further, it is subjected to neatly codified conventions, etc. In other words, for self-expression, one is allowed to set the tempo, but a desire to communicate with others or to create as art immediately sets limits on individual freedom in the interest of social or cultural exchange. The simple dictum is: you may change the tempo, but this desire must be moderated by the ultimate ideal of human exchange. The crux of the matter is that, time, as one of the ruling dimensions of life, brings into circulation a utility groove that is explored and exploited by the cultural group. If the tempo change desired by an individual is capable of maintaining a reasonable balance of 'similarity–difference' with the socially acceptable tempo, then the individual's choice is given a hearing. He is, as it were, put on trial. If the individual's perception and application of tempo answers the generally felt need for a tempo change, then he stands a chance of being hailed as an artist, creator, etc. In fact, he may then be praised for finding a new rhythm for the entire culture. In his context, the truth is rather paradoxical: To create rhythm, a change in tempo is essential, but every change in tempo cannot aspire to be a rhythm. This is why introduction of a new tempo can be both easy and frequent, but to take the next qualitative step always proves difficult. All societies are wary of tempo changes because of the omnipresent element of tempo in our life areas. There is bound to be a clash of interests if two versions of a tempo are vying for attention. There again, Plato was prophetic. He emphatically stated in *Republic*: 'Never allow rhythms in your State to change, because that spells anarchy in the State.'

It should, therefore, be obvious that change in tempo is a serious matter that has deep social implications. A new tempo brings in new divisions of time. It represents a new segmentation of life and a subsequent emergence of new life patterns. Pattern speaks of intricate interrelationship of all strands of the life fabric. Patterns, both of pleasure and pain, are nothing if not pervasive. They cannot be highly or firmly localised. Accepted patterns always tend to spread to areas adjacent to the areas of their origin. (However, patterns in different life areas cannot be presumed to be governed by the principle of correspondence alone.)

Are we today opting for new tempos because of the felt need of new rhythms? Is the well-realised circularity of the Indian *tala* idea proving irksome to our psyche? Are we pining for more collective, broad and compulsive tempos and rhythms, which make no demands on mental alertness and skill to perceive sophisticated *avatars* of temporal patterning? Is it not interesting to note that a majority of new manifestations of fusion music directly rely on tempos and rhythms employed in musical categories earlier identified as primitive, religious and folk? Are not these categories known for their capacity to bind together bodies and minds into collective wholes?

Language

This brings us to the third component, words/language. How are they being employed? For what purpose? Words/language are sounds as well as meaningful units. When music makers focus on sound as sound, one kind of song is made. The story is different when meaningfulness is the motivating spirit. Music in India sings in multiple voices in this context. On the one hand, *bhajan*s and *ghazal*s have gained a new-found popularity—and they are easily recognisable examples of a meaningful use of words and language. On the other hand, the popular category of music registers a new high in using words and language as clusters of sounds, which may provide a basis for an endless manipulation. What does the notable popular reception to instrumental music in the art category suggest? Are we not indicating a preference for sound as sound? The current overt reliance on sound amplification, the desire for sophisticated techniques of employing public address systems, concern for good acoustics and such other features point to the fact that we are intent on utilising a dimension of musical sound that so far mostly remained on the periphery of our musical sensibilities.

Craving for New Timbres

I want to suggest that today there is an unconscious shift in favour of the dimension of timbre as contrasted with pitch and volume. Popularity of instrumental renderings, vocalists' concern for amplification and such other effects in art music, the high-profile projection of certain language-backed genres, and the enthusiastic employment of novel instrumental resources in popular music are logical side effects of the present intense craving for new timbres (a fact that Indian musical cultures have been trying to bring to our notice at least from the beginning of the 19th century!). It is a known ethnomusicological feature that instrumental sounds are, culturally and emotionally, more neutral than the vocal. This is the reason why they migrate easily, repeatedly and extensively. The present situation is only an added proof of this phenomenon, which enjoys a long recorded history in India. Organology, the science of musical instruments, combined with a purposeful reading of music history as the history of performing ideas, reveals how instruments trace a career as music-making agents, as well as objects of interest. The manner in which new musical instruments hold sway, or the way in which old ones find new uses, are items worthy of more analytical study. Such investigations are likely to bring into relief instrumental symbolism, operating at unimagined levels. For example, the increasing frequency of women taking to drums and to *sushira* or wind instruments would suggest a changing of sexual symbolism in music. These changes are not confined to instrumental music alone. More and more male musicians are making a kind of music that was conventionally associated with females and vice-versa.

Visual Music

The last overall change in Indian music making is simply put: earlier, musicians' appeal was, 'Listen to me.' Now this is preceded, if not replaced, by a forceful plea: 'Look at me.' To develop an appeal for the eye has become a primary concern. I have always maintained that Indian manifestations are overwhelmingly multi-sensory. Therefore, grouping of arts, formation of art families, aesthetic theories about art mediums and their use, etc. have flowed in streams different from the ones in many non-Indian traditions. Any yet the contemporary appeal to the eye is qualitatively different. It seems to believe that more artistic information—as distinct from aesthetic significance—can be conveyed via the visual. In my opinion, the situation has been complicated because information has also been regarded to be the main agent influencing the act of making 'the judgement of taste'—so vital in aesthetic behaviour. This has resulted in a considerable clogging of information channels, as also in a marked reduction of emphasis on conveying artistic insights. Transmission of significances has taken a back seat in art activity, and more and more information is pumped in the music-making process—with unfortunate consequences.

Finally, to draw the strings together, what could symbolise the contemporary attitude of those engaged in music making? Perhaps it would both be appropriate and picturesque to say that where *bhramara*'s *gunjarava* once reigned supreme, *chitrapatanga*'s flitting fanciful flights have become the cynosure of our eyes!

The description may appear to lean a little on the negative side. That is not the intention. The eye–ear changing interrelationship is only a part of the story unfolding before us. Our sensory profile is undergoing a transformation as a whole. And as we are aware, senses in action are not five but thirteen, and thus the profile becomes a challenging spectrum of possibilities. To explore it we need some time, and more than that, a will. As has been said, most of the battles are won in the mind. A period of 50 years is less than a moment for a nation's march in time. Let us not stretch the *purusha* concept to the extent of equating a nation's career with the human lifespan. The pace of the cultural action is more than what we are used to, but it is not unnatural. I believe that the quality of our perception is changing and all our theories of art and culture will need hard and careful rethinking. We can use this occasion to take a step in that direction.

References

Deva B.C. (1977). 'The Development of Chordophones in India', *Sangeet Natak*, April–June, 10–18.

Ranade, Ashok (1992). *Indology and Ethnomusicology: Contours of the Early Indo-British Relationship*. New Delhi: Promilla Publishers.

3

Lineages of the Modern in Indian Art: The Making of a National History

Tapati Guha-Thakurta

This essay may appear off-key in a volume addressing cultural transformations in post-colonial India, for it covers a spectrum of trends that takes us back from the historical juncture of independence to half a century preceding it that saw the shaping of a new modern art history for the nation. It is, however, grounded in the urgency of our present post-colonial imperatives of a re-engagement with our colonial and nationalist pasts. In tracking the artistic developments in post-independence India, we need to take fresh stock of the long and complex modern heritage that we inherited in 1947. One of my main aims in this essay is to suggest ways of framing a meaningful history that could enhance our sense of what followed in the years since independence.

The essay was conceived around the very problem of producing a historical background for the present. In what ways can we write a larger history of 'modernity', and not just of 'modernisms', in Indian art history? What presents itself as 'a usable past' for the multifaceted persona of modern and contemporary Indian art? The questions could be put more simply: Where do we mark the founding moments and turning points in the making of national modern history? Do we sketch a backdrop in terms of the specific antecedents of the first group of artists of the 1940s and 1950s, in different art centres like Shantiniketan, Bombay and Delhi, who inaugurated the course of art in independent India? Or do we offer a wide overview of developments since the late 19th century, figuring all the trends and phases that were superseded before the nation arrived in the 1940s at the most crucial junctures of its modern art history?

The issues are not just about selection and coverage: they devolve on the more vexed question of what we designate as the 'true/authentic' history of the evolution of modern art in India. 'Authenticity' (its assertion, or the fear of its loss) is what has been most critically at stake. The contest has long been over what kind of art could qualify as both authentically 'modern' and 'national'. Since the turn of the century, both art practices and writings have revolved around a twin concern with Indianness and modernity. Even as the definitions of the 'Indian' and the 'modern' continuously changed, what remained constant was the search for a way of collating both identities. I raise this point here only to emphasise that the historical background I lay out is also a product of this historiography. It remains inextricably embedded in the contending positions over the course of artistic developments in modern India.

The challenge has been to recover a sense of the 'modern' on the one hand as a significant new art-historical period (whose beginnings can be located in the late 19th and early 20th century, in the changed patterns of patronage, practice and professions that came up under colonial rule), and on the other hand, as a powerful ideological and aesthetic category, whose changing contours have defined the form and structure of the period. Here, the main weight one has to carefully negotiate is that of nationalism: of what the nation has perpetuated and institutionalised as its 'own' modern art history. Retrieved from colonial art education, the idea of a modern artistic identity had, over the early years of the 20th century, been fully assimilated within nationalist endeavours and an autonomous national history. By the time of independence, the rejection of the colonial past was a part of a firmly entrenched nationalist history, which itself was now an object of challenge. It is widely acknowledged that for Indian artists of the 1940s, the prime struggle was less against the colonial and more against the nationalist legacy—against the baggage of 'Indian-style' painting and the tyranny of a 'spiritual' Indian aesthetic. This critique of nationalism, which activated new modernist art trends since the 1930s, came to be deeply ingrained into the entire later history of modern Indian art.

Yet nationalism, I would argue, remains the central frame of all discussion concerning modern Indian art, whether of the post- or the pre-independence period. Fifty years hence, it is only within the discursive parameters of the 'nation' that we can conceive of any kind of sequential narrative that brings together all the diverse and dispersed strands of art practices in independent India. Similarly, it is only by engaging with the various dominant layers of nationalist histories that we can access sections of a relevant past that can lead a historical context to the developments of the last 50 years. This essay does no more than offer some selective vignettes of this early past in the spirit of a continuing debate about the nature of the 'national/modern'—laying open the multiple claims over how we piece together this formative phase of the nation's modern art history. There is no attempt here at a complete or representative coverage, only the suggestions of the broadest lineaments of a past for today's modern art world in India.

Mapping the 'Modern'

Let me set out, to begin with, three working categories of the 'colonial', the 'national' and the 'modern' in mapping this historical period. While these categories closely enmesh and overlap, they have also served to conventionally define three chronological phases of this art history unfolding from the end of the 19th century through the first four decades of the 20th century. The 19th century is associated with the proliferation of new westernised forms of art practices in the country, which thrived around the British art schools and the elite circuits of Anglo-Indian patronage. This phase is seen to have had its exemplary product in the most renowned oil painter of the time, Raja Ravi Varma of Travancore (1848–1906), whose fame rested on his application of a perfected formula of western neoclassical painting to the depiction of Indian mythological and classical themes. The turn of the century saw a dramatic turnabout in artistic preferences from the 'westernised' Ravi Varma model to a new model of 'Indian-style' painting initiated by Abanindranath Tagore (1871–1951) in Calcutta. This is seen to mark the critical passage from the 'colonial' to a 'nationalist' interlude in painting and aesthetic discourse of the swadeshi years (1905–11), which generated a powerful agenda for the recovery of tradition and the renaissance of new 'national art' in modern India. The work of Abanindranath Tagore and the movement that grew around him (loosely termed the Bengal School) have become synonymous with this nationalist phase of modern Indian art.

However, it is only with the waning of nationalism and the Bengal School that the first truly 'modern' genres in Indian art are seen to have emerged since the 1920s and 1930s, in the work of artists like Gaganendranath Tagore (1867–1938) and Rabindranath Tagore (1861–1941), in the new directions pioneered by Nandalal Bose (1882–1966) at Shantiniketan, and in the novel paths charted by Amrita Sher-Gil (1913–41) and Jamini Roy (1887–1974). Here, the designation of the first 'moderns' have varied with the separate artistic proclivities of critics and art historians—and on the particular values they placed on individual stylistic innovation, on the affinities with modern European masters or on the return to traditional folk idioms. But the one decisive criterion of this new 'modern' phase was seen to lie in its break with both the 'colonial' and 'nationalist' phases—in its rejection of both western academic/neoclassical art and the stereotype of 'Indian' painting of the Bengal School.

Here, let me briefly turn to the existing art-historiographical canon, to see the ways this history of modern Indian art has been narrated and nationalised (for an elaboration, see Guha-Thakurta 1995: 7–11). Histories of modern Indian art leave us with diverse verdicts as to when the modern commenced, and as to who were its most genuine representatives. We find a interesting sample of such writings in the books of the immediate post-independence years, where the main battle seems to have been fought over the eligibility of Abanindranath Tagore and the Bengal School to fig-ure at the head of our modern art history. Some of the first post-independence histories drew strongly on the legacy of the Bengal School and on its country-wide diffusion over the 1920s and 1930s in constructing the first phase of the 'modern' in Indian art history (see, Appasamy 1968; Rao 1953; Venkatachalam, no date). In the same period, other volumes on modern Indian art, notably the one by W.G. Archer (1959: 33–41), spun out from the 1920s and 1930s the main strands of criticism against the Bengal School, whereby the nationalist movement was marked as a false start only through superseding which could more genuine modernist tendencies emerge on the Indian art scene.

Whether or not Abanindranath's art movement was accepted within the canons of modernity, these histories all shared and re-produced its mythology of the past. Like the nationalist artists and critics, rejecting their immediate colonial past in search of a distant 'great art' past that they could claim as their own, later writers continued to collapse all of the 19th century into a period of decline and degeneration—marked by the dissipation of indigenous pictorial traditions and the spread of imitative academic practices. It was only through a collapse of the historical disjunctions of this period that the Swadeshi artists could reject the period as a whole as a 'distortion' of Indian history, and place themselves on an imaginary line of continuity with the traditions of Ajanta, Mughal and Pahari painting. The compulsions have not been too different for the later practitioners of and commentators on modern Indian art. With them, too, a similar exercise became necessary in incorporating the new modern developments in Indian art within the structure of a national history—in drawing out the underlying threads linking this modernity with an inherited, indigenous past. To fully break the interim spell of darkness and mediocrity, the 'modern' phase had to clearly establish and integrate itself within the continuum of an Indian art history—it had, in other words, to proclaim as much its generic links with tradition as its novelties and innovations.

Both modern artists and writers on modern art have continuously laboured under this compulsion. Following the flickering out of the last lights of traditional Indian painting with the demise of Pahari painting in the late 18th/early 19th century (a scenario that was repeated in several books of the 1950s and 1960s [see, for example, Mookerji 1956: 13–14; Rao 1953: 5]), artists like Ravi Varma and then Abanindranath Tagore were seen to first emerge out of the long night into a new dawn. However, for most writers, neither artist nor phase could adequately carry out the transition to modernity. Such a transition was seen to have been effected only with the break with the Bengal School—with the artistic output of the 1920s and 1930s of stalwarts like Nandalal Bose, Rabindranath Tagore, Amrita Sher-Gil and Jamini Roy.

This constructed lineage of modern Indian art, thrown up by the histories and powerfully reinforced through museum displays such as that of the National Gallery of Modern Art, New Delhi, also remains the backdrop to my essay. It frames my period of study, as also the selection of artists. I wish, however, to intervene in the linear evolutionary teleology of the narrative, by arguing that each artist and trend represented a particular historical option of negotiating the double demands of 'Indianness' and modernity, and that each of these options had ideological resonances that went beyond the immediate period or the individual style. And I find, thus, each of these resisting their conventional placement along a development line under headings like 'westernised', 'nationalist' and 'modern' phases.

Ravi Varma and the Emergence of Academic Realism

To rethink this chronology and canon of modern Indian art history, let me return to the first phase of the 'colonial'—the one most hurriedly passed over in most accounts in marking the transition to the modern period. The 'colonial' has long figured as the most uneasy and embarrassing inheritance. It stands associated with the servile westernisation of tastes of a colonised elite, and the imitative adaptation of illusionist oil painting and the academic realistic style by a new group of Indian artists, spawned by British Indian patronage and new institutions of art education. The persistence of these standards of academic training in our contemporary art schools as essential aids in the making of artists goes hand in hand with our continuous disavowal of these practices within the flow of our modern art history. It becomes imperative, then, to remind ourselves that the 'modern' made its first appearance in the Indian art scene in the prestigious guise of oil painting and the primacy of new realistic, illusionist pictorial conventions. A radically new definition of 'art' and 'artist' was first produced in the encounter with colonial rule and internalised through the mastery of western academic training and new pictorial and printing techniques.

Paradoxically, the status of 'artist' was seldom given by the colonial art schools: it had to be wrested from its institutional space and staked over and above the offered job opportunities of drawing master, copyist, surveyor or draughtsman. The paradox lay in the structure of our formal art education, whose 'colonial' and 'modern' histories were coterminous, whose main purpose was to offer art as a form of technical training and respectable means of livelihood, not as a creative vocation. The academic art school training, inaugurated in British India in the 1850s, still stands fundamental to the modern artistic profession, even as the making of the modern self (with all its connotations of individuality and identity) has always required a transcendence of that training. The tensions clearly lie between the two different markers of the 'modern': one that indicated a new middle-class professional identity and livelihood in art (which constitutes an ancestry for India's entire creed of modern artists), and the other that defined new notions of talent, creativity and artistic genius (which became equally constitutive of the dispensation of a modern artist).

These dual signs of the 'modern' would be played out, partly in the career of Raja Ravi Varma, more in the nationalist belittling and rejection of his artistic legacy. Here, a strong case is to be made (as it has been made in recent times by many scholars) for refiguring a persona like Ravi Varma and his whole model of Indian neoclassical painting within any history of the emergence of modern Indian art (see, for example, Guha-Thakurta 1986, 1992; Kapur 1989; Mitter 1995). In the late 19th century, Raja Ravi Varma, a scion of the royal family of Travancore and a self-taught oil painter, epitomised the arrival of the modern Indian artist on the Indian scene. His career marked the juncture where the changing world of court painting in the south merged with new patterns of patronage, professionalism and commercial success in colonial India. It marked also the maturing and public emergence of the individual 'artist', with the full new status associated with the designation, distinguishing it clearly from those of court, 'company' or 'bazaar' painter. Ravi Varma's singular success at the time lay in his mastery over oil painting and realistic portraiture, his access to elite commissions, and his usurpation of the coveted place and status of the European artist in India.

Ravi Varma also articulated, through his choice of genres and themes, a first conscious bid for a new national identity in art, negotiating traditional content with 'modern' form. Oil painting and the academic realistic style, as they appeared in his work as the modernised art form of the time, became the means of visualising a new body of Indian imagery—a range of regional, feminine, and classical and mythological figure types, each purposefully posed as 'Indian' (Plate 3.1). Since the 1870s we see this implicit nationalist quest for typically 'Indian' images shaping the direction of Ravi Varma's work, leading him from commissioned portraiture to a series of ethnic figure compositions of Indian women to themes from Hindu mythology and Sanskrit literature (Plate 3.2).

Plate 3.1
Ravi Varma, 'Lady with a Mirror' (oil, c. 1873)

Collection: National Art Gallery, Government Museum, Chennai.

Plate 3.2
Ravi Varma, 'Hamsa-Damayanti' (oil, c. 1899)

Collection: Sri Chitra Art Gallary, Department of Museums and Zoos,
Thiruvananthapuram.

This pageantry of Indian female figure types, classical *nayikas*, Hindu gods and goddesses, and dramatised mythological episodes, all visualised with what were then the most privileged representational techniques and conventions, provide us with some of our earliest examples of the nation's modern art. Yet there is a clear problem and tension in this acknowledgement. For we find that largely the same genre of pictures have also come to typify for us specimens of a vulgarised mass-produced calendar art form that grew out of Ravi Varma's art in the same period. The problem was lodged at the core of the exceptional career of this first of our modern Indian artists: a career that moved from the exclusive portals of aristocratic patronage and salon art to engage with popular tastes and mass picture production. Here is the case of a uniquely successful princely artist, courted by the Maharajas of Travancore and Mysore, Baroda and Udaipur, feted by our early nationalists and art critics, who is also driven by the immense popularity of his mythological paintings to establish his own press in the outskirts of Bombay in the 1890s to launch the mass production of his new brand of mythological paintings. Herein lay the roots of the artist's displacement: his quick slide from neoclassical to kitsch. Mass production came with its own logic of standardisation, duplication and loss of finesse. Towards the end of his career, we see the artist producing paintings purely for reproduction by the press, we see the circulation of his mythic imagery in newer and highly distorted types of print incarnations, just as we also see the widespread piracy of his pictures by numerous other presses that cropped up around Bombay and Poona—transforming the Ravi Varma style into a brand name for a new highly marketable form of popular print picture (Plate 3.3). In many ways, this one move towards mass production both made and unmade the 'modern' artist. While it turned his model of Indian art into a mass phenomenon (the staple of a new popular picture trade), it also signalled Ravi Varma's fall from grace—his banishment from the canons of 'high art' and 'modernity' in Indian art history. The first of our new creed of modern Indian artists was lost to the mass market, largely a victim of his own success, as I have elaborated elsewhere (Guha-Thakurta 1995: 19–20).

Ravi Varma in history not only stands within a once-thriving, now largely devalued, world of our academic salon artists, his pictorial output also stands within a wider milieu of changing popular art

Plate 3.3
Ravi Varma, 'Shakuntala Writing a Love Letter to Dushyanta'
(oleograph, c. late 1890s, Ravi Varma Picture Depot, Malavli-Lonavla)

Private Collection: Courtesy, The visual archive of the Centre for Studies in
Social Sciences, Calcutta.

practices of the time, which saw the large-scale appropriation of
western techniques and new realistic norms by 'bazaar' painters
and print makers in the creation of a new religious and mythic
iconography (see, Guha-Thakurta 1992: 78–116) (Plate 3.4). Like
Ravi Varma's art, this spreading scenario of borrowings and adaptations in the domain of popular urban art (often operating outside
any identifiable circuit of western training) complicates the whole
story of the westernisation and modernisation of Indian art. It com-
pels us to interrogate the 'colonial' branding of the multiple strands
of academic/realistic art practice that came to prevail in India. It
forces us to probe deeper into the ways in which the local incarnations
of a 'realistic' style in popular religious pictures effectively delinked
the style from its alien 'western' antecedents. It also leads us to
rethink the very polarity of 'western' and 'Indian' styles in a period
that witnessed the continuous intermixing and reinvention of both
categories. It is precisely such a blurring of boundaries between
'western' and 'Indian', 'high' and 'low' art forms that have

Plate 3.4
'Hara-Parvati'
(chromolithograph, c. 1880s, Kansaripara Art Studio, Calcutta)

Private Collection: Courtesy, The visual archive of the Centre for Studies in Social Sciences, Calcutta.

compounded our discomfort with this phase of our modern art history, making it impossible to accommodate it within a smooth flow from 'colonial' to 'nationalist' options.

Abanindranath and the Bengal School

We find that it was only through a re-establishment of these crucial polarities and boundaries that a new nationalist movement of 'Indian-style' painting could effectively stage itself in Bengal at the turn of the century. Throughout the 20th century, the colonial patterns of art, education and academic art practices flourished, as did the Ravi Varma model of mythological painting, a genre which proliferated in varying versions to set the prototype of what came to be subsequently referred to as 'calendar art'. While the one survived as the underside of the world of modern professional art in the country, the other pervaded the domain of our mass visual culture. But neither could figure within the criteria of either the 'modern' or the 'national' in our art historiography. And it is only by positing a sharp shift from the allegeadly 'debased' and 'Westernised' Ravi Varma style to a new 'refined' and 'authentic' Indian style of painting of Abanindranath Tagore that India's modern art history could mark its progress from the 'colonial' to the 'nationalist' phase. The Ravi Varma/Abanindranath Tagore divide became central to the self-positioning of the new Indian art movement (see, Guha-Thakurta 1992: 185–89). Orchestrated at the time by an influential creed of orientalist and nationalist champions of Indian art (art historians and critics, like E.B. Havell and A.K. Coomaraswamy, Sister Nivedita and O.C. Gangoly), the divide has since been continually reproduced in later histories of modern Indian art.

Like Ravi Varma, Abanindranath Tagore also came from a privileged social background. By then, such backgrounds had become an essential component of the new status of the modern artist, as distinct from that of the artisan or bazaar painter. Abanindranath's background can be seen as an even greater endowment, belonging as he did to the culturally elect family of the Jorasanko Tagores of

Calcutta. But what is particularly significant is the way Abanindranath's entire self-image of an 'Indian' artist came to be fashioned
through a set of contrasts with Ravi Varma and the world of academic
art. The commission-based work and commercial success of Ravi
Varma's career now came to be pitted against Abanindranath's
romantic ideal of the artist as a genius, free of the trammels of
education and rules, professionalism and commercial demands.
And it was largely in reaction to the pervasiveness of the Ravi
Varma brand of mythological painting in the popular market that
Abanindranath's art movement strove to recover a new purified
space of 'high art' for the nation. If Ravi Varma had exemplified
a particular creed of the 'gentleman artist' and professional art,
Abanindranath Tagore offered an alternative model of the romantic
modern artist and creative art (see, Mukherjee 1942; Tagore 1944;
1946) While Ravi Varma's art set off a new wave of mass picture
production, Abanindranath and his school established for the first
time a new institutional sphere of bourgeois art practice: a sphere
where the power of the rich patron stood replaced by that of the
critic and writer, where the taint of the mass market was kept at
bay by the cultivation of a discerning middle-class art public.

Let me get back to the fundamental issue of the break in style
achieved by Abanindranath, alongside a break in the very ideology
of artistic creation. In contrast to Ravi Varma's arduous struggle
to master the techniques of illusionist oil painting, we have Abanindranath opting out of formal training and initiation in academic
art methods very early in his career. Against Ravi Varma's endeavours
to capture the full tactile presence of persons and objects on canvas,
we have Abanindranath's rejection of realistic simulations (along
with the whole medium of oil painting), and his evolution of a
counter-style (his famous miniaturised style of wash painting),
that deliberately underscored the materiality and tangibility of
the painted image. Under this new dispensation, painting became
less about the challenge of representation or the perfection of
technique, and more about the invocation of mood and feeling
(Plate 3.5).

Just as there is a great need to recover Ravi Varma art from its
'colonial/western' designations, there is an equal need to rethink
the scope and implications of the 'nationalist' intervention in art
brought about by Abanindranath and about the nature of this
new creed of 'Indian' painting he engendered. A run-through of

Plate 3.5
Abanindranath Tagore, 'Abhisarika' (water-colour, c. 1900)

Collection: Indian Museum, Calcutta.

the art-critical writing of those Swadeshi years reveals the highly
charged aesthetic and emotive connotations that adhered around
his celebrated 'Indian-style' painting. One could, however, argue
that the force of this new nationalist intervention had only partially
to do with the evolution of Abanindranath's 'Indian-style' painting—
a style whose 'Indian' pedigree was, in any case, endlessly debated,
both by contemporary opponents and by a host of later critics
and writers. It had as much to do with a new wave of orientalist

reinterpretation of Indian art history and aesthetics that sought to retrieve India's artistic past from western calumny and misinterpretations. Reversing the East–West hierarchy in art, the new art history foregrounded the ideals of the 'spiritual' and 'transcendental' as the essence of the Indian tradition. For the modern artist, too, the issue of 'Indianness' in art came to devolve centrally on the invocation of this imagined 'spiritual' aesthetic.

The return to the historical traditions of Mughal and Pahari miniature paintings or to the 'classical' art of Ajanta by these nationalist artists would be heavily couched in the language of this aesthetic. If this brought on allegations of the falsification and invention of tradition, it was the aesthetics that gave their art its privileged mark of modernity. Feeding off this sharpened ideological divide between western and Indian art traditions, the novelty of Abanindranath's work lay in its experiment with this new genre of wash painting that carried through the artistic obsession with mood and emotion—where his 'Indian style' could become a conscious vehicle of the new-found spiritual aesthetics of Indian art. Within a few years, the power of this 'Indian style' dwindled, as it came to be repeated by an all-India following and reduced to a sterile stereotype of conventions and mannerisms. The style and the movement that had bred it increasingly lost its claims to a 'national modern' status. But its vision of India's artistic tradition (as pronounced by writers like Havell and Coomaraswamy) became fixed and institutionalised within a national canon, long surviving the demise of the movement, as the most powerful bequest of the period.

There are other long-term legacies that can be drawn out from this nationalist interlude in Indian art history, pioneered by Abanindranath Tagore's movement. One prime compulsion lies in freeing the artistic personality of Abanindranath from the strictures of the movement that grew around him, and the narrow construct of 'Indian style' painting of his early years. A study of his work of the subsequent decades reveals his highly eclectic talent: his continuous play with different themes, forms and narratives, his move away from classical literary subjects to new types of fables and allegories (Plate 3.6). Since the 1920s we see the increasing retreat of the master from his once-ordained nationalist role into an increasingly private art language and aesthetic sphere, even as his image in history remained trapped within the frame of the Indian art movement he had pioneered.

There is also room for recovering other individual artistic figures from among the first group of students who gathered around the

Plate 3.6
Abanindranath Tagore, 'Red Pigeon' (*Dhakai Durey*) *Hitopadesa* series
(water-colour, c. 1940)

Collection: Rabindra Bharati Society, Calcutta.

'guru', first at the Calcutta School of Art where he came to teach as vice-principal from 1905 to 1912, as then at his salon at Jorasanko, and later at forums like the Indian Society of Oriental Art, set up in 1907. Many of these figures remain to be pulled out of the generalised fold of what has come to be called the 'Bengal School'. There was, for instance, Abanindranath's foremost pupil, Nandalal Bose, who emerged in his early career as one of the active proponents of the 'Indian style', before he launched an alternative trail of Indian painting at the Shantiniketan Kala Bhavan (Plates 3.7 and 3.8). There were also those like Asit Haldar, Kshitindranath Majumdar, Samarendranath Gupta, Surendranath Kar and K. Venkatappa, each of whom evolved their own particular form of stylised 'Indian' painting, and who carried forward the Indian art movement to new centres like Lucknow and Benares, up north to Lahore and down south to Mysore. To follow the careers of Abanindranath's followers through the 1910s and 1920s is to map the all-India spread of the Bengal School, the springing up of new centres and varieties of oriental painting all over the country, and the induction of the art schools within a new nationalist art establishment. Yet, just as Abanindranath in modern Indian art history remains inextricably tied to a given historical role, so also can all these artists find a place in this history only in their identity as 'Aban-*panthis*' (followers of Abanindranath's path) as a part of the master's Indian art move-ment. (For a good synoptic survey of this school, see, Appaswamy 1968: 46–69; *Lalit Kala Contemporary* 1962)

The nationalist art of these years had evolved its most pronounced collective identity around a style that served also as the easiest target of attack and negation in the search for new modern genres. However, I would argue that the real significance of Abanindranath's movement lay less in this increasingly devalued legacy of 'Indian-style' painting and far more in the new ideology of a modern art-istic vocation that it offered, and in the new institutional sites it opened up for modern art activity in the country. In repositioning this 'nationalist' phase in India's modern art history, we need to emphasise the lineage of a new artistic self and a new personalised model of art production that emanate from a figure like Abanindra-nath. We need also to look closely at the tensions between the per-sonal and the professional, between creativity and training, which remain central to the realm of modern art, which are played out

Plate 3.7
Nandalal Bose, 'Partha-Sarathi' (water-colour, c. 1912)

Collection: Indian Museum, Calcutta.

Tapati Guha-Thakurta

Plate 3.8
Nandalal Bose, 'Spring' ('Palash') (water-colour, c. 1931)

Collection: National Gallery of Modern Art, New Delhi.

for the first time in the alternative circuits of art teaching, patronage and practice that emerge under the aegis of the movement.

With the Bengal School we encounter the first sample of a modern art 'movement' in India, one that later loses its momentum to trail off into a 'school'. With this first movement arrives a new exclusive circle of art journals, critics and connoisseurs, a new middle-class art public, a new premium on the cultivation of tastes and initiation into art, new forums for exhibiting and viewing. With it is inaugurated a freshly empowered role of art writing and art reproductions, as the interface between a select world of modern art and its equally select public. Together, these lay out the critical new social space for modern art practice in India, establishing it as both an autonomous and exclusive domain, outside colonial institutions, well above the milieu of mass picture production. Subsequent modern trends in Indian art, even as they overtly abandoned the constricted formula of 'Indian' painting, remained firmly grounded in this institutional site.

The New Modernism

The rejection of the Bengal School and a break with this 'nationalist' phase form the fulcrum of the story of the maturing of a new modern age of Indian art. The break would be as crucial for all the changing artistic choices and identities that swung into limelight since the 1920s, as for the different narratives that emerged for modern Indian art history since this period. 'Swadeshi', we are told by Asok Mitra (Mitra 1962: 19), 'had served its turn, but served better still as it slowly retired from the scene.' Henceforth, the modern in Indian art came to be defined primarily in terms of an outgrowing of a colonial and nationalist adolescence—a freedom from the extraneous binds of 'Indian-ness' in style and theme, also a liberation from the literary and illustrative crutches of painting. On the one hand, the 'modern' in Indian painting took the course of a new openness to contemporary European stylistic invitations; on the other hand, it also sought compelling new roots in alternative sources of tradition, gleaning a different visual vocabulary from various folk and non-classical schools of Indian painting. While the idea of western art came to be expunged of its colonial, academic traits, to be associated with new modernist inspirations, a sense of the Indian tradition was recouped from its earlier aesthetic frames to be located in a new set of visual qualities—like sensual form, flat bright colouring, bold linearity, or two-dimensional imagery. In all these trends, art historians have marked a central shift: the artists' novel engagement with the internal dynamics of visual form (the pictorial language of line and colour, volume and depth) as opposed to the external demands of an Indian theme or nationalist stance. It could be argued that artists like Ravi Varma or Abanindranath Tagore had also worked, in their own ways, with this primary challenge of effective form. In both cases, however, the lessons of their formal experiments evaporated in the historical readings, even as their individual styles slid into readymade formulae for replication. Thus, an engrossment with visual language, like the concern with an individualised artistic personality, came to be seen as the distinctive characteristic only of a new creed of modern Indian artists.

In charting the move away from the 'nationalist' phase to the new 'modern' departures in Indian painting, one can offer a variety of accounts. My narrative will henceforth move somewhat jerkily through a selection of artists and genres. The 1920s, the very decade that saw the all-India spread and institutionalisation of the Indian art movement, provide some of the main turning points. Here our attention turns first and foremost to Rabindranath Tagore's new art-teaching centre of Shantiniketan, the Kala Bhavan, which he entrusted to the charge of Nandalal Bose in 1919–20. For, hereafter, if Shantiniketan replaced Calcutta as the centre of 'national art', it also marked a powerful shift away from the earlier pattern of 'Indian-style' painting. Nandalal Bose's work of these years carried forth the full force of this transformation. We confront it in an enlargening of the scale of his work, an accompanying boldness of colour, line and form, an unusual vibrancy of drawing and brushwork. These stemmed, in turn, from his obsessive interaction now with the natural environment and the physical realities of form, and equally from a new engagement with rural life and various folk art-traditions (Contrast Plates 3.7 and 3.8). Even as art was brought down from its classical, romantic pedestals to be located in the sphere of nature and everyday life, the 'nation' found a new location in the physical terrains and living traditions of 'Village India'. The charisma of Nandalal's art of these years lay in its critical positioning between the old and the new—between a 'nationalist' lineage whose meanings it sharply redefined, and a 'modern' identity which it retained within a distinctly indigenised fold. Nandalal's style (and with it, all of Shantiniketan's art) became the mark of a home-spun model of modernity, one that was purged of any obvious western referrents and parallels, rooted instead in an indigenous natural environment and a variety of eastern pictorial traditions, ranging from Ajanta and Bagh murals to Chinese brush drawings and Japanese woodcuts to the local *patachitras* (see Siva Kumar 1997).

Nandalal, as 'master-mashay' (teacher), takes over at the point where his guru, Abanindranath, left off. In the 1930s we see him commanding the space of the 'modern' in Indian art from his entrenched institutional base at Shantiniketan, riding at the helm of a new identity as both a 'national' and a 'people's' artist, his prolific output spreading from an outpour of sketches, paintings and book illustrations to large public murals. During these years, through the mural painting projects undertaken by Nandalal and his students at Shantiniketan, modern Indian art evolved a novel public arena of activity and interaction. It entered also a new zone of political prominence and participation centering around a close interaction between Nandalal and Mahatma Gandhi during the Civil Disobedience movement. We see Nandalal's national public role culminating in his selection by Gandhi to decorate the pavilions of the Indian National Congress for three consecutive sessions in 1936, 1937 and 1938. And in his famous Haripura Congress panels of 1938—a playful panorama of Indian popular life and culture—we see a rich blending of a 'classical', 'folk' and 'modern' vocabulary in producing an art that could signify the nation (Plate 3.9). In both its choice of form and theme, these panels were concerned with the imaging of village India, with presenting a spectacle of Indian popular life and culture for a national public forum. Drawing freely on the style and material of the Orissa *patachitras*, Nandalal produced this set of 83 panels of folkish figures—cobblers and drummers, ear-cleaners and sword-fighter, mothers and goddesses—in a manner that remained inimitably his own. In one sweeping gesture, a traditional folk idiom was transformed into the style of a modern master and into celebrated symbols of the nation's modern art. The painting of these pictures for a national public forum serves as a critical 'moment' in India's

modern art history. It reflects a dominant compulsion in the art
scene of the 1930s of blending the classical and the folk in the
constructing of a new modern idiom. In different ways, other artists
of the time, too, like Amrita Sher-Gil or Jamini Roy, were driven
in the same way to seek new sources of modernity in an alternative
fund of Indian traditions. Nandalal's Haripura Congress panels,
in a sense, stole the show by tying themselves in with a formal
nationalist project.

However, around the same years, it is largely outside the 'national'
and 'public' parameters of Nandalal's art that we can trace the

Plate 3.9
Nandalal Bose, 'Rati with a Bow', Haripura Congress panel
(water-colour, c. 1938)

Collection: National Gallery of Modern Art, New Delhi.

emergence of the two subsequent 'modern masters' of Shanti-niketan—Benode Behari Mukherjee and Ramkinkar Baij, both close students of 'master-mashay', but both emerging in their markedly different moulds as painters and sculptors (see, Siva Kumar 1997). The whole ambience of Shantiniketan was one that belied any set pedagogy or orthodoxy in art practice. It could allow a persona like Benode Behari (as sensitive an art scholar and writer as an artist) to emerge out of the shadow of Nandalal to indulge in his own style of landscapes, figure and foliage-studies, where he would draw heavily on Chinese and Japanese traditions of ink paintings and woodcuts to draw out of these a range of new compositional and calligraphic potentials. Benode Behari's work thrived on a new analytical awareness of the many modalities that could be tapped in nature, landscapes and these eastern art-forms (Plate 3.10).

Shantiniketan also had room for the rather different 'rustic' artistic personality of Ramkinkar and for the different art language— earthy, raw, sensual—that he developed since the 1930s in a novel genre of open-air monumental sculptures, and also in a series of powerfully stylised oil and watercolour sketches. This rustic image of Ramkinkar (which has been continuously replicated in all writings on the artist) was integral to his self-positioning in a markedly rural habitat, at one with the natural elements and the toiling world of peasants and tribals, even as his formal language opened itself to abstraction, cubism and post-cubist expressionism. With Ramkinkar's work is seen to arrive the 'modern' history of sculpture in India: a late arrival, but one which finally broke the bounds of commissioned statuary and academic realism to explore a new modernist vocabulary and a new genre of elemental and enlarged form in cement and mortar (Kapur 1995). From a romantic, ethereal motif, the Santhal figure (by now, a special symbol of Shantiniketan's art) erupted in Ramkinkar's sculptures as a restless, disquieting, primeval presence (Plate 3.11).

Nandalal Bose's Haripura Congress panels find their equivalence in the subsequent decade in these massive open-air sculptures of Ramkinkar, and in Benode Behari's splendid mural frieze on the medieval saints of India, executed on the eve of independence on the walls of Shantiniketan's Hindi Bhavan (for a detailed study of this mural, see, Chakravarty, Siva Kumar and Nag 1995). Yet, in contrast to Nandalal's work, these other exercises in public art

Plate 3.10
Benode Behari Mukherjee, 'The Tree Lover', (tempera, c. 1932)

Collection: National Gallery of Modern Art, New Delhi.

Plate 3.11
Ramkinkar Baij, 'Santhal Family', (cement and mortar, c. 1938)

Collection: Kala Bhavan, Shantiniketan.

remained distinctly outside an official national fold, seeking their own private space within their niche in Shantiniketan. While Nandalal by this period had been claimed and cast within an official 'national' canon of Indian art, Benode Behari and Ramkinkar in their distinct differences from Nandalal beckoned to the future, offering themselves to new histories of indigenous modernism. Still, we find that Shantiniketan in modern Indian art history keeps demanding its own internal unity, its own composite and collective identity, where Nandalal as 'mastar-mashay' invariably leads on to his two successors, Benode Behari and Ramkinkar— where the three can be placed together as the 'reigning trinity' of the institution.

This points to a central tension between individuals and institutions that have defined this new 'modern' phase of Indian art. Our narratives of the unfolding of fresh modern options in this period would be always centred around individuals, who broke new grounds, who defied classification within established schools and genres. Here, figures like Benode Behari and Ramkinkar (in their individualised standing within an institutional centre like Shantiniketan) hark back to other independent, non-institutional figures who are seen as the first pioneers of modernism in Indian art. Breaking chronology, we could mark other inaugural moments of our modern history in the 1920s, in an artist like Gaganendranath Tagore (brother of Abanindranath) and his series of 'cubist' compositions of haunted interiors, mystery figures and somnambulist landscapes (for a detailed account, see Ratan Parimoo 1973: 88–110) (Plate 3.12). Or we could turn back in the same period to Rabindranath Tagore's unique pictorial output of doodles, drawings and paintings in coloured ink, that present us with an exceptional instance of a purely personalised, introspective art. In either case, the most pronounced sign of the modern was to be found in the artists' independence from the surrounding genres of oriental painting (whether of the Abanindranath or the Nandalal variety) and their deep probings into the formal language of art.

The two Tagores thus laid out another route for the entry of the modern in Indian art, opening out their art for comparisons with the European cubist, futurist and expressionist painters of the time. In the one case we have Gaganendranath's versatile incursions into Japanese-style brush painting, caricature and stage decor, leading to his experiments with the splintering of space and the

Plate 3.12
Gagagendranath Tagore, 'Swarnapuri/Dwarakapuri'
(water-colour, c. 1925)

Collection: Rabindra Bharati Society, Calcutta.

prismic refractions of light and colour. In the other we encounter the strange, equally personalised and introspective, visual world that sprang out of the poet's manuscript erasures, where an array of angular designs, bizarre beasts and savage figures coexist with brooding heads and luminous landscapes. We find both artists tackling the post-impressionist innovations with light, space and depth through their own chosen medium of watercolours or coloured ink. No doubt, both drew inspiration from the exhibition of the German Bauhas group (the first exhibition in India of contemporary European art), which they organised in Calcutta in 1892. However, analogies drawn between Gaganendranath, Rodchenko and Feininger (by Parimoo) or between Rabindranath, Klee and Kandinsky (see, Archer 1959) have also served a different tactical purpose—they made the interaction with the new currents of European art the enabling condition for the shaping of India's own modernist trends.

This provides the most opportune point to bring into the picture the other celebrated exponent of a new modern Indian painting of the same period—the young Amrita Sher-Gil, freshly returned to India in 1934 from a training at the Ecole-des-Beauz-Arts, Paris, launching on a passionate rediscovery of her 'Indian' artistic self and roots. It is through her that the scenario of contemporary European art, both its academic pedagogy and a range of new Fauvist colourist trends, is seen to have made its most decisive intervention in redefining the course of modern art in India. Amrita Sher-Gil's has remained the most complex and resonant of our new modern legacies. The reasons are many: a mixed Sikh-Hungarian parentage that made of her (in her own and for all later times) an enigmatic blend of the East and West in art; a flamboyant and youthful artistic persona with her sudden death in 1941 has left eternally emblazoned in our modern art history; a gendered identity that has singularly empowered our post-independence generation of women artists; an open articulation of pictorial choices and di-lemmas that have provided the most distinctive markers of a modern artistic self-image.

Let us confine ourselves here mainly to the last theme—to see how, with Amrita Sher-Gil, the strengths of academic realism, life study and oil painting re-enter the modern Indian scene, freed of colonial guilt, open to a new engagement with Indian pictorial traditions. We can mark the refiguring of the academic tradition in Sher-Gil's bold explorations of the nude female form from live models: paintings that bear often an affinity with Gaugin's Tahitian nudes or Modigliani's figures. We also see the artist uncovering through oil painting a way of working beyond realism to capture the warm colours, flat tones, the spatial structures and compositional intricacies of traditional Indian painting. Amrita Sher-Gil, in her brief career, takes us back to the traditions of Ajanta and Pahari miniature painting, through routes entirely different from that of the Bengal School. She also sets out her own agenda for 'Indian' themes and forms—trying to evolve a particular Indian facial type and physiognomy in her posed studies of 'hill' men and women; exploring a range of ethnic figure tableaus of village girls and banana sellers, haldi grinders and storytellers (Plate 3.13). The agenda culminates in her south Indian trilogy of 1937, done under the direct impact of her visit to Ajanta—in the figures of 'Bride's Toilet', 'Brahmacharis' and 'South Indian Villagers Going to the Market' (Plate 3.14). Sher-Gil's work, like that of Nandalal or Ramkinkar, is driven throughout by the same restless urge to

Plate 3.13
Amrita Sher-Gil, 'Two Seated Women' (oil, c. 1936)

Collection: National Gallery of Modern Art, New Delhi.

embody the 'popular', to make the ordinary, village people of her country the subjects of her art. We see this compulsion growing from the sentimental melancholy of her earlier faces and expressions to the stilled iconic presence of her 'Brahmacharis'. These figures

Plate 3.14
Amrita Sher-Gil, 'Brahmacharis' (oil, c. 1937)

Collection: National Gallery of Modern Art, New Delhi.

in her oil paintings assume the same monumental and allegorical aura that Ramkinkar would impart to his rough-hewn sculpted figures.

In a period when the definitions of the 'modern' had come to devolve on the crucial site of village India—on the refiguring of its images and traditions—our discussion cannot round off without a brief turn to one more pioneering figure of the 1930s: Jamini Roy, whose career would stretch well into the 1960s and early 1970s, when he came to be established as one of the doyens of modern Indian art (one of its ready-to-hand recognisable names). It is in him that a reinvented entity of Indian painting acquires its most reified, canonical form. Here, we find a new modern phase in Indian art history being enacted through a strategical denial of its 'modern' traces. We see this in Jamini Roy's attempt at submerging his modern, art-school-trained middle-class identity within the idealised persona of the traditional craftsman—in his staged retreat from his modern, professional circuit into the nostalgic world of Bengali folk painters.

In a way, synoptically Jamini Roy traverses the whole history of modern Indian art in his early years before arriving at this juncture. We can follow him through his academic training in the Calcutta School of Art in the early 1920s to some of his early ro- mantic studies of Santhal women that carry residues of Bengal School mannerisms. Thereafter, we encounter his brilliant forays into a post-impressionist colourist genre of landscapes, and his parallel fascination with the local art forms of Kalighat painting and Vishnupur terracottas. Emerging out of this history, his negoti- ation of a 'traditional' indigenous identity is rich in modern ironies: ironies that also permeate the work of contemporaries like Nandalal or Ramkinkar. Thus, while the artist broke with various aspects of his bourgeois art circuit (abandoning oil painting, for instance, to begin grinding his own earth colours), his art continued to be figured in fully modern terms—as a part of his quest for a personal idiom, as an example of Indian primitivism or as the expression of a Left cultural ideology.

Likewise, the 'folk' elements in his art (the flat bright colours, rhythmic outlines and decorative stylisation) came to be stamped with the insignia of a special Jamini Roy style. Extracted, tamed and reduced to a neat patterning of forms, the 'folk' in Jamini Roy's paintings easily converted into a highly marketable model of middle-class art. Side by side with his toiling blacksmith, Jamini Roy's women figures—his Radhas, Gopinis, Pujarinis and mother- and-child figures—provide us with a new brand of middle-class feminine icons (Plate 3.15). It lay in the logic of Jamini Roy's great success that his art came to suffer something of the same fate that had attended the art of his predecessors Ravi Varma or Abanindranath Tagore. Even as the artist finds his secure place in our modern art canon and his paintings become by the 1940s the reigning specimens of Bengali modern art, we see his reinvented 'folk style' receding into a standardised formula, to be repeated, not least by the artist himself. The master, like his originals, would be lost in a flood of perfected copies.

On the Eve of Independence

My ending of a historical background at this point is necessarily arbitrary. It could well be alleged that my story of the emergence of modern Indian art trails off precisely at a time when one of the

Plate 3.15
Jamini Roy, 'Pujarinis' (tempera, c. 1940s)

Collection: National Gallery of Modern Art, New Delhi.

most exciting phase of this modern history erupted in India's metropolitan centres in the aftermath of the Second World War, in the new progressive art movements being forged in Calcutta and Bombay, Delhi and Madras. The move away from the nationalist past most dramatically culminates in these movements, in which internationalism was the key agenda. They discovered in forms ranging from critical realism to fauvism and abstract expressionism some of the most powerful modernist aesthetic for their times. From the growing concern with popular traditions and a people's art— that we see variously manifested in Nandalal, Ramkinkar or Jamini Roy—we move directly into the new spurt of 'social realism' of the Calcutta Group of Artists (formed in 1944), and into the period's most haunting images of human suffering in the Bengal Famine. Much of the new modern art of the earlier decade can be seen as laying the grounds of both an international modernism and a socialist ideology that reach their high point in the work of the Calcutta Group, even more so in that of the Bombay Progressives in the immediately post-independence years.

However, in choosing to look back from this point rather than look ahead—in framing a modern time-span that goes back from the pre-independence decades to the end of the 19th century— one of my main intentions has been to firmly reintegrate the sense of the 'modern' in Indian art with its 'colonial' and 'nationalist' antecedents. It is only in conceiving of this early modern history as a broadly composite unit that we can break with the teleology of the 'colonial', 'national' and 'modern' as three successive phases, and understand the complexity of their interactive engagement throughout these years. The 'colonial', then, can move out of its narrow confines of the British art schools and academic art practices to feature as the decisive condition in the making of a modern Indian art history. And all the different artists who make up this early modern period can be positioned at the other end of a funda-mental colonial watershed, where they can be seen as inhabiting a common modernised space that the ideas and institutions of colonial rule had carved out for art in indigenous elite society. Similarly, the category of the 'national' can be separated from the restricted phenomenon of the nationalist art of Abanindranath Tagore and the Bengal School—and invoked as a central constitutive force in the shaping of new artistic identities in modern India all through this period. It can then encompass as powerfully the art of Ravi Varma as that of his antagonist Abanindranath, as well as the new modernists of the 1930s and 1940s, who rebelled against the inherited canons of both academic and oriental art. In fact, in these post-nationalist years, we see the power of a national history freshly reasserting its presence in the constant attempt at dislodging modern art from its western context, in the continuous assertion of cultural difference, and in the ceaseless search for Indian authenticity. The national remains, then, the crucial mediating site where a distinctly modern art history found its unique Indian location.

References

Anand, Mulk Raj (1989). *Amrita Sher-Gil*. New Delhi: National Gallery of Modern Art.

Appasamy, Jaya (1968). *Abanindranath Tagore and the Art of His Time*. New Delhi: Lalit Kala Akademi.

Archer, W.G. (1959). *India and Modern Art*. London: Allen and Unwin.

The Art of Jamini Roy: A Centenary Exhibition Volume (1987). Calcutta: Jamini Roy Birth Centenary Celebration Committee and Birla Academy of Art and Culture.

Chakravarti, J., R. Siva Kumar and Arun Nag (1995). *The Shantiniketan Murals*. Calcutta: Seagull.

Chatterji, Ratnabali (1990). 'The Artist in the Studio: Jamini Roy and Consumer Society', in *From the Karkhana to the Studio: Changing Roles of Artists and Patrons in Bengal*. New Delhi: Books and Books.

Dalmia, Yashodhara (1996). 'The Quest for Significant Form' in *The Moderns: The Progressive Artists' Group and Associates* (Exhibition Catalogue). Mumbai: National Gallery of Modern Art.

Dey, Bishnu and John Irwin (1944). *Jamini Roy*. Calcutta: Indian Society of Oriental Art.

Guha-Thakurta, Tapati (1986). 'Westernisation and Tradition in South Indian Painting in the 19th Century: The Case of Raja Ravi Varma', *Studies in History* n.s. 2(2).

―――― (1992). *The Making of a New Indian Art: Artists, Aesthetics and Nationalism in Bengal, 1850–1920*. Cambridge: Cambridge University Press.

―――― (1995). 'Visualising the Nation: The Iconography of a National Art in Modern India', *Journal of Arts and Ideas*, 27–28: 7–40.

Jain, Kajri (1997). 'Producing the Sacred: The Subjects of Calender Art', *Journal of Arts and Ideas*, 30–31: 63–88.

Kapur, Geeta (1995). 'When was Modernism in Indian Art', *Journal of Arts and Ideas*, 27–28: 105–26.

Lalit Kala Akademi (1982). *Nandalal Bose Centenary Volume*. New Delhi: Lalit Kala Akademi.

Lalit Kala Contemporary (1962). 1 and 2 (inaugural numbers).

Mitra, Asok (1962). 'The Forces Behind the Modern Art Movement' *Lalit Kala Contemporary*, 1: 15–19.

Mitter, Partha (1995). *Art and Nationalism in Colonial India: Occidental Orientations*. Cambridge: Cambridge University Press.

Mookerjee, Ajit (1956). *Modern Art in India*. Calcutta: Oxford Book & Stationery Co.

Mukherji, Benode Behari (1942). 'The Art of Abanindranath Tagore' and 'A Chronology of Abanindranath's Paintings' *Vishva Bharti Quarterly*, Abanindra Number.

Nandkumar, R. (1995). 'Raja Ravi Varma in the Realm of the Public', *Journal of Arts and Ideas*, 27–28: 41–56.

Parimoo, Ratan (1973). *The Painting of the Three Tagores: Abanindranath, Gaganendranath and Rabindranath*. Baroda: MS University of Baroda.

Raja Ravi Varma: New Perspectives. New Delhi: National Museum.

Rao Ramchandra, P.R. (1953). *Modern Indian Painting*. Madras: Rachana Publications.

Sheikh, Gulammohammed, Vivan Sundaram, K.G. Subramanyam and Geeta Kapur (1977). *Amrita Sher-Gil*. Bombay: Marg Publications.

Sheikh, Nilima (1997). 'Amrita Sher-Gil: Claiming a Radiant Legacy', in Gayatri Sinha (ed.), *Expressions and Evocations: Contemporary Women Artists of India*. Mumbai: Marg Publications.

Siva Kumar, R. (1997). *Shantiniketan: The Making of a Contextual Modernism*. New Delhi: National Gallery of Modern Art.

Subramanyam, K.G. (1978). *The Moving Focus: Essays on Indian Art*. New Delhi: Lalit Kala Akademi.

——— (1986). *The Living Tradition*. Calcutta: Seagull.

——— (1992). *The Creative Circuit*. Calcutta: Seagull.

Tagore, Abanindranath (1944, 1946). *Apon Katha* and *Jorasankor Dhare*. Shantiniketan: Vishvabharti.

Tryst with Destiny: Art from Modern India, 1947–1997. Singapore: Singapore Art Museum, 1977.

Veniyoor, E.M.J. (1981). *Raja Ravi Varma*. Trivandrum: Governemnt of Kerala.

Venkatachalam, G. (no date). *Contemporary Indian Painters*. Bombay: Nalanda Publishers.

4

Divided by a Common Language: The Novel in India, in English and in English Translation

Meenakshi Mukherjee

Translation Studies: A New Field

Translations have always been a vital part of Indian literary culture, even when the word 'translation' or any of its Indian language equivalent—*anuvad, tarjuma, bhashantar* or *vivartanam*—was not evoked to describe the activity. The *Ramayana* and *Mahabharata* have been retold in almost every Indian language, and stories not only from Sanskrit but Arabic and Persian have also freely travelled from region to region through adaptations and modifications. Folk tales circulate in India, as they do all over the world, paying scant heed to language boundaries. In the early era of the novel in India, many English novels were indigenised in various languages, sometimes with necessary modifications to give them a local habitation and a name. Translations, adaptations, abridgements and recreations were overlapping activities, and it was not considered important to mark their separate jurisdictions. I grew up reading abridged children's classics in Bangla, ranging from the *Iliad, Sindbad the Sailor, Les Miserables, The Three Musketeers* and *Twenty Thousands Leagues Under the Sea*, many of which, I am ashamed to admit, I never went on to read either in the original or in fuller versions in later life. Neither did I feel particularly deprived.

What has changed in the situation now that we are focusing on translation as field of study rather than the natural ambience we live in? It is certainly a more self-conscious act today, which is being discussed more than ever before; it is the theme of many current seminars and workshops. In the last quarter of the 20th century an academic discipline has evolved—first in the European and North American universities, and now gradually making its way to our shores—which concerns itself with the semantic, cultural and political issues involved in the act of linguistic transfer and the history of this act through the centuries. As in other disciplines in the humanities and social sciences in India, in fact much more so, people working in the field of translation studies cannot get very far by being derivative of the western model. The complex linguistic dynamics within the country and the ambivalent position of English in present-day Indian culture (simultaneously as a local as well as a global medium) create, along with the porous language boundaries[1] and many other factors peculiar to India, a unique configuration. This cannot be analysed by existing translation theories that originate in Europe. But we need to gather a great deal of empirical data on the situation in India before theoretical tools of our own can emerge.

Decline of Mutual Translations in Indian Languages

Even without statistical surveys, certain diachronic changes in translation practice in India seem fairly apparent. In this essay I am going to look at novels only. Translation of novels from one Indian language to another, which was a major conduit of cultural transmission within the country for nearly a century, seems to have declined in recent decades. It has made way for a new activity which is fast growing in visibility—translation of Indian language fiction into English. In the early part of the 20th century, Marathi readers knew Bankimchandra Chattopadhyay through direct translations from Bangla. Hari Narain Apte, a major early novelist in Marathi would have been known in the neighbouring regions in Kannada or Telugu versions. Lalithambika Antherjanam (1909–88) acknowledges the early influence not only of Rabindranath Tagore's novel *The Home and Outside*, but of a much less known Bangla writer Sitadevi Chattopadhyay on her Malayalam writing.[2] I have met several north Indian readers who casually assumed that Saratchandra Chatterjee was originally a Hindi writer, such was the widespread availability of his novels in translation, and his grassroots popularity in regions outside Bengal! In my classroom in Jawaharlal Nehru University at Delhi, with a cross-section of students from all over the country, I used to come across even in the late 1980s, an occasional student from Kerala who knew Premchand's *Godan* or Tarashankar Bandopadhyay's *Arogya Niketan* through Malayalam translation. Such readers are far fewer in number today than they were a generation ago.

To me this decline is a matter of regret for several reasons. Transferring a text—say, from Hindi to Bangla or from Marathi to Kannada—is a far more natural and satisfactory activity both for the translator and the reader than when the same novels are rendered into English. In the latter, negotiating semantic and cultural hurdles to achieve equivalence of meaning tends to be a relatively uphill task. I say this in full awareness of Sapir's statement (1956: 69) that 'no two languages are ever sufficiently similar to be considered as representing the same social reality'. It is true that even neighbouring languages do not inhabit identical universes. Still intersecting penumbras of meaning between two languages in the subcontinent are likely to generate a richer resonance of recognition and discovery than the against-the-grain 'elevation' into the master language of the world with a certain inevitable attenuation of specificity. The target audiences are also very different in each case. The potential readers for an English translation of, say, a novel by Shivaram Karanth or Manik Bandopadhyay, would be an indeterminate and undifferentiated mass, situated either in the same region or in another part of India. Among them some may have rural hinterland in their background not entirely unlike what these writers draw from. Some may be cosmopolitan urban Indians in the metropolis with no exposure, either direct or literary, to subaltern Indian life. Or the reader may be in another country altogether, with no previous knowledge of the ethos being represented. As a result, the anxiety of communication gets reflected in an explicatory or dilutionary tendency. But the translation, say, from Gujarati into Hindi or from Oriya into Bangla, used to be undertaken for a very specific and well-defined audience and, consequently, the nervous uncertainty about decoding culture would be less evident. Moreover, when a local language text gets translated into a global and economically stronger language like English, there is an implicit and inevitable hierarchy involved in the process. As Susie Tharu and K. Lalita

(1991: xxii) have pointed out: 'Translation takes place where two, invariably unequal worlds collide, and . . . there are always relationships of power involved when one world is represented for another in translation.' Since most Indian languages in which novels were published occupied roughly parallel spaces in our culture—specially when viewed in relation to the master space occupied by English— the hierarchy of power might have played a lesser part in these mutual translations.[3]

I speak in the past tense not because such translations have ceased altogether, but because they are no longer perceived as important literary activity in the respective languages while every English publisher in Mumbai, Chennai or Delhi is hastening to add titles in translation to their existing catalogues to keep up with the times. Only in the realm of drama does the state of mutual translation continue to be relatively healthy and vigorous. Perhaps the general dearth of good plays in India makes the theatre world conscious of the need to share whatever is available. Mohan Rakesh, Badal Sirkar, Girish Karnad, Mahesh Elkunchwar, G.P. Deshpande, Satish Alekar and now Mahesh Dattani travel from language to language with ease, to be performed successfully in different parts of the country, although not all these translated scripts achieve the permanence of printed books.

But in the genre of the novel, mutual translation is by and large a neglected literary activity at present, while a growing number of people—many of them connected with English teaching at the college and university level—are trying their hand at translating Indian language texts into English. Some amount of translation activity does continue in languages like Hindi and Malayalam, traditionally more hospitable to texts from other parts of India than some other languages. Over the decades these languages have been enriched by this ready receptivity. In contrast, Bangla is a poorer language to the extent that although eager to translate from European literature, it has been stubbornly resistant to contemporary writing from the rest of the country. The alleged literary superiority of Bangla is a matter of history now, but the arrogance perpetrated by myth continues to the present day. The few available Bangla translations from Tamil, Urdu or Marathi are all officially undertaken projects, sponsored by the Sahitya Akademi or the National Book Trust. They reflect neither popular interest nor literary predilections.

The Indian Novel in English Translation

In 1996, when a three-cornered project called Kaveri-Ganga was launched as one of the many activities of the Katha imprint to produce direct translations among three languages—Bangla, Tamil and Kannada—the real difficulty turned out to be identifying bilingual translators.[4] Evidently, proficiency in two Indian languages is no longer the marker of sophistication and culture that it had once been in India. The few capable translators located after an intense search turned out to be all elderly and retired people—a vanishing breed. Among metropolitan youth today, even among those interested in literature, literary knowledge of even one Indian language—not to speak of two—is considered redundant if one has proficiency in English. Global monolingualism is the aspiration of the younger generation today.

In July 1999 the Kaveri-Ganga project succeeded in producing three slim but excellent volumes in Tamil, Kannada and Bangla. But amidst the din of publicity of books with bigger marketing budgets, not much has been heard of this modest venture, even in the respective languages. Since success depends not so much on the intrinsic quality of books but on strategies of publicity and distribution, books translated from one Indian language to another may never compete with translations into English, which have, to begin with, an all-India urban market, and potentially a bigger one in other English-speaking countries.

However, once we accept the inevitability of this change as the consequence of globalisation, we should perhaps also be looking into the positive potentials of this publication boom of English translations from Indian language fiction, instead of merely regretting the decline in mutual translations. Hypothetically, Bhalachandra Nemade's Marathi novel *Kosla* (in English translation *The Cocoon*) or O.V. Vijayan's Malayalam novel *Khazakinde Itihasam* (in translation as *The Legend of Khazak*), both much acclaimed in the 1960s in their respective languages, now become available not only to Indian readers who do not read Marathi or Malayalam, but also to readers in Australia, Canada, Britain or the USA should they want to read these books. How widely this is actually happening is a question that I would like to take up a little later.

It is not that English translations of Indian fiction are an entirely new phenomenon, but until the 1960s it had been, barring a few exceptions, a sporadic cottage industry. The author himself or his friends would attempt amateurish translations of isolated texts and bring out limited editions privately, and these were hardly ever commercially distributed. In the 1960s came a few organised ventures, done by Jaico Paperbacks, Hind Pocket Books and Asia Publishing House. There was also an excellent series sponsored by UNESCO, which made well-known novels like *Pather Panchali*, *Umrao Jan Ada*, *Chemmeen*, *Garambicha Bapu* and *Putul Nacher Itikatha* available in English. But that was a trickle compared to the spate we witnessed at the turn of the century. Except for the UNESCO project, which in any case did not originate here, Indian publishers in the 1960s did not display much professionalism in their enterprise. Very rarely would there be an attempt to introduce the author or the text or to provide a suitable frame to help the un-initiated reader. Sangam Paperbacks, an imprint of Orient Longman in the 1970s, was the only exception, and might have, without too much fanfare, paved the way to the more systematic activity we have been witnessing in the next two decades. There is now a careful selection—or at least a semblance of it—of the texts to be translated, an attempt to provide a suitable context for each text through an 'Introduction', 'Translator's Preface' and 'Notes', and a consciousness about the need for quality control over the texture of the language. The latter, however, is an activity fraught with controversy. It seems the policy of certain translators is to achieve smoothness and ease of reading at any cost while others take a deliberate position that the language of translation must contain syntactical as well as lexical reminders that the source text comes from another culture. One recalls that the editors of the influential two volumes of *Women Writing in India* were the earliest to formulate the second position:

> We have tried therefore (not always successfully) to strain against the reductive and often stereotypical homogenisation involved in the process. We preferred translations that did not domesticate the work either into a pan-Indian or into a 'universalist' mode, but demanded of the reader too a translation of herself into another socio-cultural ethos. (Tharu and Lalita 1991: xxii)

As a result of such articulation of positions, there is now a consciousness about the issues involved, and a debate about criteria in evaluating translation.

The imprints that have high visibility today in this area of fiction translation are MacMillan India, Katha, Seagull Books, Penguin India, Disha Books, Affiliated East-West, Kali for Women, Stree— not to speak of institutions like Sahitya Akademi and National Book Trust. Even a research centre like the Indian Institute of Advanced Study in Shimla has of late been publishing translations from Hindi and Urdu. The total number of Indian fiction texts available in English translation today is not negligible, even though it is only the tip of the iceberg when compared to what remains untranslated.

Salman Rushdie's breezy dismissal in the introduction to his *Vintage Book of Indian Writing* (1997), of literature in the 'vernaculars' (his term, not mine) on the grounds that he could not find good enough English translations need not concern us unduly. Surely it cannot be our responsibility to ensure that everybody in the world has easy access to all that we possess. In any case, some of the most enduring novels in each of our languages are virtually untranslatable because of their local and specific frames of reference and the play upon variations of language and dialect. These invariably suffer attenuation when translated in English, but may not suffer as drastically when translated into another Indian language. One example is Tarashankar Bandopadhyay's *Hansuli Banker Upakatha* (1947), a novel that would figure in my personal list of 10 best novels of the world in the 20th century, which has never been translated into English, perhaps because the caste/class/tribe interaction in the novel is represented partially through variegated registers of speech. Incidentally, an excellent Hindi translation of this book has been available for some years. Similarly, a Bangla novel called *Aranyer Adhikar* (1979), which to me is the best work of Mahashweta Devi, is still not available in English although some of her short stories are. But this novel has been translated into Hindi, Telugu and a few other Indian languages a couple of decades ago. There may be more such examples in languages to which I do not have access.

The totality of our fiction texts available in English translation does not compare with what actually exists in any of the major languages of India. But quantitatively it can compare favourably with, say, Indian novels originally written in English, which used to be a trickle earlier, but have become a steady stream in the last two decades, gaining in volume daily.

The Politics of Translation: Writing in English vs Translating into English

Thus, we have two numerically comparable sets—Indian novels *written* in English and Indian novels *translated* into English—and the asymmetry in their reception might be something worth looking into. The novelists who choose to write in English—at least the best of them—attract international media attention, their books sell in other countries as well as in India, and get translated into several European languages. While writers like Vikram Seth, Vikram Chandra, Rohinton Mistry and Arundhati Roy are reviewed and interviewed widely, invited for readings to different corners of the world, not many outside the borders of India have heard of Ismat Chughtai, Gopinath Mohanty, Shivaram Karanth or Shirshendu Mukhopadhyay who write in Urdu, Oriya, Kannada and Bangla respectively. But language does not have to be a barrier to accessibility because English translations of at least one novel by each of these writers is available quite easily for anyone who would care to look for them.

But who should care to look for them and why? Books do not exist in the abstract realm of aesthetic value alone. People often read books because the desire to read a specific text is created through advertisement and discussion in the media, and the books are then seductively marketed like any other consumer product. Alternatively, they are read if put on reading lists in academic courses. One of the reasons for their relative invisibility may well be that translated novels are brought out mostly by Indian publishing houses that neither have large advertising budgets nor a promotional network to project their books outside the country. The question to ask then is why is it that multinational publishing concerns—generally based in London or New York—never touch translations from India, whereas they do, now and then, publish and promote Indian novels written originally in English? The standard reason

put forward to explain away this omission—poor quality of translations[5]—does not seem adequate because translation is no longer
an entirely amateur activity in India. The entire question of who
decides the criteria for good translation throws up issues about
the hierarchy of cultures. The natural superiority of an original
novel over a translated novel cannot also be sustained as a reason
at a time when all the old adages propagating the secondary status
of a translated text have been challenged and discarded. 'Translation
is the reverse side of the carpet', 'the translator is a traitor', 'poetry is
what is lost in translation': such clichés of an earlier era are now
anathema to translators and translation theorists the world over
who see translation as a creative and interpretative act. In this al-
tered state of consciousness when the earlier metaphors of inequality
between the original and the translation (master/slave or male/
female) are being turned upside down, one has to look for other
reasons why multinational publishers do not consider taking up
translations from India. This is especially pertinent because the
same publishers have no difficulty in publishing and selling translations from Colombia, Argentina or the Czech and Slovak Republic
and securing worldwide media coverage for them.

Many will recall that in 1989 Timothy Brennan proposed and
gave currency to a new category of writers called 'The Third World
Cosmopolitans', who are globally visible, whom the reviewers in
the *New York Review of Books* and *Times Literary Supplement* hail
as interpreters and authentic voices of the third world. According
to Brennan, this group includes Gabriel Garcia Marquez, Mario
Vargas Lhosa, Isabel Allende, Derek Walcott, Salman Rushdie,
Bharati Mukherjee and a few others. These writers emerge from,
and often write about, a non-western culture, but their mastery
over the current idiom of the metropolitan metalanguage of narrative
ensures their favourable reception in the world centres of publication
and evaluation. It is interesting that even though this list includes
Latin American writers who have been translated into English,
the precondition for belonging to this club for an Indian is that
s/he must write originally in English. Implicit here is an erasure
of the diversity of India.

There is also a pedagogical factor in the dissemination of books:
when prescribed in university curricula, novels certainly get a
wider currency. Unfortunately, in Indian universities, English

departments by and large continue to be orthodox in their course of studies, and even though some might prescribe Homer or Dostoevsky or Ibsen in English translation, inclusion of Rabindranath Tagore's *Gora* (1909) or O. Chandu Menon's *Indulekha* (1889) is strongly resisted on the grounds that a student of English must be given only books that are composed in that language. I speak from personal experience of being involved in such debates in board of studies meetings in several universities.

Less explicable is the absence of translated Indian novels in the post-colonial literature courses in the numerous English departments of universities in the USA, Canada, Australia and several places in Europe. The proliferation of these courses is partly in response to the increasing multicultural components of their own population, and partly due to an ideological climate that emphasises the need to open out the eurocentric academia to the plurality of the world. These universities are far more innovative and the teachers there have greater autonomy in the selection of texts than what the system allows in India. Yet, when these courses include Indian texts, they invariably bring in R.K. Narayan, V.S. Naipual (who for some reason often qualifies as an Indian), Salman Rushdie, Anita Desai, and sometimes younger writers in English like Rohinton Mistry or, more recently, Arundhati Roy. The only two writers sometimes to be included who do not write originally in English are U.R. Ananthamurthy (only his novel *Samskara* was translated into English by A.K. Ramanujan) and Mahashweta Devi (the short stories translated by Gayatri Chakrabarty Spivak).[6] In both cases the translators' credentials in the American academy and their appropriate mediation of the texts (through commentary, interpretation and prefatory material) may be as much the reason for such inclusion as the intrinsic quality of the texts themselves, because work by these authors translated by others have not received similar academic attention. For example, Ananthamurthy's second novel *Bharatipura*, also available in English translation, to me a far more complex and nuanced work foregrounding an individual situated at the cusp of history and very different from the fable-like quality that marks *Samskara*, has hardly been critically noticed outside Karnataka. The attraction of *Samskara* to those outside its culture milieu may well be the timeless, allegorical quality of the protagonist's existentialist dilemma. *Bharatipura* on the other hand presents an intricate web of predicaments, tangled in caste and class tensions, and kinship and ritual patterns peculiar to that region of Karnataka and a specific moment of time. Although the shifting configuration of a community's public and private value systems are its major focus, the novel cannot be simplified into a bipolar tradition/modernity dialectic. The stubbornly local and regional novels in the Indian languages, at least the best of them, generally resist such reductive readings, often refusing easy accessibility to those outside the culture. This may be one of the many reasons why some of the best novels from India do not find a ready readership abroad. Novels written originally in English on the other hand do not take for granted too many unarticulated cultural assumptions because they are addressing a heterogeneous audience.

Indo-Anglian Writing: Anxiety of Communication

Indian writers in English have for a long time been engaged—though not always self-consciously—in the construction of a clearly defined and recognisable India. Long ago, in the early 1960s, Raja Rao presented an Advaitic/Brahmanic perspective on life in *The Serpent and the Rope* and called it an 'Indian' view. R.K. Narayan's Malgudi has a broadly metonymic relationship to India even though at closer scrutiny it may turn out to be a Hindu upper-caste pan-India, eternal, immutable and on the whole benign. This is very different from the towns we know from Indian language novels—Maryganj in Phanishwarnath Renu's *Maila Anchal* (Hindi, 1954; available in English translation as *The Soiled Border*) or Purnea in Satinath Bhaduri's *Jagori* (Bangla, 1946; available in English translation as *The Vigil*). Both are specifically located on the map of north Bihar, variegated in terms of caste and sub-caste, language and dialect, and in the throes of constant turmoil. Or take Shivpal-ganj in Srilal Shukla's *Raag Darbari* (Hindi, 1968; available in English with the same title), which is so convoluted in its local politics that the comfortable pastoral dichotomy between rural wholeness and urban depravity gets completely subverted. Because the original target audience of the English novel about India is different from that of the specific audience of the Hindi or Bangla novel, certain shifts in representation become inevitable. The novelist in the Indian language seems more involved with the local and the particular, compared to the national project in English, which has a greater anxiety to appear 'Indian' because the target readership is diffuse and may include those who have no first-hand experience of India. This anxiety sometimes manifests itself in a pull towards homogenisation, a certain flattening out of conflicting contours, a glossing over of the changing dynamics between individuals and groups in a fluid and plural society.

It is not only the earlier writers who felt the need to construct a unitary and recognisable India. In a book published as recently as 1997 (*Love and Longing in Bombay* by Vikram Chandra) the author calls for five sections—'Dharma', 'Bhakti', 'Kama', 'Shakti', and 'Shanti'—disembodied signifiers for India that promise to live upto the unambiguous 'otherness' of the title. *The Mistress of Spice* (1997) the second book by California-based Indian writer Chitra Banerjee Divakaruni, contains the kind of exotic colours to evoke the country that might have embarrassed an Indian language writer: 'my birthland, land of aquamarine feathers, sunset skies as brilliant as blood'. In this tale of a mysterious eastern woman, the distinctly 'Indian' flavour of the title is intensified by naming the sections 'Turmeric', 'Red Chilli', Peppercorn', 'Lotus Root' and ending, for good measure, with a climactic chapter called 'Maya', in case the seasonings have not been sufficiently cooked in! Since English is used in many regions across the globe, there is perhaps an urgency to announce the specific Indian location fairly early in a novel, if not in the title itself. This might explain why even a promising first novel like *The Madwoman of Jogare* (Sohaila Abdulali 1998) begins with the following clichèd sentence: 'The koel sat in the tamarind tree and called urgently.' To reader from a temperate climate, 'koel' and 'tamarind' would quickly establish the novel's 'otherness'.

Certain words, objects and concepts are associated with India in the popular imagination outside the country, which the writer in English may be tempted to deploy as short cuts to create an ambience. Any project of constructing a national identity is predicated upon two simultaneous imperatives: an erasure of differences within the border and an accentuating of differences with what

lies outside the border. The English writer in India automatically
achieves the first because s/he does not have an obvious regional
or linguistic constituency within the country, and the second is
facilitated when a recognisable Indian essence is pitted against
an equally unitary and similarly constructed 'West'. The imperative
to essentialise India through evocation of local colour or standard
signifiers is naturally less perceptible in the Indian language novel
where intricate tensions of community, religion, caste, language,
region and class assume a greater immediacy and the question of
Indianness is seldom addressed. In this context, Jorge Louis Borges'
comments on how 'what is truly native can and often does dispense
with local colour' is worth remembering. U.R. Ananthamurthy
(1979: 105) quotes this passage from Borges as an epigraph to
one of his essays:

> Gibbon observes that in the Arabian book par excellence, in
> the Koran, there are no camels; I believe if there were any
> doubt as to the authenticity of the Koran, this absence of camels
> would be sufficient to prove it is an Arabian work. It was written
> by Mohammed, and Mohammed, as an Arab, had no reason
> to know that camels were specially Arabian; for him they were
> part of reality, he had no reason to emphasise them . . . he
> knew he could be an Arab without camels.

Had the *Koran* been written originally in English, the presence of
camels might have been unavoidable. While all generalisations in
literature are hazardous, and one always looks forward to exceptions
that would challenge truisms, Borges' camel might, for the sake
of convenience, serve as a suitable metaphor for the differential
representation I have been trying to describe. In India the constituency of readership is determined by the language of original
composition. Even when a Hindi or Bangla text is translated into
English, the subtext of assumptions and references do not always
get easily transferred to another culture. Thus, the fates of the
Indian novel in English and the Indian novel in English translation
might continue to be dissimilar in the global market. But there is
a potentially large domestic market to justify the present surge of
translations into English.

Notes

1. For example, the poet Vidyapati is claimed both by Bangla and Maithili, and Meerabai's language has elements of both Rajasthani and Gujarati.
2. 'A Woman Writer's Reply' in *Cast Me Out If You Will: Stories and Memoirs* (Antherjanam 1998: 53). The translator in her introduction to the volume informs us that the Malayalam translation Lalithambika read was done by B. Kalyani Amma in 1921.
3. It would, however, be simplistic to assume that Indian languages, either in their own self-perceptions or in the perceptions of each other, had equal partnership in a common literary endeavour. The discrepancy in the numbers of translations from and into a particular language is one of the indices of this inequality. For example, many Bangla novels were translated into Kannada, Malayalam, Telugu and Marathi, but very few novels from other Indian languages were translated into Bangla. This, however, does not substantially alter my argument in this essay.
4. My data about this is derived from conversations with Enakshi Chatterjee, the Bangla coordinator for the project.
5. Dilip Chitre expressed this view categorically in an earlier version of his paper in this volume.
6. The data for these comments on the courses of study is based on my experience of interacting with students and researchers during my teaching assignments and lecture tours in the USA in 1990, 1997 and 1999, in Canada in 1992 and 1997, and Australia in 1993 and 1996.

References

Ananthamurthy, U.R. (1979). 'Search for an Identity: A Viewpoint of a Kannada Writer', in Sudhir Kakar (ed.) *Identity and Adulthood*, pp. 105–17. New Delhi: Oxford University Press.

Antherjanam, Lalithambika (1998). *Cast Me Out If You Will: Stories and Memoirs*, translated into English from Malayalam by Gita Krishnankutty. Calcutta: Stree.

Rushdie, Salman (ed.) (1997). *Vintage Book of Indian Writing*. London: Viking.

Sapir, Edward (1956). *Culture, Language and Personality*. Berkeley: University of California Press.

Tharu, Susie and K. Lalita (ed.) (1991). *Women Writing in India*, Vol. I. New York: The Feminist Press.

Part 2

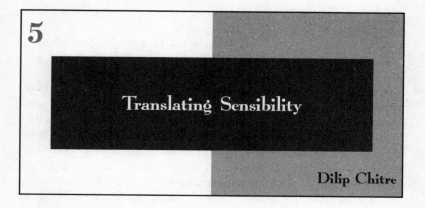

5

Translating Sensibility

Dilip Chitre

I speak as a translator and not on behalf of translators. I am neither a philosopher of translation nor an expert theoretician of comparative literature. I am simply a practising translator, and mostly I translate poetry from Marathi to English and vice versa. I am also a poet in both languages. I state this at the outset so that nobody expects from me anything loftier than what follows.

A statement about my background might help. I am a product of a pluri-lingual cultural environment. I was born in Vadodara, Gujarat, and although my mother tongue is Marathi, as a child I spoke Gujarati equally fluently. The Marathi spoken in Vadodara is, in fact, a distinct dialect of Marathi coloured by the Gujarati of the former princely state of Baroda. As a child I learnt two more languages: I picked up Hindustani—the lingua franca of Gandhiji's undivided India—from the streets, and English from my first school, which was run by Jesuits. I love languages and kept acquiring and losing them during my adolescence and throughout my adult life. This love has shaped my life both as a creative writer and as a translator. Behind my love of language is an instinctive curiosity and attraction for all others who communicate and wish to be communicated with. Perhaps there is even an empathy or a metalinguistic telepathy behind all this. I do not think that my background makes me unique. A large number of people in India and even in the rest of the world are like me. I also believe that with increasing mobility and speed of communication, the inborn pluri-lingual abilities of more and more human beings will be stimulated and awakened in the future. In other words, I see a great future for literary translation, out of which may emerge a

truly pluralistic global literary tradition. At present, no such tradition exists. But during this century, as English developed into
an international language sweeping across the world, it adapted
itself to a vast variety of 'native' and 'vernacular' idioms and language habits. It has already become different from what it used
to be in England in the 19th century. As for American English,
its idiom is the 'melting pot' of the former languages of its immi-
grants, and in the near future the 'globalisation' of English will
facilitate the entry of more and more languages and literatures of
the world into English. This is going to cause a lot of dismay to
literary and linguistic purists, and one imagines that it will be
comparable to the situation created by the emergence of *dalit*
literature' in Indian languages. These speculations excite me and
give me the optimism necessary for one who initiates translation
projects, some of which take decades to complete. The translation
of poetry is in itself an eternally contested concept. It is also a
hazardous practice with doubtful rewards, if any. Though many
of the most creative literary minds of every era in all major literatures
have engaged in translation with a consuming passion, philosophers,
linguists and literary critics have regarded the activity with deep
suspicion or scepticism. I mention this only to define the climate
of opinion in which a translator must continue to function.

One can now turn to the theme of my article: translating sensibility. By 'sensibility' one means 'cultural sensibility', which consists
of a complex set of responses to or in a given situation. When I
translate from Marathi into English, in technical jargon the Marathi
text I translate is the SLT or 'source language text' and the English
text I produce is the TLT or 'target language text'. My SLT is
'situated' in a culture whose sensibility is different from the new
text I produce in the target language culture, which is located or
situated elsewhere and has its own distinct sensibility. My SLT is
uniquely positioned in space and time, has its own historical trajectory and course of development, and is a unique modification
or 'embodiment' of a universal concept and category, namely 'poetry'.
There is a Marathi concept of poetry and an English concept of
poetry, just as there is a Marathi concept of music or architecture
and an English concept of those arts. The fundamental similarity
between a Marathi home and an English home is the fact that
both of them are human dwellings. However, they are and look
different because they have been built by different communities

in different environments. It is only when such different communities cross paths, confront one another, overlap or converge that a dialogue develops between then and they discover that they share the concept of home even though their actual homes differ in detail, and for very good reasons. Once they understand the reasons for the difference, they not only appreciate the ingenuity of each other's homes, but are ready to imagine themselves in the other's place, and thus enjoy the other's unique world-view. Translation is thus a complex inter-cultural negotiation that goes on continuously between and among different cultures that are historically thrown together in an ongoing intra-specific process of adaptation and cross-fertilisation, and throws up a variety of mutations. They are symbolic and symptomatic of what happens during evolution. It implies that languages and literatures continuously and inevitably interact. This process reflects the historic progress of mankind itself, in a nutshell.

I will now try to put into perspective two of my translation projects in the context of a historically developing interaction between Marathi and English as languages and literatures. I have translated the 13th-century Marathi poet Shri Jnandev's (A.D. 1275–1296) text *Anubhavamrut*. The first point to be noted here is that Marathi culture had not started interacting with English culture in the last decade of the 13th century when Shri Jnandev produced this text, which is a 3200-line poem articulating a mystical doctrine and a spiritual experience at its core. There is nothing in English or any other western literature known to me that renders such a theme and its conceptual components as poetry on such a massive scale. The sheer architecture of this text is awesome. The content and the form of *Anubhavamrut* can be comprehended only after considerable foregrounding not only in Sanskrit poetry and poetics in general, but also in religious philosophy and the world-view of Shaivite cults such as the Natha order as well as the Kashmir school, which preceded Shri Jnandev by at least three centuries. An English reader 'entering' the poetic text of *Anubhavamrut* is in the same situation as an English art lover discovering the Kailash caves at Ellora. That the rock carving involved great architectural and sculptural creativity would be obvious to the English art lover chancing upon the caves. The human forms represented in the sculptures would also have immediate as well as deep significance of a universal nature. Yet the cultural ethos of the sculptures and the architectural design, and the nuances of 'meaning' carried by it would escape the English art lover. He would have to revise his eurocentric concepts of art and modify his artistic sensibility to accommodate this newly revealed 'foreign' vision of art. The English reader of poetry would have to make similar revisions and modifications in order to 'place *Anubhavamrut*' in his literary experience, awareness and knowledge. This can take years and generations of continuous cultural interaction and critical evolution. Perhaps it will also take generation after generation of translation to internalise Shri Jnandev and *Anubhavamrut* into the English awareness of literature. Until this happens, it will remain an exotic text with an element of 'otherness'. This applies generally to all translation from any language into any other because there always is an element of 'otherness'—of different degrees—between cultures that translation attempts to reduce and bridge.

Marathi and English started interacting some time by the end of the 16th century and during the reign of Shivaji in the latter half of the 17th century translation between the two languages took root. Thus, Tukaram, an older contemporary of Shivaji, was not familiar with English literature. Turakam, incidentally, was born in the same year as John Milton (A.D. 1608). But within the same century, the English East India Company (founded in London at the end of the 16th century) developed a flourishing trade with India and found opportunities to become a major political player in the subcontinent. Eventually, the Marathas and the English contended for subcontinental hegemony. The latter lost decisively only in 1818. By this time, the English had begun in earnest to study and translate from their foe's tongue. They compiled the first modern dictionary of the Marathi language, which translators like me still consult. The first major literary work to be translated into English under their own initiative was the collected poems of Tukaram, and this was accomplished at the beginning of the 20th century. Anglo-Marathi cultural interaction, of which translation is a central feature, has gained momentum during the last 150 years. My own recent translation of Tukaram's selected poems is a tiny event in this vast ongoing process.

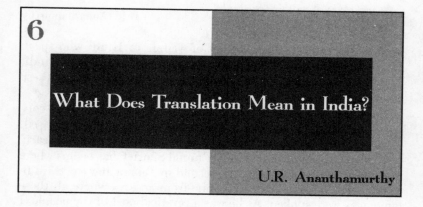

6

What Does Translation Mean in India?

U.R. Ananthamurthy

I must try to change our academic notion of the word 'translation' and make it more homely if I want to make some sense of what I want to say here. Let us look at ourselves in our everyday speech activity. Most of the time we are translating from one language to the other. Many of us use at least three languages, one at home, another on the streets, still another at our office. When you narrate to your old mother what happened in your office, you are translating. And vice versa.

This is not just an aberration of contemporary urban life. I can imagine Adi Shankara using two languages, Malayalam in Kaladi and Sanskrit everywhere he went. And he travelled quite a lot, from Kanyakumari to Kashmir through a complex web of languages. Anandateertha in Udupi must have used three languages, Tulu at home, Kannada on the streets and Sanskrit everywhere else. Ramanuja was inspired by the low-caste saints, the Alwars of Tamil, but he used Sanskrit for his metaphysical speculations.

We live everywhere in India in an ambience of languages. The term 'mother tongue' does not mean what it means in Europe. Conrad is an exception writing in an alien tongue. We can count such geniuses in Europe on our fingers. But many of our writers in Kannada, some of them the best in our times, spoke a different language at home. Masti and Puttanna spoke Tamil at home, and the great poet known for his magical use of language, Bendre, spoke Marathi at home. As he once related to me, in his formative boyhood years, he was not even conscious that he spoke two different languages.

This is true of a large number of writers in Hindi who speak Rajasthani, Bhojpuri and many other languages related to Hindi. The characters in their fiction may be actually speaking these languages, and they are rendered for us in Hindi.

More significant than this in our understanding of what constitutes a text is a unique Indian phenomenon often bypassed. Kalidasa's *Shakuntala* is not a text in a single language. An early poet of our times in Kannada, Shishunal Sharief, has poems where the first line is in Kannada, the second in Telugu and the third in what may be called Urdu. He came from an area where all these languages were spoken. As he was a mystical poet of the people, I am sure his immediate audience would have understood all these languages whose co-presence in the same poem must have made unique sense to them. They were listening to the silence beyond the spoken word, especially to the silence celebrated in a variety of words.

This free play of languages existed in an ambience allowing for shifts and mixtures. Because of such free play, aside from hegemonic indications that languages carry with them, the poets of the past could acquire the territory of Sanskrit for their vernaculars. The use of vernaculars never seemed to threaten free communication with others. It did not isolate each language group in its own territory. Such a process of cultural inclusion and quiet synthesis has gone on in India for more than a thousand years. First it was the language of the gods making way for the languages of the common people. Now it is the official domain of English making way, however reluctantly, to the vernaculars in the process of the empowerment of the people. Translation, oral as well as textual, was the principal mode in the past as well as the present for such negotiations.

When languages that do not travel (as they lack imperial power) still undertake spiritual and intellectual journeys into the experiential richness of other languages (that travel and therefore assume universality), then we in India do not seem to bother much to remain literally true to the languages from which we translate. We have to digest these languages of power, lest they dominate us. We rarely translate the Sanskrit 'word-as-mantra' in which the *shabda* is supposed to be both sound and sense to the believer. But we unhesitatingly adapt and change the narrative texts, even when they are composed in the language of the gods or of the white men who ruled us. In Kamban's Tamil *Ramayana*, the cursed Ahalya becomes a stone and not a disembodied voice as in Valmiki's version. And it was not Dryden alone who tried to make Shakespearean tragedies into comedies; our early writers in Kannada did it, too. That is why I would like to propose that if India has been able to digest several influences through its long history, it is mainly because of these vernaculars, the unquenchable imaginative hunger of the people who speak these languages.

I must also add here that these are languages with a difference: they have a front yard of a self-aware literary tradition, as well as a backyard of unselfconscious oral folk traditions that have never been discontinued during our millennium. The oral traditions that flourish in the backyard have vigour as well as an unfailing sense of what is alive on the tongues of men and women without which a literary language can become heavily artificial.

I want now to take up some concrete examples in support of my ideas. Coastal Karnataka has a small town called Udupi, a name made familiar by its inhabitants who have opened restaurants all over India. There are at least three languages spoken in and around Udupi. Tulu is the language of a large number of its inhabitants, the peasants and workers, and it is also a language rich in folklore. Not only do the lower castes speak it, but a Sanskritised version of it, considered impure by the native Shudra speakers, is spoken as mother tongue by the Brahmins as well. Next to Tulu is Konkani, mainly the language of the trading castes.

Kannada exists in Udupi along with these languages. One could say it is perceived as the language of high culture, whatever that means. Kannada is also the mother tongue of a large section of people. However, the point I want to make is this. A large body of Kannada literature in the past as well as the present has come from this coastal region. If one encounters a stranger on the streets, the language used for communication is Kannada. But a Tulu or Konkani speaker encountering other speakers of those languages would invariably use the language native to the speaker. Otherwise it would be considered arrogant behaviour. And almost everyone of the native Tulu and Konkani speakers would understand Kannada *and* if s/he happens to be a writer, most probably the language of choice for writing would be Kannada.

Thus *Chomana Dudi*, a celebrated novel in Kannada by Shivaram Karanth, is written in Kannada. Choma, the hero of the novel is an untouchable, and in real life he would be mostly speaking in Tulu. In fact, one could say that much of the novel takes place in the language of Tulu, and the author Karanth, while writing the novel, is truly translating from Tulu into Kannada.

I wonder if this is not true also of much of the good fiction in English written by us in India. Isn't Salman Rushdie translating from Bombay Hindi in many of his creatively rich passages? The best effects of Arundhati Roy, I feel, lie in her great ability to mimic the Syrian Christian Malayalam. Raja Rao's path-breaking *Kanthapura*, although it is written in English, is truly a Kannada novel in its texture as well as narrative mode, both deriving from the oral traditions of Karnataka. Regarding most of the truly creative Indian novelists in English, who seem to have made a contribution to the way the English language is handled, I would venture to make this remark: for them to create a unique work in English is to transcreate from an Indian language milieu.

I want to conclude with a few comments on what is a topic often written about these days. I mean, 'the politics of translation'. What do we choose to translate from among the Indian texts into English? We often think that we choose the best. This may be so. Yet there are notions of the 'best' that need to be interrogated.

We not only write in a language, but write into an ethos. Kumara Vyasa, a great poet of the past in Kannada, would have made sense to a contemporary of Chaucer, but today, if translated into English, he would be read by a few interested European scholars only. Kannada has a thriving modern literature that would interest a common reader in the West, but Kumara Vyasa is also a part of the literary ethos in Kannada. But Chaucer isn't a part of the living literary ethos in England. As a matter of fact, a non-literate in Karnataka would respond to Kumara Vyasa more genuinely than to a modern writer like me. This makes me feel humble as a writer because Kumara Vyasa has Shakespearean strength in his use of language and is a greater writer than many of us writing into a modern ethos.

A.K. Ramanujan is the best of our translators and when he chose to translate from the past, either from Tamil or from Kannada, we should ask the uncomfortable question: was he influenced by the ethos into which he was translating? Would not a lot of great literature in our languages remain untranslatable if what is good is determined by the literary ethos of the language into which we are translating? I do not know what we can do about it, or honestly speaking whether we should do anything about it. For us writing in India, it should never matter what is translatable into English and what would be acceptable in the literary ethos of the West. If we begin to think that what is good is that which is eminently translatable into the modern western ethos, we cannot be forgiven. Indian literary ethos has space for the ancient as well as the modern, the written as well as the oral. In the silent process of translation as I have defined it earlier, much more of Europe is coming into Indian languages as living literature than in the other direction. I read Saul Bellow as literature, but Premchand is read in the universities of United States of America for sociological purposes. That is their problem, not ours. But that may well become our problem, too, if we should also globalise and become prisoners of the homogenised modern world system.

7

Inter-culturalism and the Question of Body

Anuradha Kapur

The voice of inter-culturalism has a sort of family tie with multiculturalism. The multiculturalist/inter-culturalist voice is in response to monoculturism, which is in some senses the ideological common sense of the 20th century that seeks to homogenise political and cultural entitlement rights, and replace the pre-modern concept of honour with dignity, moral authenticity and equal recognition (Appiah 1994).

Multiculturalism critiques monoculturism on two main grounds: (*a*) that a single standard of universal truth supplants local standards and local knowledge in the name of rationality and egalitarianism; and (*b*) that an abstracted notion of equality allows for a tolerance of difference, which is instrumental in managing and containing economic difference by paying lip service to cultural distinction/difference (see Taylor 1994).

Inter-cultural projects articulate themselves within the boundaries of the following ideas; recognition of collective identities, inserted within that, a recognition of individuality down to its detail, through the body; and framing both these, a desire for a survival of cultural traditions.

In inter-culturalism the recognition of difference is set within a celebratory style, but identities as we know from the long history of race and gender relations can be exclusionary as well. Those who do not belong are denied certain privileges, even rights. And apart from that, identities, though they see themselves as being forged by affinities, may also entrap, make people stay in even when they do not want to. For certain sorts of inter-culturisms constitute groups as givens, but also entrench them as being historically unchanging.

As against the overt problem of delineating Asian bodies in the international context, there is in India an unstated problem of depicting an Indian body intra-culturally, that is, terms of the internal differences that fissure any totalising sense of the nation. This project is spelt out within the terms set up by the official versions of Indian culture, including the inscription of modernity in actual practices.

I wish to work through these ideas with the body—the body in performance—as site of the argument.

'Bodies'—one of the most significant sites on which and by which meaning is made in performance. What are the markers that make a body on stage specific? Costume, movement, gesture, stance— these add up to what would be thought of as standard character, individual, person and, on occasion, even symbol. Yet characters, individuals, persons are located in a *misenscene* and carry corporeal techniques proper to their cultural traditions. For instance, *mudra*s, cultural markers inscribed on and through the body, to make it a more or less readable hieroglyphic functioning within specific conventions and scanned for meaning. The ensemble of naturalistic gestures that actors in the West have interiorised are also part of such conventions.

If aesthetic collectives transfer meanings (which may in time transform and retransform themselves) and these are manifested in actor's bodies, what are the meanings that an inter-culturalist body carries? A body where two corporealities (enactments) are visible at once—cultivated body discipline on the one hand, and cultural habit that has been suppressed, repositioned and reconditioned to allow for the other on the other hand. Thus, the international body produces characterisation, in the main, of one sort alone. Where 'depth' of character is jettisoned for body training, and discourse for cryptic language. A body that has taken on skills, codifications and disciplines from 'other' cultures, and enacts these skills, not as being, but as culture.

To illustrate my point further, let me put before you some very brief thoughts on Peter Brook's *Mahabharata*. In this, bodies of the actor are made Indian first by the costume, then by gesture, by posture (sitting on the ground, for instance), by music, and then by less specific cultural markers.

Of these, location is the least specific and the most mysterious. What geographical, temporal or cultural spaces do these actors inhabit? Where, in specific terms, do these characters live? When I saw the *Mahabharata* I could only read that they were located in a space other than space conventionally coded as European; the atmosphere totalled 'difference'. What needs to be noted here is that specificity does not obligate a strict naturalistic answer; specificity here can mean a particular form from which a gesture is relocated or quoted.

Specificity then puts in place regional details and produces an image that may not be receptive to universalisation. What Peter Brook achieves is a 'feeling' of India, a particular (as opposed to specific) atmosphere that can be sensed as being part of a universalist typification of quaint pre-modern cultures. Dealing with culture as *form* leads in some senses to segregating a particular detail to make that function a *sign* of the whole.

Ariane Mnouschkine's productions are similar to the Peter Brook project in that culture is seen as form, especially to rejuvenate existing European theatrical traditions. Mnouschkine has used Indian theatrical language, ranging from make-up to sylisation quoted from, for instance, *kathakali*, to make a reading of Shakespeare. Stylisation might liberate Shakespearean texts from the grip of naturalism and relocate them within the theatre of blood and thunder reminiscent of Elizabethan performing styles, and whereas this might be seen as producing a 'new' Shakespeare, it might just as well be read as a sort of cultural nostalgia.

Cultural nostalgia, as Rustom Bharucha has so incisively shown, is a sort of reinvention of tradition: heralded as novelty or even innovation, it is almost always set on achieving intelligibility though establishing a continuity with the past. The project to represent Indianness on stage especially promoted by government funding policies of the 1970s has been depicted both as innovation and as excavation of a past.

Mapping the argument again, the body in inter-culturalist terms remains mysterious; its temporality, nationality and temperament are hazy, much in the same way that projects to represent Indianness on stage remain indeterminate. There is, as we know, no pan-Indian costume, language, even gesture. The internal differences themselves fissure any totalising sense of the nation. Even within our own terms today, we can scarcely make a national identity on stage.

I should like now set before you some problems I encountered while directing with Tara Arts[1] in England.

In 1988–89 I worked with Tara Arts to prepare a version of Gogol's *Inspector General*. It was a text that charted its return to the West after several transformations. We based our work on a Hindi rendition of the English text (done by Mudrarakshasa and B. Kaul), and on this version was based the new English text. As the story was located in India, Hindi was also used in the narrative. We wished to work with a narrative that was post-Brecht, as it were. This was a way to designate the making of cultural identity against obvious odds: a scenario where we would be inevitably seen to manufacture oriental versions of ourselves but through and beyond which we, in our own turn, would expose the dominant versions of Indianness abroad.

I wanted to work with a performing style that allowed the actor freedom of movement outside the limits of motivation, but which kept historical causes in place. This was a way of rethinking pre-modern theatre forms still alive in India through the lens of Brechtian theory. We were talking to our traditional forms and the interlocutor was Brecht.

In a sense, this was a reworking of the individuality of the performer, and that means the way that the self is organised on the stage. Whether it is cogent and bound by a thorough individuality or whether it is distributed across narratives, narration, music and stylisation. The structure of the narrative determines that. In this case, it was ballasted or tamped by the chorus that dispersed or focused speech through repetitions, prompts and repartee; the stylised body of the performer implemented gags and circus routines.

But how to read this body? I decided that such a body must not docket into a sort of pre-expressive category reconstructing once again a divide between speech and action. Third world actors are often primitivised when their energy and spontaneity are valorised: the body is a given, the speech is to be learnt. But this was equally a way of resisting the theatrical traditions that were institutionalised in mainstream British theatre as well as in training, which is especially directed towards speech and articulation.

Thus, what sort of voice would emerge from such a body? The question becomes all the more complicated when the Asian actor performs in the English language. From her/his mouth may emerge speech that can range from English drama school style to English working-class slang. The language explodes dominant images of Asianness in England, but the stylisation of the body can yet pull in another direction.

The speech that was finally scripted was 'hybrid, sly, witty'. These words themselves are a stereotype of the strategies of survival available to the post-colonial. But whether they were able to confront the kind of volatility of that existence on edge, I am not certain. Do stylised bodies confront their situations by wit alone—or, put another way, is wit the main tool of transgressing the codes of genteel behaviour produced by western drama school training and etiquette? What form of real hard irony can we produce as post-colonials?

I come now to the discussion of work done in India. In India, of course, the body—speech relationship functions at a different register. At the National School of Drama where I teach, students take a three-year training in, among other things, acting. A modern institution as opposed to traditional structures of learning, which include long-term apprenticeship, already produces different expectations in them. What they seek to learn are ways to explore consciousness, which is another way of saying their individuality, history and social environment. They seek to represent *themselves*, as it were. By doing that, they make an absolutely contemporary body for and *in* India, seeking to reduce the distance between art and life, fixing the body in the temporal frame of our vexed and sullied urban space. Their relationship with modernity and city life is both complicated and strong. They see themselves as urban young persons who do not solicit any pastoral nostalgia.

They do not want to fashion themselves only by the tool kits of traditional stylisations, nor by any omnipresent aura that might be obtainable from popular philosophical and cultural readings about Indianness. For them to make a contemporary reading of gender and character in modern India—a character/body buffeted by displacement, transnational pressures and ruthless machismo—is of passionate importance.

The materiality of this contemporary body is manifested not through changes in the soul, but on the surface, in actions. This is as much to do with pedagogy of identity within a national frame-work as it is to do with acting. By nationalist identity I mean the process of becoming what we are today; how we have been composed and recomposed, as views on nation and community have changed.

The landscape on which this enactment is played is one of debate, confrontations and revisions. The body–nation–identity discussion in which we engage today as one in which Indianisms are inhabited, tested and sometimes rejected for being too tyrannical or accepted for being dignifying. Skin colour, political preference, religious conscription are forces that make up nationality, the nation. Such collective identities may choke off individual autonomies, but that is a debate that we work at every day.

Thus, the inter-cutural in the theatre is something that we battle every day in our practice. We may not recognise it as such, but the task of making a contemporary body in and for India is indeed that task.

The intra-cultural then refers to the search for national traditions, sometimes forgotten, repressed, misrecognised, in order to reassess the vocabularies with which we can represent ourselves today. It is an attempt to recognise the transformations of our vexed cultural traditions.

Imaging Contradiction on Stage

In *Romeo and Juliet*, which I did at the National School of Drama, the students were given two possible acting options to work with: being yourself on stage or finding a being for yourself on stage. Both are about actor control, but both pull in different directions.

Being yourself requires presenting yourself as a model; somehow you have to leaven or refashion yourself. You have to make a life script, or appropriately revise one to suit your story. This one is an enormously fraught demand, and by that I mean one that assumes wholly contemporary and indigenous set of governing factors. On the one hand, contiguity between time, place and milieu of the dramatic action and the dramatic performance; therefore, a closing of distance between art and life. There are no references to hedge the dramatic action back in time from where it is being performed. No brackets that filter you off from your viewers. It is wholly secular, in the broadest sense, as it allows no agency other than yourself to make your script. It is then about recognition, not as Indians, Punjabis, Kannadigas, Tamilians, but about qualities or temperament you choose to mobilise to represent yourself: witty, cunning, passionate, generous, reckless, stylish.

As for the second option: finding a being through models, identification, personalisation even impersonation.

When my students routinely perform Michael Jackson numbers for the entrance audition of the National School of Drama, I wonder whether this is some sort of imitation, or a desire to find a body to house a soul. It might just as well be a brazenly secular authoring of oneself without the markers of specific geographical distance.

In *Romeo and Juliet* the intention was to reduce the classical universalist burden of playing Shakespeare. The translation had many languages, classical Urdu, Sanskritised Hindi and urban slang. Such a language 'set' on the bodies of the actors as if it was their own. They played the language and the situation, not the character.

Teaching Conflict

Pedagogically then, it is necessary to teach conflict. Teaching conflict requires the unmaking of universalist conceptions of identity and also destabilising the notion that certain political and cultural communities are historically changing. (Such is the reading of Asian cultural traditions when they are understood as being perennially poised, spiritual and sacred.) In such a case the performing body is made transcendent—or at least it is sought to be made so. Cultural and historical specificities are cast aside and a pre-national state of cultural/human togetherness is desired. But such embodiment, I suggest, is a masquerade. It is like speaking through the actual material body and voice, a *metalangauge* that is a contradiction in terms.

Bodies are carriers of culture—joy, pain, suffering, loss are scripted on historical bodies. They breathe in temporal moments and often in very local atmospheres. Which means that the actor must see herself or himself as always in the making, being made, responding to the vulgar and many demeaning pressures.

These are the markers, of course, of our contemporary worlds. Teaching conflict means disburdening actors of universalist baggage and making them recognise their individuality, however besieged it might be, however sullied and unremarkable.

But the questions still remain on how to represent this temporal body on stage.

The fixity of the body, its contours, its movements, are fully material, and they will not make sense apart from when they are materialised before us. Gender or temperament thus are not simply what one has, it is not a static description of what one is; it is the way in which we become visible at all. From here we are culturally intelligible.

Mobilising such a body (character, temperament) produces identification, of course, but also dis-identification. Perhaps in theatre practice today this dis-identification—with soap opera characters, mythological beings, classical representations—in a sense produces a re-articulation of our changing selves; it is also a recognition of the rules that bind us into certain preset characters or representations (read poise, tranquility, grace, acrobatic ability, improvisational freedoms, spontaneity).

If characterisation is a social construction, enacted on the surface of the body, then it is in some senses a fiction, perhaps even a fantasy. Inter-culturalist practitioners and we too have to be alert to the various fictions of regional and nationalist identities as they form and reform in our times.

I am not, despite and beyond the above argument, advocating a strictly local cultural politics that proscribes the travel of texts. A great deal of modern Indian drama has been literally built upon Shakespeare or Brecht or Ibsen. These texts are not material to rejuvenate our theatrical traditions, but to joust with our modernity and 'our time'. Perhaps because of our colonial experience we may well have a better grasp of texts that are western than is possible the other way around.

As we know from recent histories, specially colonial ones, transactions are not always a two-way process. So that the same rules do not apply when western intervention/appropriation of say Asian drama/theatre takes place. They may have to undergo a historical procedure and a contextualising effort that would then take inter-culturalism beyond hybridity and eclecticism and global access. By virtue of keeping historicity in place, we may keep theatre from becoming some universal performative mode. Travelling theory, travelling texts and travelling bodies should at least suffer the normal conditions of insecurity, exile and painful translation, after which there is a way to speak and to inhabit. By that stage the local is everywhere because it is a stake in location and the inter-cultural is a fully annotated way of adult/intelligible communication—perhaps on a global scale, but not in a global style.

Note

1. Tara Arts is one of the most distinguished Asian theatre companies in England, and has been active for more than 25 years.

References

Appiah, Anthony (1994). 'Identity, Authenticity, Survival: Multicultural Societies and Social Reproduction', in Charles Taylor and Amy Gutman (eds.), *Multiculturalism*, pp. 149–63. Princeton, NJ: Princeton University Press.
Taylor, Charles (1994). 'The Politics of Recognition', in Taylor and Gutman (eds.), *Multiculturalism*, pp. 25–73. Princeton, NJ: Princeton University Press.

8

Inter-culturalism and Intra-culturalism in Theatre: A Personal Response

Vijaya Mehta

Instead of presenting a statement, I would like to offer my comments and share some questions that arise in my mind.

The discussion on theatre is part of a series organised to commemorate 50 years of independence. The title of the discussion—'Journeys from Inter-culturalism to Intra-culturalism'—therefore presupposes a definite *new*, post-independence awareness reflected in Indian theatre's journey from its regional origins to a pan-Indian entity. It also implies that the journey is always from inter-culturalism to intra-culturalism and does not consider the impact of intra-cultural influences in embellishing and redefining inter-cultural sensitivity.

But, first, a definition of these terms. I comprehend their meaning as follows. 'Inter-culturalism' seems to indicate a process of cultural evolution whereby all performing, visual and plastic arts become an integral part of the lifestyle and cultural fibre of a region, giving rise to a distinct regional character.

'Intra-culturalism' on the other hand seems to refer to conscious efforts with political connotations such as 'unity in diversity'. It is an inevitable outcome of the ongoing contradiction in our society of progress versus tradition.

The concept of inter-culturalism does not need much explanation. Each of us is a living embodiment of our own cultural, social and ethical (regional) traditions, which in fact etch our distinct individual identities. I shall, therefore, concentrate more on the process of intra-culturalism.

I would like to deal with some of the implications of these two concepts by referring to the history of Marathi theatre, which has been my field of work for many years, and, in its context, offer my personal reflections.

The history of Marathi theatre dates back to the latter part of the 19th century and reveals a fascinating web of British influences and their interaction with and acceptance in regional theatre. Exposed to the performances of visiting British theatre companies, Marathi theatre accepted Shakespeare as a part of its repertoire. The Marathi musical emerged as a form, influenced by operattas. These influences were not directly replicated. They were imbibed through drawing from play texts from Indian mythology, religious folk theatre and classical music. Thus, Marathi theatre created its own genre. One can cite *Saubhadra* as an example. Yet another play, *Zunzarrao*, has the storyline of Othello (minus his poetry) and characterisation with local colour, which can vibe with the Marathi middle classes.

All this took place during colonial rule, during a period of political oppression and socioeconomic exploitation. Consciousness of political identity led to political revolt. Yet, on the other hand, the English language and British theatre ushered in a renaissance in Marathi theatre.

During the 1920s and 1930s, an already well-established theatre tradition in Maharashtra region reflected the communities' own ethos. For example, the progressive reform movements of the time were captured in *Sharada*, and the political upheavals by *Kichakwadh*.

This brief glimpse into Marathi theatre suggests an ongoing process of interaction between intra- and inter-cultural forces; it reflects an intrinsic need of the Marathi mind, which found expression in its theatre. It constantly reached out for external influences and imbibed them in its own fibre, thereby enriching its own traditions. In the context of Marathi theatre, therefore, the interaction between inter- and intra-culturalism was at play even during colonial rule. It is not a new phenomenon.

In the post-independence era, the Nehru government, in its effort to create awareness of a pan-Indian culture, established three academies and the National School of Drama. A series of endowment programmes were launched and cultural scholarships established. The institutes were all Delhi based, and the endowments and scholarships were handled by the Department of Culture in Delhi.

Perhaps the reason behind centralisation of all cultural efforts—what I term intra-culturalism—was to create an awareness of a new pan-Indian culture, 'unity in diversity', as the slogan declared.

The central government's conscious efforts did not create any noticeable ripples in Marathi theatre of the 1950s. Despite spurts of innovative theatre work such as *Andhalyachi Shala* in the 1940s, the 1950s remained a lacklustre period for Marathi theatre for various reasons, the emergence of cinema being cited as one of them.

However, with no correlation with the new officially declared cultural institutions and schemes, but due to Marathi theatre's own need to revitalise itself, annual drama festivals were organised in Mumbai. The younger generation started a parallel experimental theatre movement to cope with its own cultural vacuum. Rangayan, the theatre group, was part of this movement. None of these happenings had any connection with the central government's cultural policies.

It was in the 1960s that the Sangeet Natak Akademi held a competition of regional 'play-texts' with the winning texts to be translated into 13 languages. The scheme was an instant success. With availability of translated plays, a movement of inter-regional language plays gathered momentum—initially under the Sangeet Natak Akademi's schemes and later on independently. Plays by Badal Sarkar, Mohan Rakesh, Vijay Tendulkar, and later by Girish Karnad and Mahesh Elkunjwar were translated and performed all over India in different languages.

The crossing of the language barrier led to a new and more significant role for theatre directors. The directorial concept and interpretation of a playwright's text came to the forefront in the presentation of plays. There are three basic factors in the development of the role of the Indian director. First, with an increased level of translation within Indian languages, the same play was presented in different languages by different directors. A qualitative comparison of their work was inevitable and posed a new challenge to the director's capabilities. The second and more important reason was the widening of international horizons. The innovative contributions of directors such as Peter Brook, Grotowsky and Brecht were constantly discussed and analysed, and the role of the director as the prime spirit in theatre presentations emerged on the Indian scene. Third, directors had to take on a new challenge of defining Indianness in their own work in the context of international theatre. Habib Tanvir, Ratan Thiyam, Kavalam Panikker, B.V. Karanth and myself, among others, were recognised as directors with an Indian sensibility. Our work, however, had distinct regional qualities.

Once again, it proved that a forced governmental effort to generate intra-culturalism, as I have defined it, is truly realised only in the regional theatres, through what I call inter-culturalism. For the same reason, the Ford Foundation's efforts to fund and create an Indian theatre identity for international reference created only a temporary ripple. It was directors who had already created a niche in their own regions, well before the Ford Foundation's funding commenced, who survived after the Foundation withdrew its support.

In conclusion, I would like to say that it is the inner need of regional inter-culturalism that generates a process of intra-culturalism, and not an imposed effort by government or international agencies. In this process, regional theatre reaches out for newer horizons and sensitivities, and enriches its own distinct theatre tradition. The composition of the panel on theatre at the Asiatic Society of Bombay illustrates this point. Samik Bandyopadhyay with his Bengali theatre background, Anuradha Kapur representing the Delhi theatre scene and the National School of Drama, and myself as part of Marathi theatre—our works represent distinct regional identities. Yet we have been influenced by each other and have borrowed freely, reaching beyond our regional sensitivities and imbibed diverse influences to make our own theatre repertoire richer.

Inter- to intra-culturalism, therefore, is not a one-way journey but a creative ongoing process of redefining theatre. It is a process that has been going on for 150 years in Marathi theatre. In the 50 years of post-independence theatre, the same process was evident, reflecting the challenges that theatre in each region had to face.

Part 3

9

Stri Shakti: Dimensions of Woman Power in India[*]

Vimla Bahuguna

Indian tradition gives women a high position. The seven vows of marriage emphasise equal partnership of the couple in life. Unfortunately, with the spread of consumerist culture, woman came to be regarded only as an instrument of entertainment, as a commodity, as a procreator of children.

My thoughts go back to Gandhiji's ideas and his work. He was not just fighting for freedom from alien rule. He was in fact constructing a new India. He had radical views on every sphere of life, including that of man–woman relations. In his *ashram*, a man was addressed as *bhai* (brother) and a woman as *behn* (sister). Upliftment and equality between men and women, and togetherness in living (*sahajivan*) were important components of his constructive programme.

Gandhiji had an English disciple named Katherine Hillman whom he had given the Indian name Sarla *behn*. In 1940, on his instructions, she came to Kausani in Almora to escape from the heat and Malaria at Sevagram. She established Lakshmi *ashram* there. This was the time of the nationalist struggle and the young men from the hills also were wholeheartedly with Gandhiji's movement. Sarla *behn*, born in England, had earned the title of being the most dangerous person in the 1942 Quit India Movement and had been imprisoned twice. To understand the situation of the families of imprisoned activists and to extend help to them, she used to travel on foot to many areas far away from the villages. She found that women were not frightened when their sons and

[*] The author wrote this article in Hindi and it was translated into English by Usha Thakkar.

husbands went to jail. They managed the smooth running of their farms and homes with self-confidence. But they were not aware of their inner power. When Sarla *behn* talked about it to them, they used to reply, 'Sister, what are we? We are passive animals.' Sarla *behn* used to feel very upset on hearing this and she decided that she would work to unearth the power hidden within the women of the hills. So she established in 1946 a school for girls named Kasturba Mahila Utthan Mandal in Kausani. Here, to awaken the power and energy of the women of the hills, she started training girls through the method of *nai talim* (basic education) in accordance with the norms supported by Gandhiji. The educational course included agriculture, animal husbandry and health. Along with this, she used to take the students with her to neighbouring villages for practical education. Sitting with the villagers, they would get an opportunity to study their difficulties and problems. Rural women would thus get a chance to become educated and self-reliant. In this way Sarla *behn* trained and prepared a group of young women workers who formed service centres in different parts of the hills and started working there. The results of Sarla *behn's* work became visible after 20 years, when at several places women came out of their homes for picketing liquor shops. This was the first public manifestation of their suppressed hatred and anger towards liquor. They were harassed by the misbehaviour of drunken husbands at home and the rowdy behaviour of drunkards in the villages and on the roads.

The movement against liquor was on continuously from 1965 to 1971. Thousands of women participated in it and around 100 women were jailed with their young children, some as young as one and a half years of age. We organised picketing of liquor shops at Tehri, Dehradun and Saharanpur. I went to jail with my son who was 6 years old. My mother also went to jail. To break the morale of the women, the government put the women in faraway jails, but we did not bend. Ultimately, we succeeded. As a result, prohibition was introduced in five hill districts, which lasted for several years. Later some shops selling foreign liquor opened for permit holders. But the women's movement against liquor is still going on. They could get the shops that had opened at Dhansali and Dhanyaganj closed. Now they are struggling against the shops opened in New Tehri town.

The Chipko Movement was the next movement and the most successful one. It generated a new perspective towards the tree in the minds of the people. Trees in the hills prevent soil erosion. They protect earth and water. The entire economy of the Tehri area was based on natural forests and this was destroyed with the commercial exploitation of forests. The Chipko Movement began as an economic movement to end the *thekedari* or contract system of exploitation of forests to provide raw material from forests to locate small industries and to establish people's rights over forests.

But women had a different way of looking at the forest. For them, the forest was the source of life, from where they could get fodder, grass, fuel, wild herbs and fruits for satisfying daily needs. Water streams arose and flowed from the forest. So, for the women, the forest was like their mother's home.

During the movement to save the trees, women stood with their arms around the trees to be felled. The official slogan of the forest management was:

What are the bounties of the forest?
Resin, wood and commerce.

Challenging this, the women from the hills said:

What are the bounties of the forest?
Soil, water and air.
Soil, water and air,
The basis for staying alive.

This was a scientific truth that they expressed. Women clung to the trees saying:

The axes may shine forth, but we will stick to the trees.
We will face sticks and bullets and save our trees.

They sang:

If you wish to live in happiness,
Let each child hug a tree.

In this way, Chipko was accepted world-wide as the first of the people's movements in the rural areas for the protection of forests. It spread to many states in India and also to many countries. The government was forced to make changes in its policy. Nowadays more attention is given to planting trees and to protecting them rather than to cutting them.

The roots of the Chipko movement lie in our culture, which equates trees with life. The *samskar*, the temperament and training to see divinity in trees is kindled and nurtured from birth. In 1730, in Khejad village near Jodhpur, a Bishnoi woman named Amrita Devi led 363 men, women and children to face the axe of people who came to cut their trees. They died saving the trees from being chopped. Before giving up her life, Amrita Devi said:

If our heads are chopped off but the tree remains,
Know that this is no great price to pay.

Now, a new problem has come upon us in the hills: the building of big dams on the rivers, drowning settlements and displacing people. The tallest dam of Asia—260 m high—is being built at Tehri on the Bhagirathi. Fertile valleys will be submerged because of this and 100,000 people will be directly affected. There has been a struggle going on against it for the last 25 years. Here, too, women have played a major role. They have taken direct action to stop work on the dam and have tolerated the miseries of jail for this. People who were displaced 15 years ago due to this dam and made to settle in the ground areas, which is a big contrast to their natural, social and cultural surroundings, find that life for them in their new environs is hell. Women are the worst hit, so their voices of protest have not subsided.

Now a new age of globalisation for economic progress has commenced in India. The state and multinationals have usurped control over the natural resources of water, forests and land. Women are the worst victims of this because they have to suffer the hazards of displacement. Women play an important role in the movement against displacement.

The basis for women's collective action in the Tehri region is not religion or culture. In the hill regions, people share certain conditions of life. Soil erosion or big dam construction affects all of them. Women as upholders of life are sensitive to this connection. There is a certain sense of connection—*samuhikta*—which brings people together and is the basis for collective action. The culture of sharing is very strong in the hill region.

Women's movement in India is not limited to ending discrimination based on gender. It has a wider meaning. Vinoba Bhave, the exponent of *bhoodan* has named it as *stri shakti*. It means feminine qualities such as empathy, friendship, compassion and love. When these qualities are developed in the whole of society, only then will violence, corruption and inequality end. A society will emerge where everyone will enjoy happiness, peace and contentment.

10

Vimla Bahuguna and the Legacy of Gandhian Politics

Usha Thakkar

Decline of Gandhian Politics

What followed the burning of a train compartment on 27 February 2002 at Godhra was more violence throughout Gujarat, sending danger signals to the very foundations of civil society and democratic polity, and posing the anguished question, 'How could this happen in Gandhi's homeland?' The upwardly mobile and middle classes in the state displayed insensitivity and even support to the pervading communal hatred and violence, thus marginalising the Gandhian legacy. On the one hand Gandhi's name continues to be invoked the world over as an icon for inspirational purpose by alternative movements and people's struggles; yet Gandhians and Gandhian institutions in India today do not seem to have been able to sustain the vibrancy of pre-independence times. Their ability to respond to the overwhelmingly changed scenario and to mobilise the masses on the path of service and sacrifice seem to be limited. The recent communal violence in Gujarat has once again made us aware of the inadequacy of civic and political institutions—traditional, contemporary and Gandhian—to cope with the crisis created by the ruptures of the secular fabric of our democracy.

Indian democracy, right from its inception, has been experiencing tensions arising from the struggle for political equality against the background of social hierarchy and from the interface between the nation-state and emerging ethnic and community identities. Over the years the size of the electorate has increased and the

aspirations of the people have soared; but the political and administrative systems have not been able to provide adequate and appropriate responses. By the end of the 20th century, the Gandhian
ideals of wiping the last tear from the eyes of the poorest man
and establishing an egalitarian society have been overpowered by
a bizarre kind of populist politics with the emergence of the 'vote
banks' (like 'Dalit votes', 'Muslim votes' and 'Rajput votes'). New
market forces with their emphasis on profit-oriented management
are influencing the contours of national development; and the
people, especially the poor and oppressed, are remembered mostly
in election manifestoes. Promised schemes do not bring qualitative
changes in the lives of ordinary citizens. The frustrations of the
people often result in the spurt of violent conflicts around regional,
religious, caste and community identities. The number of such
violent conflicts is alarming. (For a succint analysis, see Varshney
2002).

Gandhi's vision of a non-violent society seems to be a utopia in
these times and his concept of oceanic circles (which establishes
link between the individual, the society and the community) a thing
of the distant past. Gandhi's ideology itself has evoked critiques
from various perspectives. There is a huge body of critical and re-
flective literature on the topic (see, for instance, Parekh 1997,
1999). He is called an idealist who used religion for political purposes, who favoured the policy of compromise instead of confrontation and change, who supported the bourgeoisie, who used women
for his political movement, and a leader who could not visualise
the coming economic and political changes at national and international levels. This, however, does not mean that Gandhi's legacy
is to be found only in the annals of the past. Gandhi lives on.
Organisations such as SEWA and individuals who embody and
extend the Gandhian spirit in their lives and work do exist and
they reassure us about the existential reality of Gandhi's life and
work. Usha Mehta, Ratan Shastri and Sushila Nayar, to name a
few, represent for me such persons who till the very end continued
to live out the Gandhian way of life. Chunibhai Vaidya, at an advanced age, has done commendable work of healing after the recent
riots in Gujarat. Women from Kasturba Ashram do not hesitate
in organising peace marches in the troubled areas of Assam. Many
young activists in rural and urban areas as well as professionals

and common persons draw inspiration from Gandhi's ideas, though all of them do not carry the label of being Gandhians.

Vimla Bahuguna is a Gandhian who has impressed me in her own serene way.[1] Her work with the community and especially with the women of the hills of the Himalayas makes us aware of the fact that such crusaders, in sufficient numbers, can be influential enough to bring about a deep-seated change in India.

Though fragile looking, Vimla Bahuguna has in her life displayed grit and determination that result from a long and continuous struggle for the welfare of people and the environment. Initiated into social activism at the age of 17 by Sarla *behn*, a European disciple of Gandhi, Vimla sees close links among the struggles of individuals, groups and communities, and strives to strengthen them. She represents the spirit of those women in India who made a conscious decision to bring change in their surroundings by putting Gandhian values into practice, especially the values of austerity, non-violence and deep concern for the deprived. She has not seen Gandhi, but as she says she is very much influenced by him in her life, like women participants in the freedom struggle in earlier times and women constructive workers in contemporary times.

Gandhi's Impact on Women's Status

It will be useful here for a better understanding of Vimla's work to touch upon Gandhi's views on women and the impact he had on their lives. Gandhi had a special rapport with women from all backgrounds, regions, religions, castes, classes, professions and age groups. He wrote in *Young India* (Gandhi 1930: 121), 'If non-violence is the law of our being, the future is with woman.' His ideas and work relating to women have, however, not been free from criticisms. It is argued, for example, by Patel (1988: 377–87) that Gandhi's reconstruction of women helped the political struggle led by him, but did not challenge patriarchy. Gandhi recruited women to channel the energies of an emerging women's movement into the political movement he controlled and created a new myth of Indian womanhood. She must be Sita-like in her devotion to service and self-sacrifice, whether to her family or to her nation. The forces of nationalism and feminism, in fact, have remained closely intertwined in pre-independence times. Movements of social reform and freedom widened the horizons of the Indian woman, yet supremacy of home in her life was never questioned. According to Partha Chatterjee (1990), the central problem for Indian nationalism was the problem of modernising the nation on western terms and simultaneously retaining an essential national identity. Nationalist thought dealt with this contradiction by distinguishing the spiritual/inner sphere (meant for women) from the material/outer one (meant for men). The external/public could be influenced by the modern West, but the inner/private had to remain pure, traditional and Indian. For most Indian women the home became the site of resubjection.

Realising the importance of family and home for women, Gandhi devised ways through which women could play a crucial role in the public sphere from their homes. Life stories and testimonies of women who participated in the freedom struggle provide ample evidence for this. Gandhi effortlessly turned traditional symbols and ideals into a source of energy and inspiration for thousands of women. By participating in activities like organising morning processions, spinning and selling *khadi*, picketing of liquor shops and shops selling foreign cloth, holding literacy classes, and spreading the nationalist message of freedom, women could become active agents in the public sphere without uprooting themselves from their homes and without intimidating their family members. They realised that to be powerless is not an obstacle; what is required in the struggle against inequality is inner strength rooted in non-violence and freedom from fear.[2] In his study of women and the anti-colonial struggle in Delhi, Legg (2003) points out that the spiritual space of home was Gandhi's domain and it is within his writings and speeches that one finds the home depicted as a site of agency, not just subjection. Talking to women participants in the freedom struggle, Thapar-Bjorkert (1997) found that a large number of women during the nationalist movement retained their traditional roles and still made significant contributions from within the domestic sphere. Sharing their experiences of participation in the freedom struggle, many women from Maharashtra have said in interviews with me and my colleague Rohini Gawankar that it was possible for them to contribute to the struggle from the precincts of their homes.

Vimla Bahuguna's Life and Work

Vimla's life and work also bring to the surface the blurring line between the private and the public domains. Family and home are important for her, and so are the community and the environment. She is aware of her responsibilities to her home as well as to the community in general and women in particular. The fine-tuning between the two may appear to be submerging her 'self' in her famous husband's work, but a little probing into her life shows that she has a mind of her own, and decisions having an effect on home and family are taken by both of them together. Vimla, in her own life, made the important decision of marrying Sunderlal Bahuguna only after a careful weighing of pros and cons. Young Vimla had found the purpose of her life in her work with Sarla *behn* for the rural deprived and had already been with Vinoba Bhave in his *padayatra* for a year. At that stage she did not want any interruption in her activities. Her father, however, wanted her to get married and had found a suitable match in Sunderlal who was a leading social activist and the secretary of the local Congress Party. Vimla and Sunderlal knew each other since both were working in the same area. Sunderlal accepted the marriage proposal, but Vimla wanted a year to make up her mind. Reflecting on the implications of marriage, Vimla had realised that Sunderlal was involved in party politics and lived in a town, but she was living in a village and could not give up her work among the rural poor. Responding to Vimla's views, Sunderlal took the decision of channelising his own energy also for rural reconstruction. Thus, her inclinations and activities were not disturbed by their marriage in 1950.

The couple started a new chapter in their lives by setting up their little home in the remote and backward village of Silyara, about 31 km from Tehri. They established the Parvatiya Navjivan Mandal and dedicated their lives to people of the area:

We made our hut in the village. There are stories of *Ramayana* and *Mahabharata* in the village. There is Ayurveda. But there are also superstitions. But we had decided to stay in the village. The villagers used to give us a little from their produce. Sunderlal became a journalist. We made our life a laboratory for life in the hills. We did not indulge in lectures.

All these years they have been able to abide by their decision of not taking any grant from the government, but to sustain their work on voluntary help and contributions. Running a low-income rural household has never hindered Vimla's activities related to improving agriculture, providing and propagating a balanced diet with home-grown vegetables and fruits, educating girls (there is now a college for them in the area), working for the entry of *dalits* into temples, and curbing the evil of liquor. It was again their joint decision that Sunderlal would devote more of his time in the villages for spreading the Gandhian message and mobilising people, while Vimla would run their *ashram* at Silyara. This has meant that the bulk of the household responsibilities have fallen on her, but she has carried the burden with dignity and without creating a fuss.

Vimla feels inspired by Gandhian ideology. Talking to women like her, one realises how so many Indian women have discovered their potential and strength under Gandhi's leadership. As Devaki Jain (1986: 255–70) has pointed out, though many of Gandhi's statements on women may seem jarring when read today, Gandhi seems to have been intuitively attuned to women, and to have seen women's potential more clearly than any other political or religious leader in any part of the world. He perceived women to be equal; different. In their difference, Gandhi himself identified with women.

Vimla believes that people, and especially women, have tremendous energy within themselves. But in order to release it for the development of the nation and society at large, they have to be freed from the oppression, drudgery and misery that are present in their daily life. She is, however, aware that the traditional set-up cannot be demolished overnight. She knows the plight of women living in the hills from the experience of living with them. She says: 'I had decided long back that if I wanted to work for them, I must live like one of them.' She and Sunderlal have lived a life of voluntary austerity. Her children studied in the village school like the children of the villagers. She and her husband were busy with the movement and had neither the time nor inclination to give them special treatment. She says, 'I believe in living with voluntary poverty. One does not have to sleep hungry but one has to keep Gandhi's touch alive. There has to be a sound economic basis to life which is not commercial.'

Natural resources and forests have been the lifeline for the people in the hills. The Chipko Movement was a spontaneous response of the people to save them.[3] Vimla has been an important participant in the movement. She remembers those heady days on 1979 when a difficult and prolonged confrontation took place in Badiyargar. At that time, many women were present with Vimla, who stayed in the forest for a month in bitter winter, on the alert, to protect the trees from the axe men. Vimla recollects the impact of the Chipko Movement:

> The awful feeling of hill women that they were considered to be like animals, passive and unchanging, (something that had distressed Sarla *behn* so much) has begun to change. Women have realised that they can change the government's policies if they are organised. They now feel that they are as strong as men, in fact even stronger, because their strength lies in *non-violence*.

The mobilisation of women has been important. But it has also resulted in a situation of conflict regarding their own status in the society. As they increasingly demand a share in decision-making processes, their involvement has generated some questions.

Vimla has been a source of inspiration for women in the hills. The area is infested with the effects of the money-order economy. The men are away somewhere in the cities, earning and sending some money to the women back home, and the latter are managing homes and children on their own. It is no longer a secure place for women. They have to walk miles to get fuel, and have to run their homes with extremely meagre resources. Vimla strives to bring change into their lives by making them aware of the need to preserve forests and environment. She is convinced that if forests vanish, women's independence will be snatched from them. The strategies evolved by Vimla and other women are indigenous, innovative and non-violent, hugging the trees being the most striking among them. They sing, coin slogans, share experiences and make collective decisions. Once, during the hectic days of the Chipko Movement, Vimla and several other women went to the government officer at noon with lanterns to convey the message that the government does not see the obvious. Since 1990 Vimla has been very active in the agitation against the Tehri dam. The earthquake in Garhwal in 1991 almost destroyed the Silyara *ashram*. Without any self-pity, Vimla got busy with the work of repair and relief.

Vimla and Sunderlal have evolved their understanding of nature through Gandhian principles. They firmly believe that nature is not a commodity for consumption. The consumerist culture that is eroding the very basis of the hill region has to be curbed and an alternative culture has to be created. The couple has faced innumerable difficulties, but both have continued their journey in mutual harmony, undeterred. Yet, interestingly, they have grown independently. Vimla has evolved through her unique way of expanding from self to community. She has been the moving spirit behind the Parvatiya Navjivan Mandal, nurtured by both of them over the decades.

When women influenced by Gandhian ideology protest against inequality and injustice, their protest does not acquire the form of direct confrontation with social norms. Gandhi's ideas and way of working have made it possible for women to traverse between their private world of home and public world of political and social activism as well as to earn social acceptance and credibility for their participation. They work without directly challenging traditions, but through their deeds they remould their traditional roles, pushing, extending and even transforming them from within. They create freedom and mobility within these traditional spaces. They invoke some traditions as sources of empowerment, but take care to steer clear of the problematic aspects and also oppose the discriminatory elements within these traditions. Decades after independence, women still have to struggle for equality and justice. This, according to Vimla, calls for educating girls, making women self-reliant, curbing the evil influence of liquor, striving to save forests, working for Gandhian ideals of self-reliance of villages, and resisting injustice with non-violent methods. Without any jargon or grandiose talk, Vimla Bahuguna, the recipient of the Janakidevi Bajaj Award in 1995 for outstanding work for women, practises what she believes in and speaks about; and effortlessly presents a grassroots perspective of the women's movement and people's struggles.

Notes

1. The profile of Vimla Bahuguna was written based on several interviews and interactions with her.
2. For an insightful analysis of Gandhi's views on women see Kishwar (1986).
3. Chipko is one of the most widely known and appreciated people's movements. For details of the Chipko Movement, see Dogra (1992) and Weber (1989). For women's significant role in the movement, see Sundarlal Bahuguna (1984). For Vimla's involvement, see the interview of Vimla Bahuguna by Madhu Kishwar in *Manushi* (1992). For a critical assessment of the impact of the movement on the women's lives, see Jain (1984), Joshi (1984), Sharma (1984) and Weber (1989).

References

Bahuguna, Sundarlal (1984). 'Women's Non-violent Power in the Chipko Movement', in Madhu Kishwar and Ruth Vanita (eds.), *In Search of Answers: Indian Women's Voices from Manushi*, pp. 129–33. London: Zed Books.

Chatterjee, Partha (1990). 'The Nationalist Resolution of the Woman's Question', in Kumkum Sangari and Sudesh Vaid (eds.), *Recasting Women: Essays in Colonial History*, pp. 233–53. New Brunswick, NJ: Rutgers University Press.

Dogra, Bharat (1992). *Forests, Dams and Survival in Tehri Garhwal*. New Delhi: Published by the author.

Gandhi, M.K. (1930). 'To the Women of India.' *Young India*, 12(15) (10 April): 121–22.

Jain, Devaki (1986). 'Gandhian Contributions Toward a Feminist Ethic', in Diana I. Elk and Devaki Jain (eds.), *Speaking of Faith*, pp. 255–70. New Delhi: Kali for Women.

Jain, Shobita (1984). 'Women and People's Ecological Movement: A Case Study of Women's Role in the Chipko Movement in Uttar Pradesh', *Economic and Political Weekly*, 19(41): 1788–94.

Joshi, Gopa (1984). 'Slandered by the Community in Return', in Madhu Kishwar and Ruth Vanita (eds.), *In Search of Answers: Indian Women's Voices from Manushi*, pp. 125–29. London: Zed Books.

Kishwar, Madhu (1986). *Gandhi on Women*. New Delhi: Manushi Prakashan.

Legg, Stephen (2003). 'Gendered Politics and Nationalized Homes: Women and the Anti-colonial Struggle in Delhi, 1930–47', *Gender, Place and Culture*, 10(1): 7–27.

Manushi (1992). Interview of Vimla Bahuguna by Madhu Kishwar', 70 (May–June): 12–21.

Parekh, Bhiku (1997). *Gandhi* (Past Masters Series). Oxford, New York: Oxford University Press.

Parekh, Bhiku (1999). *Colonialism, Tradition and Reform-An Analysis of Gandhi's Political Discourse*. New Delhi: Sage Publications (revised edition).

Patel, Sujata (1988). 'Construction and Reconstruction of Women in Gandhi', *Economic and Political Weekly*, 23(8): 377–87.

Sharma, Kumud (1984). 'Women in Struggle: A Case Study of the Chipko Movement', *Samya Shakti*, 1(2): 55–62.

Thakkar, Usha and Rohini Gawankar (1998–2002). *Interviews with women freedom fighters* (unpublished manuscript).

Thapar-Bjorkert, Suruchi (1997). 'The Domestic Sphere as a Political Site: A Study of Women in the Indian Nationalist Movement', *Women's Studies International Forum*, 20(4): 493–504.

Varshney, Ashutosh (2002). *Ethnic Conflict and Civic Life: Hindus and Muslims in India*. New Delhi: Oxford University Press.

Weber, Thomas (1989). *Hugging the Trees: The Story of the Chipko Movement*. New Delhi: Penguin Books.

11

Heritage of *Bhakti*: *Sant* Women's Writings in Marathi[*]

Vidyut Bhagwat

After a prolonged neglect by Indian as well as western intellectuals, the *bhakti* tradition is at last getting the necessary critical attention. Both as a part of this newly found interest in general and due to the impact of the post-1975 women's movement and women studies programmes, a good body of work on *bhakta* women, particularly *sant* women,[1] is now being published. As is natural, the assessment of their collective and individual work is carried out in terms of competing theoretical and ideological paradigms. The search by contemporary feminism in India for indigenous roots and the mobilisation of *bhakta* women's poetry to fill this need is one such effort. It is fraught with several dilemmas. Nonetheless, one could see it as part of a pattern in a range of fields in post-independence India, which have trained the searchlight on past traditions in their quest for an identity. It is in this context that the present article focuses on *bhakta* women who were a part of the *bhakti* tradition prevailing in the Marathi-speaking areas in the later medieval period in Indian history.

The initial part of this article consists of a brief review of the *bhakti* tradition specific to the Maharashtra region in the period between 13th and 17th centuries. It then goes on to trace key interpretations of the Varkari Sampraday (as the *bhakti* tradition is known in Marathi) and the Varkari *sant*s by scholars. Contextualising the neglect of *sant* women's lives and writings, the article moves on to note the key elements in the post-1980s feminist scholarship on

* I would like to thank Kamala Ganesh for her patience, and Ram Bapat and Sharmila Rege for their valuable help. Swati, Anagha and Vaishali were a constant source of encouragement in my struggle to complete the paper.

the contributions of women *sant*s. In conclusion, the article suggests that *sant* women's resistance to patriarchies and resistance to caste hierarchies were inseparable. It underlines this early feminism in India as having a predominantly *dalit–bahujan* character, that is, representing non-Brahmin peasant and artisan groups.

The Varkari Sampraday of Maharashtra

Spanning a period of over five centuries, the *bhakti* tradition in Maharashtra began with the generation of *sant*s like Dnyanadev and Namdev, Muktabai and Janabai, and reached its zenith with Tukaram and Bahenabai. Its spread and impact covered the entire space of political economy, culture and language occupied by the Marathi-speaking world, and included even parts of Karnataka and Andhra. The *sant*s entered almost every home through Vithoba— a domestic deity par excellence.

The Marathi *sant*s were neither sectarian conservatives nor Shaktas practising *tantra–mantra*. They were open to all castes, including untouchables and women, and insisted on sharing the language of the masses. *Sant*s were very much a part of the peasant communities of their time. Jayant Lele (1981: 107) notes that they were 'a community of active producers . . . . Jnaneshwar explicitly rejects the renunciation of productive life and ridicules the claims of liberation through rejection of activity'. The *sant*s, while celebrating human productive activity, were a part of the community of the oppressed. They consciously preferred to write in a language that highlighted the everyday practices of common people. Their idiom of writing was direct and dialogic, thus reaching out to women as well. The women of the period, especially those who were in search of creativity and freedom, realised that the doors of the Varkari Sampraday were open to them.

Romila Thapar notes the historical role of *bhakti* as a departure from the earlier indigenous religion. *Bhakti* soon became a new vehicle of religious expression. The main features of the *bhakti* tradition lie in its drawing from the Puranic tradition of Saiva and Vaisnava *bhakti* and from the Sramanic religions, a deep sense of God-centredness, and the worship of a specific icon or idol. Some sects rejected brahmanical *sruti* and *smruti*, and insisted on the equality of all worshippers in the eyes of the deity (Thapar 2000: 970). A.K. Ramanujan (1989: 9–10) clarifies that:

> There are many kinds of bhakti though we speak of it in singular . . . . One way of looking at bhakti movements is to see them as a counter system, opposed to classical, orthodox systems, say in their views about caste, gender or the idea of god. For example, the Vedic Gods are not localised, but in bhakti they are worshipped in local forms in temples. The Gods . . . are as human as they are divine.

If modernity is seen as the first social philosophy that allows ordinary people to dream of freedom and self-determination, then it is not surprising that *bhakti* paved the way for India's early modernity. Lele has pointed out that given the nature of India's peasant economy, the direct producers were battling for sustaining their economy as a moral economy. He examines the role of *bhakti* in this light as an expression of that modernity (Lele 1995: 53). The radical *sant*s challenged brahmanism, caste hierarchy, untouchability and Islamic orthodoxy. They built a broad unity of the masses, cutting across class, caste and gender lines. It is well known that the dialogue between Islam and earlier indigenous religions is reflected in various *bhakti* and *sufi* traditions. Though some of the leading *bhakta*s were Brahmans, its broad following consisted of Shudras, in particular the middle castes. *Bhakti* was thus neither elitist nor cultist. *Bhakti* in Maharashtra always remained a mainstream movement of peasants and artisans offering a most potent source of critique of brahmanism.

If we look at the variations in the expression of *bhakti*, north India produced *nirguna* (abstract) *bhakti*, whereas south India adopted *saguna* (concrete) *bhakti*. Maharashtra represented the confluence of the northern and the southern traditions.

What then are the salient features of the Varkari *bhakti* tradition? What features constitute the specificity or peculiarity of Marathi *bhakti*? One of the striking features in this context is the range of castes and occupations that came together within the Varkari Sampraday. Their articulations were in the idiom of their caste-based occupation, their everyday life practices. Sena Nhavi (a barber) would carry his critique of caste discrimination by upholding his occupational skill: 'We are the barbers, we do "*hajamat*" minutely.'

Gora Kumbhar was from the potter community, Savta was a gardener, Chokha Mela was a Mahar,[2] Narhari was a goldsmith, Bahira came from Jatved, Jagannath from the Vadwal sub-caste. Jnaneshwar and his sister Muktabai belonged to an excommunicated Brahmin family. Namdev was from the Shimpi (tailor) caste. His disciple Janabai, from a Shudra caste, was a part of Namdev's household as a bonded domestic servant. The community of *sant*s in Maharashtra, therefore, were from the artisan and service *jati*s, and the *bhakta* community included women from both high and low castes. The crucial feature of this formation, therefore, was the fact that every caste contributed to the knowledge building process on equal terms.

Thus, Chokha Mahar analyses the discriminatory system, saying:

While for one there is only food for subsistence
For another sweetmeats.
Some do not get even grains despite asking
For one there is wealth and titles of kingship
While another begs for alms from village to village,
This is the law of the 'home' you created
Says Chokha, O Hari this is my karma! (My translation)

Chokha often asserts his 'Mahar' identity and states, 'They curse me as a Mahar and blame me for polluting the deity.' But then in open defiance argues:

Who is pure and who is untouchable?
My Vitthal is different from both of these
Who gets polluted by what?
Everything of birth is pure.
If five senses pollute the one body
In which they are housed
Who in the world is pure then?
Says Chokha my Vitthala is different
Formless and different standing on the brick. (My translation)

Sant Eknath (1533–99), a Brahman from Paithan, notes:

God baked pots with Gora
drove cattle with Chokha

cut grass with Savta Mali
wove garments with Kabir
colored hide with Ravidas
sold meat with butcher Sajana
melted gold with Narhari
carried cow dung with Janabai
and even became the Mahar messenger of Damaji. (Zelliot 1987)

Varkari *sants* composed in various folk meters like *ovi, abhanga, bharud, virani and palna*, collectively developed by women and men. Generally, the *ovi* meter is treated as Dnyaneshwar's contribution and the *abhanga* as Tukaram's. The *ovi* originates in the rhythm of the songs sung by women at the grinding stone. Janabai, Soyrabai and Bahenabai had used *abhanga* meter for their free and hard-hitting compositions. Tukaram had imbibed this tradition. *Virani* were songs of pain of separation, and *palnas* or lullabies were also a favourite form of articulation for both men and women *sants*. Eleanor Zelliot (1987: 91) has noted:

A great many of Eknath's three hundred bharuds are in the persona of untouchables, passing Muslim fakirs, acrobats and travelling entertainers, religious personages from unorthodox sects, prostitutes and unhappy women—a wide sweep of the non-sanskritic world around Eknath.

Bhakti was centred on Vithoba, the God who was more or less like any one from the toiling class, man or woman. Vithoba was seen as a common Marathi peasant, free from excesses of miracles. He did not expect any kind of sacrifice, in animal or other forms, and was a friend, a motherly figure. Irawati Karve even sees him as her 'boyfriend'. Right from Dnyaneshwar, all the *sants* talk to him in a conversational mode. For Janabai, he becomes a helpmate in carrying domestic chores. Vithoba was no doubt a homely god. Varkari Sampraday built up a strong egalitarian, democratising, anti-hierarchical ethos of Vithoba *bhakti*. Celebrating earthly joys, their *bhakti* had a robust peasant like directness of expression.

Modern Interpretations of the Varkari Sampraday

The arrival of colonialism marked the rise of print culture and, in consequence, a new intelligentsia. The new rulers—Elphinstone, for example—as well as a band of Christian missionaries needed to know Marathi for the implementation of their desired projects. The evangelical missionaries began to distribute translated scriptures on a massive scale. The new intelligentsia's response appeared in the form of printed texts of key *sant*s like Dnyaneshwar and Tukoba. The process began in full vitality from 1844. Sadanand More (1996: 225) points out that Tukaram's writings appealed to the religious as well as literary taste of the missionaries and colonial officials as his writings were direct and simple, lucid and trenchant in their critique of brahmanism. A leading liberal British official like Alexander Grant confessed in the Royal Asiatic Journal that Tukaram's poetry revealed a high sense of morality and authentic spirituality based on *bhakti*.

Missionaries treated *bhakti* as a bridge to Christ for commoners in Maharashtra. Eminent social thinkers like Justice M.G. Ranade turned to *bhakti* as an alternative to utilitarianism. He also argued that *bhakti* provided the energies that resulted in the rise of Maratha power under Shivaji. His own Prarthana Samaj initiative drew its sustenance from the *bhakti* tradition and above all from Tukaram.

Mahatma Jotirao Phule had a complex relationship with the Varkari Sampraday. He founded the Satyashodhak Samaj as an alternative to the Prarthana Samaj. But he knew the potential of the Varkari Sampraday in resisting casteism and untouchability. More has demonstrated that while Phule kept himself aloof from the Varkari tradition for reasons of his own, his *akhanda*s are in fact organically linked with Tukaram's *abhanga*s. Lokmanya Tilak's interpretation of the *Bhagavad Gita* is a confluence of *bhakti* and *karma*. Tilak stood against the rituals of the Varkari Sampraday and followed Sant Tukaram in his forthright critique of hypocrisy.

Anthropologist Iravati Karve countered Rajwade's and Ketkar's denigration of the Varkari endeavour as unscientific and backward. She in fact participated in the *vari* or pilgrimage to Pandharpur and then defined Maharashtra as 'that region where people visit

Pandhari' (Karve 1962). G.B. Sardar refuted the charge of the
Varkari Sampraday being non-intellectual and praised Tukaram
for his honesty and transparent self-expression (Sardar 1969).
D.K. Bedekar, an eminent and creative Marxist scholar, read
Tukaram and the Varkari Sampraday in a democratic, secular
framework.

Jayant Lele argues that in order understand the revolutionary
potential of Varkari Sampradaya, one must enter the world-view
of the peasant with gentle humility and alertness. He sees Varkari
Sampraday as an example of an immanent critique of brahmanism.
'It rejects both counter culturalism and ritualism. As a discourse
of the underprivileged, it penetrates the falsehood of an ideology
through the eyes of suspicion but it does so in order to extract
and expose the encrusted truth of that ideology through the sensitive ears of a believer' (Lele 1995: 80). For him the *sant* poets of
medieval Maharashtra offer a most important methodological lesson
of unmasking the hypocrisy and falsehood of orthodox beliefs,
but they also teach us to develop the art of listening. Sadanand
More considers the Varkari tradition as the core of Maharashtrian
culture and sees Tukaram as a social critic and a poet of a high
order with matchless clarity of expression and an utter fidelity to
his own integrity as a free and radical human being and *bhakta*.

Sant Women and Their Poetry

Almost till recent times, women's *bhakti* writings were more often
than not studied only in terms of literary expression. The rigorous
critique developed by them to challenge all kinds of caste and
gender ideational hegemonies were either altogether neglected or
pushed into the background. In reality, the Varkari women had
dared to enter the Varkari movement as equal partners. They drew
fearlessly from their domestic life-world and wasted no opportunity
to challenge the unequal order that subordinated them. We have
a long line of woman *sant*s full of radical intent, critique and expression. Mahadaisa, Baisa, Ausa, and then Muktabai, Janabai,
Soyara-Nirmala, Sakhu, Premabai and Bahenabai. From the 13th
to 17th centuries, there is an uninterrupted tradition of radical
women *sant*s and *sant* poets.

Some writings of *sant* women were translated and printed in the early 20th century. For example, Justine Abbott's preface mentions that the first printed edition of the 17th century *sant* poetess Bahenabai's work was edited by Dhondo V. Umarkhane which appeared in 1914 and was soon out of print (Abbott 1985: 9). Eventually in 1929, Justine Abbott published a translation of chosen portions of her autobiography. 'To introduce to the west a name there absolutely unknown but worthy of being known', he had chosen such portions 'as seemed best adapted to give to the English reader the thoughts of this Indian woman that found expression in her verses nearly three hundred years ago.' (ibid.: ix).

It would be apt to say that this writing of women *sant*s was seen for a long time, in fact up to 1975, only as a part of the spiritual realm, and women *sant*s like Muktabai and Janabai were treated as women who had already transcended the physiological division of humans into 'man' and 'woman'. But in this process it was ignored that women *sant*s were very much a symbiotic part of the Varkari masses. They were also a part of the social historic reality of the Marathi-speaking region. After the rise of women's movement in India, gender-sensitive academic and political discourses made conscious efforts to write women into history. Initially, women *sant*s were treated as add-ons to the list of male *sant*s. Muktabai, Dnyaneshwar's sister, was designated at one level as '*mahayogini*', highlighting her spiritual status, but her very complex writing is yet to be analysed seriously. Thus, these historical accounts did not recognise the agency of women *sant*s. Moreover, mainstream history was preoccupied with 'women in early India' as enjoying a high status, a position of honour and dignity. This homogenisation had created a category of 'women in India' with Gargi and Maitreyi being seen as exceptional women seers and knowledge makers. The predominance of this homogenised category further blurred the agency of *sant* women of the medieval period. Their expressions were relegated to the sphere of '*bhakti*' as only devotion, contrasted to the sphere of 'knowledge'. Women *sant*s' lives as well as writings were either not contextualised or rendered a tokenist treatment.

There have been serious controversies as to whether there was one Dnyaneshwar or two. Namdev is acknowledged for his organisational brilliance and skills. But the women *sant*s were always clubbed together with the male *sant*s as their dependants. As I have observed elsewhere, 'we always talk of Mahadaisa of Chakradhar, Jani of Namya, "little" Muktai of Dnyaneshwar, Bahenabai of Tukaram . . . . This is a classic instance of how the hegemonic order manages to reappropriate emancipatory drives for its own legitimization' (Bhagwat 1995: ws-25). As a result, as late as 1957, Neera Desai acknowledged the *bhakti* movement as an important movement, but concluded that the *bhaktas*' 'total conception of woman's status was not quite free from the admixture of the then prevailing attitude towards womanhood'. Hence, in her opinion, the overall effect of the movement on women was rather limited (Desai 1957: 34–47).

During the 1980s, in the overall context of 'gender politics' and the second wave women's movement in India, there seems to be a proliferation of scholarly writings on *sant* women. A.K. Ramanujan in 1973 translated love poems and published the *Classical Tamil Anthology* (Ramanujan 1973). In 1989 he talked extensively about *sant* women in an interview for *Manushi*. He began studying the detailed history of Mahadeviakka, a Virasaiva woman, and an extraordinary picture emerged before his eyes. He saw 'marriage' as an issue in the lives of Indian women *sant*s, in a way that it was not for male *sant*s, both upper and lower castes. He saw the women going through five phases: (*a*) early dedication to God in the form of a particular deity; (*b*) denial of marriage; (*c*) defying social norms; (*d*) initiation by the guru; and (*e*) marrying the Lord. He notes, 'The upper caste male's battle is with the system as a whole, often internalized as the enemy within, whereas a woman *sant's* struggle is with family and family values.' The woman *sant* remains feminine because 'she has nothing to shed: neither physical prowess, nor social power, nor prudity, nor even spiritual pride. She is already where she needs to be, in these saints' legends' (Ramanujan 1989: 324).

Since *bhakti* movements, radical in their beginnings, eventually got routinised, Ramanujan suggested that the *sant* writings have to be constantly reinterpreted and rescued from the domestication that they undergo. In his opinion, *bhakti* writings do offer alternatives, humane and creative ways of being and acting. Hence, he gave immense importance to the lives and poems of women *sant*s for studying Indian women's voices, for finding alternative conceptions in Indian civilisation (Ramanujan 1989: 14).

Jayant Lele in his edited work on *bhakti* movements (1981) makes pertinent observations about women *sant*s in the context of the tradition–modernity debate. He argues that when *dharma* speaks only as an oppressive moment, as a duty from which the joy of performance has been stolen, it becomes coercive. He sees *sant* women's rebellious posture vis-à-vis the social order in the context of their reality as communally exchanged young brides in an alien patriarchal/patrilocal family, in an often hostile household. He points out:

> A sensitive woman under conditions of oppression, looks upon god as an alternative to her husband, she does not, I think, look upon the former as a mere alternative, but a determinate negation of that very being which a husband is not, but should be. The worldly husband symbolizes the lure, the bondage, the oppressive reality of family life, while the god as husband and lover signifies liberation . . . . Their involvement with the lord was an all-consuming affair . . . . They rejected repressive marriage and not marriage, oppressive sex and not love making (ibid.: 12).

According to him, women *sant*s' love transcended the prison gates of legitimised duty, false modesty, enforced honour and oppressive kinship.

Feminist Engagement with *Sant* Women's Poetry

In the 1980s feminist scholars of the second wave of women's movement were grappling with an extremely troubled situation in India. The statistics of deteriorating women's status; the experience of Indian women's overall victimisation and sexual exploitation complicated by their locations in different communities, castes, classes; an absence or invisibility of women's collective resistances in historical narratives; an urgent need of writing cultural historiography in order to combat naturalising or essentialising 'the woman question': all these presented immense complexities. A nuanced understanding of recasting of Indian women during the colonial period (Sangari and Vaid 1989) was attempted. This also led to researching 'women in early India' and challenging the myth of the 'Golden Age' (Chakravarti 1989). The search for women's voices in Indian history sought to make them audible as specifically women's voices. This was the context within which women *sants'* lives and writings were foreground and studied by feminist scholars of different ideological dispositions.

In the late 1980s feminism emerged as a critique of biologism and the sexual division of labour. It rested on the assertion of the right to chosen political affiliation and social identities above birth-bound ones. Women's membership of any community and even of the state was seen as problematic due to their patriarchal modes. The roots of misogyny were rightly traced to traditional as well as modern male-dominated cultures. The stereotypical abuse of the weaker sex along with deep-seated phobic anxiety about the woman's body and its reproductive ability was critically analysed by feminist scholars and activists. Sexism was defined as a process providing a rationale for the disempowerment of women in all spheres of life, secular and spiritual.

In this milieu, it is not surprising that the special issue of *Manushi* celebrating its 11th year sought to resurrect women *sants* as exercising individual choice and creating alternative tradition. Women *sants* were seen as 'extraordinarily courageous and creative women who asserted right to their own life as they defined it'. Their writing was seen as a celebration of their individual choice and their religious path as an escape from the narrow confines of domesticity (Kishwar 1989: 7).

Uma Chakravarti situates gender relations within the context of caste, class and delineates the issue of the control of female sexuality as the central issue. Chakravarti acknowledges *bhakti* as a rich tradition

> particularly significant for women both for variations and com-
> monalities in its social and religious implications. Here the
> dominant brahmanical ritual world is attempted to be turned
> upside down, boundaries operating in the social world collapse,
> and the shackles imposed by rigidly hierarchical social order
> are stretched to provide breathing space for some men and women.
> (Chakravarty 1989: 18)

She warns against homogenising *bhakti* into a neat unified tradition and simplifying its social content, and suggests that the

extent to which *bhakti* dissolved gender lines needs to be investigated further.

Kumkum Sangari provides an analysis of *bhakti* thus:

> In an economy where the labour of women and the surplus production of the peasant and artisan are customarily and 'naturally' appropriated by the ruling groups, high Hindu traditions sought to encompass and retain the management of spiritual 'surplus' and to circumscribe its availability along lines of caste and gender. In this spiritual economy, the liberalising and dissenting forms of bhakti emerge as a powerful force which selectively uses the metaphysics of high Hinduism in an attempt to create value grounded in the dailiness of a material life within the reach of all. (Sangari 1990: 194)

Susie Tharu and K. Lalita compiling an anthology of *Women Writing in India* (1995: 35) argue that, 'We might indeed learn to read them not for the moments in which they collude with or reinforce dominant ideologies of gender, class, nation, or empire, but for the gestures of defiance or subversion implicit in them.'

Tharu (1991: 57) observes:

> The path of devotion set up no barriers of caste or sex. The women poets of the bhakti movements did not have to seek the institutionalized spaces religion provided to express themselves and women's poetry moved from the court and the temple to the open spaces of the field, the workplace and the common women's hearth.

Tharu and Lalita do acknowledge *sant* women's writing as expressing a new sense of self-worth, new dignity to domestic chores, new self-confidence and even their access to a wider world, but note that their options were limited. They, too, doubt whether patriarchal controls were radically questioned and lives of ordinary women changed.

Vijaya Ramaswamy's work *Walking Naked: Women, Society, Spirituality in South India* appeared in 1997, mapping the spiritual history of women in the context of societal structures though historical time and space. Her study looks at the issues of gender inequalities in the context of dominance and power, and the debates over female sexuality and education.

In Marathi, Indumati Shevde's *Sant Kavayitri* (Women Saints) was published in 1989 under the guidance of Suma Chitnis, the editor of the series of books *Stri Muktichya Maharashtratil Paulkhana* (Footsteps of Women's Liberation in Maharashtra). It was, in Shevde's own words, an effort to search for the seeds of contemporary women's movement in the past in order to create an understanding of the struggles of contemporary women in search of 'self'.

During those years I, too, was engaged in researching the complex weave of *sant* women's compositions in Maharashtra. 'Man–Woman Relations in the Writings of the Saint Poetesses', written in 1991, is an effort to show how women *sant*s were talking differently as women and hence even as *sant*s. 'Marathi Literature as Source for Contemporary Feminism' (Bhagwat 1995: ws-24) argues that:

> The feminist movement in the [Maharashtra] state ignored its own tradition of a succession of women saints and other women writers who had inverted, and occasionally even subverted, the classical ideals of womanhood embodied in the hegemonic texts. The movement paid a price for this failure; it appeared to be based on dry, upstart ideas lacking roots in the soil.

Postscript: Personal Reflections on *Sant* Women's Lives and Poetry

The last decade has posed several challenges to feminist scholarship in India, and new directions and issues have been opened up. As Rajeshwari Sunder Rajan (2000) has argued, feminist scholarship's move from victimisation of woman to resistance and agency of woman has emerged in the context of majoritarian religious politics and its mobilisation of women, and the failure of the state and its laws to ensure women's safety or rights. The other important context of the 1990s, at least in western India, has been the challenge posed by *dalit–bahujan* feminist perspectives and organisation to feminist and non-Brahman historiography and epistemology. These challenges have led us to reflect on questions like: What constitutes resistance? Can the resistance to patriarchies and brahmanism/ caste hierarchies be neatly separated even if only for analytical purposes? We are impelled to reflect on what we hide when we privilege the voices of women *sant*s as voices of female resistance, as if they are unmarked by their caste location. For instance, Soyarabai, a Mahar *sant*, questioned untouchability: 'O God, every human being carries impurity along with purity, then why should some human beings be treated as untouchables?' she sang (Pawar 2003). Or Janabai, as a bonded slave, as a *dasi*, that too of a Shudra caste, consciously stated, 'I am low-born and kept outside the temple.' Her declaration that Chokhamela, the Mahar *sant*, was the only true Vaisnava is important in understanding her as a member of the Varkari community. When we read their voices as voices of specifically female resistance, we edit out the fact that early feminism in India had *dalit–bahujan* beginnings and that these women were resisting the principles of brahmanical patriarchy. In fact, their consciousness, expressed through their poetry, spanned different locations of gender and caste, and thus offered a universalist and humanist critique of oppression.

No doubt there has been important feminist historical research and emancipatory interpretations of the lives and works of women *sant*s. However, the caution that most feminists express about reading 'too much' into these voices may be at least partly explained by the fact that there has been very little work on the 'living tradition'. The meanings that these women *sant*s have in the lives of contemporary *bahujan* women as well as the co-option of the egalitarian tradition by the latter needs documentation. The imprint of the egalitarian practices from the Varkari movement in the literature of the early decades of the 20th century are apparent, for instance, in the autobiographical accounts of *dalit* women. Shantabai Kamble, for example, in her 1990 work *Mazya Jalmachi Chitterkatha* (A Kaleidoscopic Story of My Life) recalls early childhood memories of practices of untouchability in the movement. Her dismay at being asked about her caste and then served water from a distance by a fellow Varkari and her disappointment after being told by her mother that the untouchables could pay respects only at the steps of Chokhoba and Namdev at Pandharpur is a case in point.

I would suggest, therefore, that the essentialisation of *sant* women's writing as 'women's writing' has often rendered invisible their resistance to brahmanical patriarchy and that this needs to be brought to the foreground. I do not suggest thereby that there is some readymade indigenous *dalit–bahujan* feminist solution in *sant* women's writing that can deal with multiple patriarchies of the contemporary situation. An analysis of Bahenabai's contributions can help explicate the argument in this context: Bahenabai (1628–1700) was the last great woman *sant* in this tradition. Born in a poor Brahman family, married at the early age of 3 or 4 to a 30-year-old Vedic *pandit* of a Shakta cult, beaten up by her husband, Bahena chose a Shudra guru and actively participated in *bhakti* by becoming a Varkari. Her writing consists of historical accounts of the Varkari Sampraday, a commentary on *Vajrasuchi*, a Buddhist text attacking dogmatic brahmanism by Ashwaghosha, an auto-biography that is an important source for the social history of Maharashtra and almost 729 *abhanga*s. As Dilip Chitre (1998: 5) notes, 'The crisis that arose in Bahenabai's life was noted simply as bhakti of "the god vs. duties of the *pativrata*" kind.' 'Her struggle was a complex weave of questions on *varna* hegemony, self-perception of brahmanism, true meaning of the Veda and the discipline of ritualism. This Marathi Brahman woman changed the conservative frame of mind of her husband, redefined the concept of *pativrata-dharma* (wifely duty) from 'loyalty' to 'pursuing a higher goal' for both men and women, chose a Shudra guru and actively participated in the Varkari Sampraday. In university courses in Marathi literature, we were taught to read her texts and underline her skills in drawing a balance between the fulfilment of her wifely duties and achievement of spiritual excellence. The context of her times was thus completely lost. There is a need to highlight the system of her times, which treated women as subordinate beings having no right over material or spiritual property and no right to the knowledge-making discourse. Her whole life then is a quest of building an open community. She thus redefines the concept of a Brahman not as born, but as one who understands truly 'Brahma', that is, truth that is universal for the whole of humanity.

Bahena challenges brahmanical patriarchy through a subversion of meanings of the pillars of its coercive structure. Her '*brahm*' is '*karma*' that is, active intervention. 'Wifely duty' for her is recognising her own self. She takes a Shudra guru and challenges the very presence of god in brahmanism.

She writes (and I have translated the following songs from Javdekar's *Sant Bahinabaicha Gatha*) (1979: 126):

> One who recognises her own self
> She is the true pativrata
> One who treats worldliness and other worldliness on par
> She is the one who holds the sky.

She tells us about the beatings that she suffered.

> Whenever it pleases him, he beats me a lot, binds me like a bundle of sticks.
> (*abhanga* 161)

She tells us that:

> The husband says we are Brahmans
> We will always recite Veda
> Who is this Shudra Tuka?
> My wife is spoiled by him.
> (*abhanga* 32)

Bhakti was her chosen path towards bringing freedom and equality for both women and shudras. She raised questions like:

> My husband earned a living through practising Veda
> Where is God in this?
> (*abhanga* 575)

She tells her God that her body was tortured in the hands of her husband:

> But my mind has taken a vow
> I will not leave singing for devotion
> Even if I die.
> (*abhanga* 588)

She had a large following of people. Her husband detested this popularity. She says

> Every moment his hatred grows
> Will she be possessed by the God?
> Will she be fed by the God?
> Baheni says this is how he worried
> The God understood all this.
> (*abhanga* 31)

She challenges brahmanical patriarchy's vicious propaganda about the sinful birth of women and Shudras, and refuses to be deceived by the mirage of rebirth. She says:

> A pativrata when she serves her husband
> Blesses both the families
> Baheni says my soul is rested eternally
> By my husband putting a stop to
> The cycle of birth ad death.
> (*abhanga* 38)

Bahenabai lived on for many years after her husband's death and worked till the end for the suffering community of Varkaris. She actually managed to convert her husband to the Varkari sect and persuaded him to accept Tukaram as his guru.

I suggest that woman *sant*s were very much a part of the early modernity of India. Hence, their struggles and negotiations within their cultural context will have to be understood and reinterpreted as emancipatory cultural histories. Drawing them out solely as women's voices often excludes their agency in challenging the political priesthood of their times and blurs their historical relevance as early voices against brahmanical patriarchy. Their voices more than being 'specific voices of women', are expressions of freedom and equality emerging from their lived experiences as women in specific communities. Their message thus has universality. These voices against patriarchal political priesthood are a demand for a new world, to be realised not in the next life through *karma*, but in the empirical world. This heritage of *bhakta* women's voices as renderings of nascent modernity has several clues for today.

Our present is marked by a world order that collapses capitalism into democracy, equating freedom with choice and equality with access. Third world women's issues are thus being equated to issues of poverty and their agency is being collapsed into efficient management of poverty and a mirage of 'choices'. In India majoritarian fundamentalism opposes the ideas of secularism and equality, labelling them as 'Western'. This challenge has underlined further the limitations of several academic trends, which pose undifferentiated 'collective tradition' against the 'modernity' of the West. Feminist scholarship that seeks to redefine democratic politics must, in retrieving emancipatory collective traditions, separate the brahmanical and the non-brahmanical, and inegalitarian from egalitarian aspects. The voices of freedom and equality of the *bhakta* women, which were at once directed against the intrinsically inter-linked caste system and patriarchy, contained an urge to transform the world. It is this tradition of equality and rights in the 'early modern' period that provide a rich heritage and can become a resource for redefining feminist democratic politics.

Notes

1. '*Bhakta*', literally means 'devotee', refers to the community of believers and worshippers in the *bhakti* tradition. '*Sant*' or saint refers to the leaders of the movement whose devotional poetry became emblematic for the *bhakti* movement. Marathi words like *bhakta*, *bhakti* and *sant* are popularly used and understood by English speakers in India.
2. Mahar is an ex-untouchable caste in Maharashtra which until the 14th century was compelled to drag dead animals. But under Malik Amber's regime, after the decline of the Yadav period, the Mahar caste became known as the Vatandars and later as a part of Shivaji's military.

References

Abbott, Justine E. (1985 [1929]). *Bahinabai: A Translation of her Autobiography and Verses*. New Delhi: Motilal Banarasidass.
Bedekar D.K. (1978). *Adhunik Marathi Kavya: Udgam, Vikas ani Bhavitavya* (Modern Marathi Literature: Origin, Development and Future) Bombay: Lokvangmay gruha Pvt. Ltd.

Bhagwat, Vidyut (1990). 'Man–Woman Relations in the Writings of Saint Poetesses', *New Quest*, 82 (July–August): 223–32.

—— (1995). 'Marathi Literature as a Source of Contemporary Feminism', *Economic and Political Weekly*, 30(17): Review of Women's Studies, ws-24–29.

Chakravarti, Uma (1989). 'Whatever Happened to the Vedic Dasi?: Orientalism, Nationalism and a Script for the Past', in Kumkum Sangari and Sudesh Vaid (eds.), *Recasting Women: Essays in Colonial History*, pp. 27–87. New Delhi: Kali for Women.

Chitre, Dilip Purushottam (1998). *Baheni Mhane Hat Ghatala Mastaki* ('Baheni Says I Have [Earned] Blessings'). Shri Kshetra Dehu: Bhagwat Prabodhan Sanstha.

Desai, Neera (1957). 'Impact of Bhakti Movement on the Status of Indian Women', in *Women in Modern India*, pp. 34–47. Bombay: Vora and Company.

Javdekar, Shalini (ed.) (1979). *Sant Bahenabaicha Gatha* ('Story of Bahenabai'). Pune: Continental Prakashan.

Kamble, Shantabai (1990). *Mazya Jalmachi Chitterkatha* ('Kaleidoscopic Story of My Life'). Pune: Sugava Prakashan.

Karve, Iravati (1962). *Marathi Lokanchi Sanskruti* ('Culture of the Marathi People'). Pune: Deshmukh.

Kishwar, Madhu (1989). *Manushi*, Sp. 10th Anniversary issue, January–June, New Delhi.

Lele, Jayant, (1981). 'Community, Discourse and Critique in Jnanesvar', in Jayant Lele (ed.), Tradition and Modernity in Bhakti Movements, pp. 104–12. Leiden: E.J. Brill.

—— (1995). *Hindutva: The Emergence of the Right*. Madras: Earthworm Books.

More, Sadanand (1996). *Tukaram Darshan*. Pune: Gaj Prakashan.

Pawar, Urmila (2003). 'Hidden Behind the Curtain: Women in Maharashtra Who Made History Too', article translated by Kunda Pramila Neelkanth, and excerpted in *IAWS Newsletter*, pp. 26–30.

Sunder Rajan, Rajeshwari (2000). 'Introduction: Feminism and Politics of Resistance', *Indian Journal of Gender Studies*, 7(2): 153–65.

Ramanujan, A.K. (1973). *Speaking of Siva*. Harmondaworth: Penguin Books.

—— (1989). 'Talking to God in the Mother Tongue', *Manushi*, 50–52: 9–14.

Ramaswamy, Vijaya (1997). *Walking Naked: Women, Society, Spirituality in South India*. Shimla: Indian Institute of Advanced Study.

Sangari, Kumkum (1990). 'Mirabai and the Spiritual Economy of Bhakti' *Economic and Political Weekly*, 25(27): 1464–75.

Sangari, Kumkum and Sudesh Vaid (eds.) (1989). *Recasting Women: Essays in Colonial History*. New Delhi: Kali for Women.

Sardar, G.B. (1969). *The Sant Poets of Maharashtra: Their Impact on Society*. New Delhi: Orient Longman.

Shevde, Indumati (1989). *Sant Kavayatri: Stree Muktichya Maharashtratil Paulkhuna*. Bombay: Popular Prakashan.

Thapar, Romilla (2000). 'Imagined Religious Communities? Ancient History and the Modern Search for a Hindu Identity', in Romilla Thapar (ed.),

Cultural Pasts: Essays in Early Indian History, p. 970. New Delhi: Oxford University Press.

Tharu, Susie and K. Lalitha (eds) (1991). *Women Writing in India: 600 B.C. to the Present*, Vols 1 and 2. New York: The Feminist Press.

Zelliot, Eleanor (1987). 'Eknath's Bharuds: The Sant as Link Between Cultures', in Karine Schomer and W.H. Mcleod (eds), *The Saints: Studies in a Devotional Tradition of India*. Religious Studies Series. Delhi: Motilal Banarasidass.

12

Feminism and Feminist Expression: A Dialogue

Devaki Jain*

Introduction: Feminist Theory and Practice

Feminism has constantly been evolving—it has been described, bound, unleashed and enacted in many ways. Elastic, flexible, mutated, searched for, found, doubted. Sometimes it is said that there are as many feminisms as there are cultures. The concept of 'many feminisms' is not plastic: it suggests separate pieces, not a soft, malleable whole. In the desire to be inclusive, accommodating, reverential to difference and diversity, in the concern for rejecting the rigid, authoritarian shades of patriarchy and of male regimens, defining feminism tends to become a chase. So sometimes it is said, feminism is a quest not a platform, a vision not a practice.

But feminists abound, and the claim to being feminist by the articulate is comprehensible both locally and globally. At another less articulate level is the phenomenon of 'feminist expression' both in thought and action. It may be self-acknowledged or recognised from the outside as feminist.

Can these two phenomena—feminism and feminist expression—be viewed together? Can there be a dialogue, if not convergence? Is there a need for such dialogue or confluence? This article will give consideration to these questions. The lens it will attempt to use is the aspiration and perspective of women—poor, less visible,

*Assisted by Supriya Seth.

disadvantaged or deprived women. Without such an ideological lens, the discourse can become an infinite enquiry, a journey without end. However fascinating and fair the journey, however kaleidoscopic the landscape, the openness might vapourise it.

There is immense literature in this area. However, in sum, the dialogue is between those who see difference and its articulation as an important characteristic of the feminist movement, and those who attempt a common identity. Coming as it does from a foundation of oppression and discrimination, feminism is necessarily idealistic. This very idealism inhibits it from practising exclusion, hence giving boundaries. But within all this accommodation is also the concern that the unified stands, unified actions and notions of solidarity built around womanhood will evaporate if 'difference' becomes the platform.

There has been a political need for affirmation of different streams. For example, Vidyut Bhagwat's presentation elsewhere in this volume recalling feminist expression in Maharashtra from the 13th to 17th centuries is a vivid pointer that feminism was not born in the West. The concept of indigenous feminism has been emerging over the last two to three decades, partly out of the need for 'naming' varied expressions of women's collective strength. This concept is part of a language that would not like to define feminism too narrowly or to affirm that there is a universally acceptable ideology called feminism. Kumari Jayawardene (1982: 2) explains it thus:

It is variously alleged in the Third World by traditionalists, political conservatives and even by certain leftists that feminism is a product of 'decadent' western capitalism that is based on foreign culture of no relevance to women in the Third World, that it is the ideology of women of the local bourgeoisie and that it either alienates women from their culture, religion and family responsibilities on the one hand, or from the revolutionary struggle for national liberation and socialism on the other. In the West, too, there is a Eurocentric view that the movement for Women's liberation is not indigenous to Asia or Africa but has been purely a West European and North American phenomenon and that where movements for women's emancipation or feminist struggles have arisen in the Third World, they have been merely imitative of Western models.

My dialogues with feminists from the North and at a meeting in Athens in 1985, pre-Nairobi (the third UN conference on women), is another illustration of this 'need'.

'But why do you women in the so-called third world separate yourselves? We are struggling against the same system of patriarchy and the same dominant discourse,' said a Dutch feminist to me.

I replied, 'We are struggling against two dominant discourses— the one you are struggling against and the one you are generating. They are strong and powerful, highly disseminated; you flood us. We need to consolidate, know ourselves before we join you.'

'What is your stand?' she asked.

'We don't know, we know it is not only the "male", nor is it "imperialism, capitalism, Zionism". It is something else. We will find out by dealing with it,' I said.

It is my perception that feminist theory—as different from feminist practice—is still not a body of knowledge in India. This statement implies that feminist practice is widespread. In India and perhaps in other similar countries the reflections or even early statements on theory are emerging from the empirical field: from activist knowledge and dialogue. The theory is grounded in user's language, it is derived as a response to the needs of grassroots activists.

The goal of several of the exercises in theory building in India is predominantly to find a basis for solidarity—feminist solidarity, a united women's movement, a common politics. This is because in India—and other developing countries as well—there are strong roots in an indigenous feminist consciousness. Thus, the 'dialogue' or interlocking is already in process. But as theory develops, it tends to emphasise the linkages with the broader political framework, the cultural contexts and the socio-political needs, and then 'difference' has to be emphasised.

On the other hand, if we take a definition of feminism that is built around practice and not around 'isms', there is a case, built through women's ways and methods of handling, what can be called a 'Common Minimum Programme' on which we can build solidarity, namely, some kind of 'standpoint'.

To give some glimpses of feminist theory, I would draw on some 'discussions' I have participated in.

My first resource is the national conference held in December 1985 in Bombay called 'Perspectives for the Autonomous Women's

Movement in India'. Some 85 women's groups and several individuals from different parts of the world attended. All of them, some 300 in number, came on their own initiative and expense. The conference was structured to have two workshops per day. Presentations were made in the morning, and for each workshop, sub-groups were formed for discussions. A plenary session was held towards the end of the day for a general reporting to all participants. Cultural programmes—plays, singing and audio-visuals—followed. On the last day a variety of small workshops suggested by the participants were held.

The method of convening this conference was feminist—several prior consultations had been held on venue and themes, and decisions had been taken by representatives from women's groups. Attendance was self-supported and self-motivated. All roles of moderator, rapporteur and so on were developed at the conference itself. Some crisp formulations came out of the conference:

The term feminism needs clarification. Do you accept that sexual bondage is a stronger one than class bondage? Is it possible to bring all women together on the same platform? Or should there be separate demands for separate classes?

These dialogues led to the whole issue of defining feminism. While some felt that feminism as a tool is sufficient to explore oppression and inequalities in all its forms, others disagreed with this definition. 'Who is a real feminist? they asked. Some participants felt that at times women became feminist chauvinists who look down on women who have to do housework, childcare, etc. These articulate middle-class women tend to dominate feminist groups. And in such groups, if expected behaviour patterns are not visible, then they question the feminism of the others. This opinion was not shared by many. However, some women continued to argue that a women's organisation is not a non-class organisation. Women's organisations had neglected the class issue in the same way as left political organisations had neglected the gender issue, they felt, and this had led to the exclusion of the large mass of poor women.

However, the principle concern of the conference was alliances, consolidation, illustrating the earlier point that the grassroots activists have a 'yen'—a pull towards unity. These are understandable preoccupations in a plural, multi-region, multi-caste, multi-language, multi-party, unequal but secular democratic nation. The concern related not only to alliances with existing forces from without, like political parties and ideological movements, but also alliances from *within*. For example, alliances of women with women as individuals; of women's groups of one kind, say, activists, with women's groups of another kind, say, researchers.

Another concern was that women's groups claiming to work as collectives had often empowered an individual, not the group. Feminist research had been no better in its interest than inherited man-made research. Dichotomies such as activism and research, class and caste persisted. Where was the breakthrough? the meeting asked. No movement—left, reformist, Christian, Gandhian—had been able to accommodate women's voices. If all the existing political forces are not appropriate vehicles, then what is the alternative? We need our own politics, was the answer. What is that politics? asked this large non-party critical formation, leading again to the quest to give content to feminism and its political, philosophical underpinnings.

The other strong concern was consolidation. The two, finding a politics and consolidation, are of course closely related quests, but not the same. Consolidation of this dynamic, self-conscious, widely dispersed, representative women's movement has become a real preoccupation in its every part. Simple aggregation does not make it into a political force. Yet the potential is there—a tantalising situation. The need for consolidation is acute because of the happenings in the Indian polity—reassertion of separatism, violent expressions of hidden angers over language, religion, caste and gender differentiation.

Why this sliding back to 'old barriers'? Poignantly bringing out the issue in analysing the ethnic conflicts in Sri Lanka, Kumari Jayawardene, who was present at the conference, said:

Ethnic consciousness has overpowered class consciousness. One reason is the scrambling for the cake: a mix of unattainable and untenable consumerism on the demand side and accelerated but distorted growth of output on the supply side. In the midst of these shattering experiences, feminist consciousness seems to flicker like lamps still alight before getting snuffed out.

Kumari Jayawardene described the spontaneity with which in the previous years, that is, the early 1980s, women from different classes, religions and politics took a united stand against ethnic riots, undertook peace marches, peace actions. The group then suggested that feminist consciousness was alive, and was replacing class consciousness and class solidarity as the focal point of progressive causes. The burning question then was how to prevent feminist consciousness from withering away or from being subordinated as has happened to class solidarity. What can we learn from the history of the deterioration of class consciousness? How to resist the decline? Again, consolidation seemed to be the first step, and that needs a politics, a common frame, a theory.

What theory can enshrine this quest? Could one trace the roots of the tangible unity and solidarity that seemed present in the room, but which escaped agreement when expressed? Feminist theory in India has to find an answer to these questions. This conference was a beginning.

My second illustration is from the thinking behind the founding of DAWN,[1] a third world women's network that brought in macro perspectives on women and development. The DAWN process analyses poor women's experience of development in the third world, in the context of the macro situations in their region like the food crisis in Africa, debt in Latin America, poverty and hunger in Asia. The DAWN analysis revealed both the impoverishing nature of 'development' and also the validity of the several survival strategies of women in poverty.

The root of this devastating development, which emptied oceans of fish, forests of tribal communities and women of wage and food, created enslavement of the South to the North, seemed to be not merely in the dubious intentions of the North, but in the theories and practices of development in the South, too—the legacy and language of the North, with the standard arguments in favour of growth.

In the alternative development programme that DAWN set in motion, what is challenged is the very process as well as the goals of development. Most revolutions talk of structural change—usually based on production and its ownership and organisation, linked to class and its power relations. The alternative path also requires a structural change but in *values*, and in conceptual and implementing *processes*. DAWN brought in the debates on political economy into the women and development discussion. It emphasised class, that is, poor women's perspectives as well as the crucial role of macro policy. It also underscored the vital importance of method/process. Thus, it could be said that DAWN, in arguing for a feminist development paradigm, suggested an ideological underpinning for the use of the term feminist: namely, identification with more than goals, with means, process. The means almost naturally are democratic, open, accountable, representative institutions, foregrounding the life experiences and perspectives of poor women.

My third illustration is from an inter-religious dialogue among feminists co-sponsored by the group 'Women, Religion and Social Change' at Harvard University, later brought out as a book, *Speaking of Faith* (Eck and Jain 1986) by an Indian feminist publishing house Kali. This dialogue leads to the view that while discrimination against women exists in all faiths, since women are the primary practitioners (of religion), there must be a strengthening and bonding aspect of religion, along with all the rest of the package of discrimination and bigotry. On what basis would women of faith bond? Feminism, it was suggested, and an illustration was provided by the feminist deconstruction of Christianity and its reconstruction by feminist believers in Christ. However, while Christology and feminism have begun to dialogue, this has not happened with non-Christian religions to the same extent.

Fatima Mernissi in a book called *Women in an Islamic Paradise* (1986) shows the clear role allocation for women and men in an Islamic heaven. A collection of profiles of women in Hindu, Buddhist, Christian and other paradises would reveal that paradises are not gender neutral, and also what they could be, if feminists remoulded them.

In an essay in *Speaking of Faith* (Eck and Jain 1986), I suggested that religion empowered women, given the context and the method. I illustrated my point with Gandhi's practice of meeting tradition halfway: *drawing on it*, so that those who have been caught in its web can step out; leading into it to keep the value of the core, of the individual ethic, the morality of self, enshrined in every religion. I referred to *bhajan*s and *sarva dharma* (all-religions) prayers to reveal both the mobilising and educating roles of religion. I showed how following an ethic of self-effacement can be a step to annihilate difference of all kinds—gender, class, caste, religion, 'me' and the 'other'. Becoming the other in a conflict situation was part of an etiquette derived from religion. Gandhi's form of secularism (*sarva dharma*), I suggested, was not agnosticism, but acceptance that there were many paths to the divine. I went on to suggest that women were the best vehicles for providing this leadership in religious practice—thus leavening, healing and sublimating conflicts in society.

There are several moving illustrations of women in struggle and women in grassroots organisations needing some form of 'unity'. For example, the chronicling of women's participation in national struggles in Palestine by Amrita Basu (1995) and by Islah Jad (1995) brings out what has been virtually a worldwide phenomenon, namely, 'the heroism of women in the struggle' not matched by concrete improvement in the status of women. Basu shows how, as a result of this negligence by the leadership, as a result of their not acknowledging in post-liberation times the work of women before the liberation, there grew a deepened feminist consciousness of the women's committees. They began to realise the necessity of both returning to women's programmes and creating new agendas for women.

While the uprising had brought together women from different 'spaces', the feminist consciousness arising out of the neglect drove them to draft a women's bill of rights. It is to be noted that the preamble says, 'We, the women of Palestine, from all social categories and various faiths'. It is inclusive because of the recognition that unity was necessary to overcome the male position of dominance and authority. The preamble continues:

> ... including workers, farmers, housewives, students, professionals and politicians, promulgate our determination to proceed with our struggle to abolish all forms of discrimination and inequality against women, which were propagated by the different forms of colonialism on our land, ending with the Israeli occupation and which were reinforced by the conglomeration of customs and traditions prejudiced against women, embodied in a number of existing laws and legislations (Jad 1995: 245).

This is the reality, and it is from this reality that we have to judge the discourse, the dialogue between feminist theorists and the practitioners. It is from this perspective that we have to see the importance of defining and giving substance to both feminist consciousness and feminist method.

The relationship between consciousness and activism is indeed difficult to establish, but in itself, consciousness too is neither uniform nor monolithic. Often women's experiences of their identities as gendered subjects do not assume a feminist form. Naihua Zhang (Basu 1995: 17) reports that since the 1980s, Chinese women have challenged the androgynous ideals of the past by emphasising their femininity. In the United States, the growing consciousness that identities are multiple rather than singular has often led women to emphasise race, ethnicity and sexual orientation as much as gender.

'Identity politics flourishes at the same time that a unified women's movement has declined' (Basu 1995: 17). This statement takes us back to the third world situation reflected in my dialogues. Christine Sylvester (1995) puts it this way:

One features feminism settling into its many philosophical and identity differences and defending an absence of consensus as appropriate for this era. Following closely on this first tendency is considerable feminist worry about issues of power and solidarity in a fragmented era and accompanying debates about the merit of this versus that specific feminism. The third tendency is in the direction of effecting some feminist amalgamations that merge or cross-fertilize the differences.

I would like to see a new trend emerge that takes the current emphasis on difference and turns it into 'something else' that is 'not an ascribed trait' or a feminist 'lifestyle' but a 'politics'.

I would like more emphasis on methods of speaking in, through and across differences—methods by which different identity feminisms and geo-spatial locations within them become mobile in ways that juggle and cross borderlands.

Barbara Cooper (1995: 853) says:

Women in Maradi share with women in feminist struggle else-where the necessity of living and working with what Ann Sintow has referred to as the 'recurring feminist divide'. In feminist discourse a tension keeps forming between finding a useful lever in female identity and seeing that identity as hopelessly compromised. Maradi women draw upon their common position as women while simultaneously calling into question the unity and stability of the category of 'woman'. They have played subversively upon the local category 'married woman' in order to make possible greater female public visibility, but their invocation of that category inevitably reinscribes local norms that stigmatize female sexuality outside of marriage.

Feminism as a 'Method'

One of the most fertile territories for pursuit on this journey to give boundaries to feminism is the issue of method or 'ways'. While even this has been contested, it can be linked to another discourse, which is on theories and practices, and how theories can be built and practice often gives content to theory. For example, an interesting dialogue among feminist scholars took place at the IAWS National Seminar at Baroda in 1997 over Periyar's Self-Respect Movement in south India . A paper by V. Geetha (1997) provided the context for the discussion. Periyar or E.V. Ramaswamy Naicker initiated a movement to build the self-esteem of the downtrodden. He emphasised rationality, the mind over the heart and emotion. He posited radical views on the roles of women, supporting their singleness as well as their autonomy in the lives they wished to lead. Periyar challenged Gandhi, arguing that the latter's attention to the spirit, and appeal to emotion, love, forgiveness, etc. was a façade for sustaining the unjust social structure of India, whether injustice on the basis of caste or gender.

In retrospect, looking at it from 1997, it was also suggested at the same seminar that Periyar's ideals have been so corrupted in today's Tamil Nadu that his idea of a rational society has been converted into a Tamil fundamentalism of the most limited kind, leading actually to the Backward Castes oppressing the Dalits. His ideal of motherhood has been distorted into 'mother' as Tamil nation and thus circumscribed women's autonomy. In other words, his principles have been misrepresented in practice.

On the other hand, for all the ambivalence of Gandhi's principles, their practical and moral values still persist. Could this be because Gandhi's theory emerged from practice and went halfway to meet Indian aspirations?

Gandhi's 'this-worldly' approach to revolution was especially appropriate to women's experience. He demonstrated this during India's freedom struggle. Women were significant participants in economic struggles—in the boycott of foreign textiles and in the salt march. For women in the freedom movement, spinning meant self-reliance and identification with the unskilled and unemployed.

In their biographies, many women leaders of the national movement have described how Gandhi's call to *satyagraha* (literally 'truth-force') opened the door to them for their own liberation from oppressive social modes. The code of his *ashram*s included simplicity in dress and reverence for women. The rules of the *ashram*s made it possible for women to come out of the narrow worlds of their homes to participate in a wider community.

> I am uncompromising in the matter of women's rights. In my opinion, she should suffer under no legal disability not suffered by man. I should treat the daughters and sons on a footing of perfect equality.
>
> Today the sole occupation of women amongst us is supposed to be to bear children, to look after her husband and otherwise to drudge for the household. This is a shame. Not only is the woman condemned to domestic slavery but when she goes out as a labourer to earn wages, though she works harder than men, she is paid less (Jain 1981).

In a sense, Gandhi met Indian tradition halfway. He directed it away from its establishment 'structures' and towards its 'dynamics' of change. It was this method that facilitated the emergence of women from the grip of orthodox tradition. However 'reformist' or 'middle-path' such an approach may seem, it is tactically effective, because it provides vehicles and options for change (Jain 1986: 285).

Feminism as Ideology

Many attempts have been made to see if, apart from the methodological, an ideological content too can be given to feminism. Formulations that method is ideology are not being considered here. One such is standpoint theory, which suggests that being a woman leads to developing a point of view—a view from where you stand as a woman. This standpoint overrides the divides of location, time and social stratification.

Helen Longino (1993: 201–2) puts it this way:

The problems of knowledge are central to feminist theorizing, which has sought to destabilize androcentric mainstream thinking in the humanities and in the social and natural sciences. Feminist standpoint theory has been one of the most distinctive and debated contributions of contemporary feminist thought to the theory of knowledge. While some feminist theorists extend its range to natural phenomena, the theory was developed in a social science context and has been advocated primarily by feminists in one or another of the social sciences or by feminists emerging from the Marxist tradition. Provisionally standpoint theory reflects the view that women (or feminists) occupy a social location that affords them/us a privileged access to social phenomena. This root notion has had various expressions, ranging from the romantic idea that women come, by nature or by social experience, to be better equipped to know the world than are men to the modest proposal that a social science adequate for women must proceed from a grasp of the forms of oppression women experience. Associated with standpoint theory was the concept of successor science, a science that would supercede male-centred science. Since feminist standpoint theory was introduced in the 1970s, postmodern theorizing which calls into question not only the very possibility of knowledge but also the possibility of the category of women, has influenced a growing number of feminist thinkers.

Again, for feminists located in countries of a high level of poverty and inequality, the need for ideology seems obvious: an ideology that contains the commitment to removal of poverty and injustice, inequality and discrimination. As I have discussed elsewhere (Jain 1996), for me, feminism is contained in Gandhi's talisman in which he says, 'Whenever you are in doubt, or when the self becomes too much with you, apply the following test. Recall the face of the poorest and weakest man or woman whom you may have seen and ask yourself if the step you contemplate is going to be of any use to him.' Gandhi referred to the poorest man as *Daridranarayana*. I would change it to *Daridranarayani*, the final *ni* giving it a feminine gender.

Into the 21st Century

Today, in the first decade of the 21st century, the 'corner' from which I view my world is somewhat influenced by the threats that I see. This century offers a challenge and demands greater solidarity and more politically significant collective action.

This century has been anticipated and characterised in many ways—positive and negative. Information technology has crossed all barriers—national boundaries, corporate empires, intellectual regimes. So in a sense it has levelled. It has also seen an increase in social fragmentation apart from acceptance and affirmation of social diversity. Difference, pluralism, multiple identities and self-determination are keywords. Feminists associate themselves with these affirmations—the rights movements, the ecology safeguarding movements, as well as the celebration of diversity and self-determination as it empathises with their cultural aspiration for democracy, for space, for equality, for a discrimination-free society.

However, this very current also mutes the power of broad-based solidarity. Feminists would argue that while difference needs accommodation, unified action on specific issues is possible when necessary. I have elaborated on this elsewhere (Jain 1997).

However, there are other aspects of the current century that are horrific and that cannot be contained by periodical spontaneous actions. They require careful, systematic, well-organised, strategically planned action that can create the pressure to resist, to push back.

What are these horrors?

Threatening erosion of nature—and therefore greater disease/ imbalance between soil, air, water and humans. The possibility of new mutants in humans and plants. The fragmentation of society and its old foundations—family, community, class, etc. Individual- isation. The overpowering economic influence of 'unaccountable' finance and its warlords. Hence, an abrogation in national sover- eignty; hence, accountability of nations to their citizens. A world order without a world, footloose-ness of all peoples, cultures, eco- nomic giants and lilliputs, and therefore a blurring of purpose and responsibility. And last, but not least, an increase in disparities between people—rich and poor, men and women, place and place— often leading to conflict. Hence, a more warring society, even if wars are little and local.

A shapeless planet in an awesome century.

In such a situation what seems necessary is intense counter- mobilisation with a clear purpose of retrieving and reclaiming the earth, water, air, humanity, justice, cultural order, identity, responsibility. The women's movement can do this; they are the largest stakeholders for a healthy planet: giving life, they do not want it corrupted or wasted.

But they require sustained and organised action plans with agendas. Not only for women, but for society, state, market. Today it seems that there is a case for finding some form of similarity within these differences. As I have reflected elsewhere (Jain 1996), Beijing showed to some extent that it is possible to 'feel' a sense of unity as a woman, even though such statements have been legitimately challenged in feminist discourse. Some of the 'sense of unity' experienced at the United Nations Fourth World Conference on Women (FWCW) are as follows.

A united sense of political will. It was as if the worldwide women's movement, including those who are spokespersons of women at the official conference, were functioning, to use the Zen concept, as one 'Big Mind', and were determined to bring women into formal political leadership.

Relating to the above, a new consciousness, which could be called a political consciousness. This is not only about politics, but about a consciousness—feminist consciousness—that women's perspectives, women's struggles are a political issue.

The third is what Naila Kabeer (1994) calls 'reversing relation-ships'. The power centres for change are moving from the govern-ment not only to the market but also to civil society. The abrogation of the state and the increasing of an undefinable autonomous and unaccountable process called globalisation is provoking reaction from citizens' groups. These elements could be summarised as Beijing's 'Big Mind'.

Fourth, the sense of discomfort with the concept and march of globalisation.

In India, the issue confronts not only the daily interaction with acute poverty, inequality, deprivation, but also cruelty and violence, especially to women and children. The statistics, however poor in quality they are, make it impossible to relax as a member of the women's movement. Yet no significant dent has been made by women on public or private policy in relation to women and girl children.

In this context, it seems important to develop an identity within the multiple identities around the consciousness of women. I give below some women's voices, culled from my own earlier work (Jain 1982)—some of whom are angry with men, some of whom want to fight with men and some who want to affirm that women have different ways than men. I suggest that these are very similar to the voices I have heard in Latin America, Africa, USA, UK, Scandinavia. Apart from Asia, I suggest that based on this 'similarity' we need to unite in action and that action has to be supported by thought and literature, which extols the common consciousness of women as women and therefore goes back to the narrow definition of feminism like the one I started out with.

Forty-five year old Kempamma works in a coffee curing shed in Chikmagalur in Karnataka. Packing coffee seeds into sacks. 'What do they know?' she says, in pointing out to her male supervisors. 'We are to do nothing but bow our heads all our lives. I have a sick child. I am late. I am not given work—the family eats nothing that day. I bow my head. The union strikes for better wages. We starve for 15 days and we go back for 10 paise more. I bow my head.' Like a swan dipping into water, Kempamma demonstrates her words, bending her head down to touch the floor, with her hand on her forehead.

Haseena Begum and many others like her live in the Jama Masjid area but are also distributed across Delhi, Agra, Lucknow and many other cities and villages. They are Zardosi workers. At a meeting of SEWA, Delhi, where the women were discussing the fact that their daughters came home with babies as their men divorced them. She said—'Yah, Allah, why did you create men?'

In rural Ahmedabad district the eminent workers' union SEWA had a project for rural women associated with the equally famous National Dairy Development Board known for what is called the White Revolution. A woman was being trained and shown the technology of artificial insemination. After the class was over she drew aside the young technician who was demonstrating how he could upgrade cattle stock, and asked him if there were a similar technique by which she could have higher quality children as the men folk in their village were weak and useless. She belonged to a social category where women cover their heads and never speak to a man except through the sari veil.

Here are some voices of the women in the local government (Jain 1997):

I am a better representative of the people than men. I can always be found in the kitchen, whereas the men cannot be traced—they are in the liquor shops or in cinema halls or loafing.

Suman Kolhar, Vice-president,
Zilla Parishad, Bijapur, Karnataka

I inherited a ward nursed by my husband but now the people come to me, not to him, as I am accessible.

Ms. Nayak, Mayor, Ponda, Goa

Many thought that being a woman I could be pushed over and they could drive from the back seat. But after a few months that feeling has changed.

A.K. Premajam, Mayor, Kozhikode

Some of the elected women who came to my workshops were very forthright:

Thirty-three per cent is not enough. We should have 50 per cent. The men treat us with disdain. We should have the strength of numbers.

Train the men—not us. Train them to step back, give them psychological training in relinquishing power.

Are they indigenous feminists? Or feminists?

Thus, I come back to my earlier proposition that the cutting edge for both defining as well as giving purpose to feminism is the 'grassroots' need of the mass of women. Classifications such as indigenous and western do not, in my view, serve any purpose. I would even deny such 'differences'.

The difficulties of using 'woman' as an identity are present in all cultures and circumstances. Whether one acts in subterfuge as the women of Niger do, consolidates feminist consciousness as the women of Palestine do, or combines an agenda across party lines as the women of *panchayati raj* institutions do, there is in my view the underlying gender-derived identity. Feminist consciousness presupposes the consciousness of the identity of woman as woman. Feminist method is a form of affirming that women have specific ways of dealing with power, with structures, with ideas.

There is a crying need for women to unite on issues. A video documentary by Friedrich Ebert Stiftung of the Andhra women's anti-arrack struggle is called 'When Women Unite'. No need to say more. Leadership, especially in governance—political, economic, cultural—is in an abysmal state. 'If women unite' can be the most significant factor of change in the 21st century. But it is a big ' if' unless feminist consciousness and being a woman is seen as a basis for identity.

Note

1. Development Alternatives with Women for a New Era (DAWN) was founded in August 1984 at Bangalore by a group of women representing all regions of the world.

References

Basu, Amrita (ed.) (1995). *The Challenge of Local Feminisms: Women's Movements in Global Perspective*. Boulder, San Fransisco: Westview Press.

Cooper, Barbara, M. (1995). 'The Politics of Difference and Women's Associations in Niger: "Prostitutes", the Public and Politics', *Signs*, 20(4): 851–82.

Eck, Diana L and Jain, Devaki (eds.) (1986). *Speaking of Faith: Global Perspectives on Women, Religion and Social Change*. Philadelphia, Pennsylvania: New Society Publishers.

Geetha, V. (1997). 'Periyar, Women and an Ethic of Citizenship'. National Seminar of the Indian Association of Women's Studies, Baroda.

Jad, Islah (1995). 'Claiming Feminism, Claiming Nationalism: Women's Activism in the Occupied Territories', in Amrita Basu (ed.), *The Challenge of Local Feminisms: Women's Movements in Global Perspective*, pp. 240–46. Boulder, San Fransisco: Westview Press.

Jain, Devaki (1981). 'Gandhian Women Workers'. Paper presented at a Seminar, 25 May, New Delhi.

———— (1982). 'Indian Women: Today and Tomorrow' (Padmaja Naidu Memorial Lecture). New Delhi: Nehru Memorial Musuem and Library.

———— (1985). 'Dialogue with Feminists from the North: A Conversation', Athens; June. Mimeo.

———— (1986). 'Gandhian Contribution towards a Feminist Ethic', in Eck and Jain (eds.), pp. 255–70.

———— (1995). 'Minds, Not Bodies'. Bradford Morse Memorial Lecture. Beijing: UNDP.

———— (1996). *Minds, Bodies and Exemplars* (book of 10 lectures). New Delhi: British Council Division, British High Commission.

———— (1997). 'Note for Anti-Arrack Meeting'. Unpublished, India International Centre, 18 April.

Jaywardene, Kumari (1982). *Feminism and Nationalism in the Third World: History of the Women's Movement in the 19th and Early 20th Centuries* (A Lecture Series, Part II). The Hague: Institute of Social Studies.

Kabeer, Naila (1994). *Reversed Realities: Gender Hierarchies in Development Thought*. London: Verso.

Longino, Helen E. (1993). 'Feminist Standpoint Theory and the Problems of Knowledge', *Signs*, 19(1): 201–12.

Mernissi, Fatima (1986). *Women in a Muslim Paradise*. New Delhi: Kali for Women.

Sylvester, Christine (1995). 'African and Western Feminism: World-travelling the Tendencies and Possibilities', *Signs*, 20(4): 941–69.

13

'Re'inscribing the Past: Inserting Women into Indian History

Uma Chakravarti

Women have a dual relationship with history in India as they are simultaneously present and absent in the historical accounts that have come down to us. Because women are both invisible, especially from a feminist standpoint, and relatively visible from the point of view of the concerns of nationalist history, especially in the context of ancient India, the task of the feminist historian today is doubly difficult. Unlike many other parts of the world where women have had to be inserted into history, here history has, in a sense, to be rewritten. Further, rewriting history from a woman-inclusive standpoint requires historians to not only explore (and re-explore) sources and social processes, uncover evidence (which has been ignored or marginalised because of existing biases) and thereafter insert issues of gender into new historical writing, such writing has also to uncover the many histories of suppression, resulting in history having become a flattened and unidimensional account of a few men. Historians writing in the last 20 years or so in India have, therefore, *necessarily* had to shift the focus on to the neglected segments of our society, thereby broadening its ambit. Under this new focus, a gender-sensitive history is now beginning to be possible, although we need to note that this new field was not an automatic consequence of a shift of focus but the conscious product of feminist interventions. What also needs to be noted is that among the first tasks to be addressed by feminist scholars, even before launching into the writing of a new kind of history, was the attention that had to be paid to analysing what had gone before: a feminist historiography has, therefore, preceded a feminist rewriting of the past. And finally, when the new feminist history began to be written it had to go beyond the concerns of colonialists and nationalists to explore the structures and ideologies that have contributed to the particularities of South Asian patriarchies.

Search for Alternative Sources and Interpretations

Despite the surfacing of new concerns and a new will amongst a section of historians, there are many inherent problems in writing a history that is genuinely inclusive of women. The sources of history, here as elsewhere, reflect the concerns of those who have wielded power. It is sometimes argued, with justification, that the notion of time, and therefore of history, in the dominant Indian tradition, the brahmanical, has been cyclical and not linear, making for a crucial difference in the understanding of history (*cf.* Devahuti 1979; also Thapar 1997). One implication of this view is that the contemporary discipline of history in India is a derivative of the western, linear, tradition, and violates the spirit of the 'authentic' Indian tradition. The further implication is that, therefore, it cannot be subjected to certain kinds of scrutiny. What is ignored in this argument is that the cyclical notion of history is as much the product of those who have wielded power as the linear view of history is. It might be useful to note that unlike archaeological evidence, which may be loosely described as the 'garbage' of history, as the incidental remnants of material culture, and therefore not associated with the conscious decision to leave something to posterity, written records are *self-conscious* products and are closely tied to those who have exercised power. The *Rajatarangini*, the *Harshacharita* or the *itihasa* portions of the Puranas are unambiguous narratives of power even if they may reflect a cyclical view of history.

It might also be argued that these sources constitute only a small fraction of the sources we have for ancient India, and the bulk of the sources are not conventional historical sources at all but a variegated collection of myths, religious texts and other types of literary productions.[1] Nevertheless, the textual sources that have come down to us, even when they are religious, cultural, social or concerned with the political economy, are products of a knowledge system that was highly monopolistic and hierarchical, and thus narrowly concentrated in the hands of a few men—a group that was even narrower here than elsewhere.

In this context it might be useful to explore the manner in which scholars have tried to break out of the limited concerns imposed by the 'recorders' of history who have, in a sense, refracted history for us. In contemporary times it is possible to use oral history as a way of countering the biases of 'official' history. But the relationship of orality to textuality is very complex in the case of our early history. In a sense, all 'texts' were orally transmitted and then 'written' up much later. Though these texts only ultimately became prescriptive, or were regarded as sacred, they were treated as authoritative and therefore worthy of formal handing down in the traditional way, which was oral precisely because it could be carefully controlled. 'Oral' texts are not in and of themselves counter-hegemonic. Further, certain oral traditions that had been brought into the ideological field of the religious literati but nevertheless circulated largely among the humbler folk, and were therefore more widely shared as they were narrated to a heterogeneous audience, such as the *Jataka*s or the *Panchatantra*, though significant in terms of yielding a different kind of evidence on women and the lower orders, are not necessarily the compositions of such sections, at least in the versions that have come down to us. The *Jataka*s, for example, comprise a rich repertoire of narratives and often describe the experiences of ordinary women and men with great poignancy; they are, nevertheless, firmly located within a Buddhist world-view. As they stand, the *Jataka*s are the product of mediations between high culture and 'low' culture; framed by the *bhikkhu*s these narratives cannot be termed 'folk'. While they are an alternative to the brahmanical texts, they cannot be regarded as the dichotomised 'other' of elite texts (Chakravarti 1993a).

Similarly, the *Therigatha*, verses or songs of the *bhikkhuni*s, a work that is probably one of the earliest compilations of women's poetry anywhere in the world, while very definitely the compositions of women, have not escaped the editorial hand of the Buddhist monastic compilers (ibid.). These factors have complicated the use of oral sources and the writing of a gender-sensitive history from below. There are further problems because of the difficulties of dating oral texts, which therefore cannot easily be collated with other evidence available for specific periods. While we gain from the point of view of the richness of the data, we lose from the point of view of specificity of time and region. Nevertheless, despite the many problems inherent in the sources, the newer generation of historians, writing from a 'history from below' standpoint, including feminists, have begun to use these sources creatively. Using strategies such as reading against the grain and between the lines, especially in the case of prescriptive texts, or looking at the way myths and narratives change in a diachronic context, they are raising new questions and bringing in fresh insights, but more of this later (Chakravarty 1983, 1993a).

Nationalist, Marxist and Subaltern Histories: Where is Gender?

It might be useful at this point to examine the factors that led to a shift in the writing of history and thus acted as a catalyst for gender history. In the Indian context, nationalist history dominated the scene until the late 1950s. Nationalist history was primarily focused on political history (kings, conquests, invasions, as in the case of the earlier colonial history; liberal and imaginative administrators, political institutions and so on) and cultural history (mainly a detailing of achievements on the cultural front). Apart from an obsessive concern with locating and outlining idealised images and golden ages, there was almost a conscious steering away from examining internal contradictions, hierarchies along different axes, and oppressive structures.[2] This was part of a move to present the imperial government with a united front, but also a product of middle-class myopia obsessed with a single axis of deprivation, between the colonial power and the nation's *bhadralok*—the elite—in relation to them.[3]

Meanwhile, going back to the late colonial period, social history made its appearance. Here, as elsewhere, in the early stages, social history was a kind of residual history with politics and economics left out. Some of the issues explored under this rubric were the history of social reform, and religious and revivalist movements, mostly within the framework of biographical narratives of the men spearheading the movements.[4] Finally, in the decades after independence and under the influence of Marxist approaches, social history became the history of social formations. D.D. Kosambi pioneered this field with two brilliant and wide-ranging books and a series of imaginative papers published from the mid-1950s onwards (Kosambi 1956, 1962, 1970). His formulations were the basis for detailed analyses on various epochs of Indian history and the relationship between modes of production and other political and social institutions. By the late 1970s and 1980s there were raging debates on whether or not there was feudalism in India (see, for instance, Mukhia and Byres 1985; Sharma 1985), and while the issues thrown up in the course of this debate were important, there was absolutely nothing on what happened to women in the feudal mode of production, or where they figured in the new relations of production.[5] The underlying presumption was that history for women was the same as history for men. No attempt was made to move into the field of the modes of social reproduction while continuing to explore modes of production where class and gender could be combined making for a connection between gender structures, ideologies, and social and economic power structures. Similarly, although there was a welcome shift towards exploring the history of the lower orders, such as the *dasa-karmakaras*, *shudras*, and *chandalas* (see, for example, Chanana 1960; Jha 1987; Sharma 1958), bringing in issues of caste and class and unequal power relations, this did not include an examination of unequal gender relations. In any case, a shortcoming, in my view, of the history of social formations is that human beings as individuals, whether men or women, and their experience of different social processes, seemed to be missing from it. Since it centred on modes of production, the primary issues that were explored were the ways in which surplus was extracted, the particular forms of labour exploitation, and the role of technology in transforming relations of production; human experiences, mentalities and emotions tended to be left unexplored. In some ways, then, such a history was as distant as the earlier dynastic or administrative histories had been. This lacuna has to some extent been rectified by new trends in history writing under the label of 'subaltern' studies, but these scholars, too, have neglected women as a category.[6] While they brought into the frame of history the lives and struggles of ordinary people such as peasants and tribals, they also focused on peasant *men* and tribal *men* without even being conscious that there could be subalterns within subalterns. Their writing was as male centred as earlier nationalist or Marxist history had been. It is ironical that even as a certain space was opening up for a history of the 'powerless', the most powerless among the powerless remained outside the framework of new historical trends.

Writing Women's History: Impulse from Activism

How, then, did the shift occur in terms of the writing of women's history? I would unqualifiedly attribute this to the women's movement of the 1970s, which provided the context and the impetus for the emergence of women's studies in India. As Sarkar (1996) has pointed out, women's history as a sustained and self-conscious tradition developed from the 1970s since many feminist scholars were themselves involved in the vigorous and turbulent movements against rape, dowry and domestic violence. In my view, it was here that the contours of the multiple forms and structures of patriarchies, and the cultural practices associated with them began to be outlined through the experiences of women on the ground. These years, during the heyday of an explicitly political women's movement, and the insights derived therein, provided feminist scholars with the experiential material on the basis of which they formulated gender as a category of analysis. (The recent phenomena of mainstream scholars cashing in on the space created for women's history, without addressing the existence of patriarchies in their writing, for example, Chakravarty [1994], is an explicitly anti-political and deflective agenda, marking a sharp break from *feminist* scholarship.) And since the 1970s also witnessed other political movements of peasants, workers and tribals, turning our attention onto the marginalised and the oppressive conditions under which they lived and struggled, historians were *forced* to broaden the ambit of history; the content of history has thus been dramatically democratised and we are now happily moving in a direction that is making history the most dynamic discipline in the social sciences. But it is important to recognise that historians, and only some of them at that, respond to grassroots assertions: they do not lead the new trends but merely follow the agendas set by our people, which is why a gender sensitive history had to wait for the women's movement and was not an automatic or logical trend following from Marxist history or subaltern history.

Women's History: A Critical Review

In moments such as these, it is apt that a review of the main trends in women's history is undertaken.[7] Beginning with tentative formulations and simple rereadings, it is by now fairly evident that despite a weak institutional base, women's history has taken off. During the last decade some very fine work has appeared in the field of women's history, forcing mainstream historians to recognise and sometimes even cash in on the 'market' created by feminist scholarship as we noted earlier. It is unfortunate that this upbeat gender market is coinciding with a decline in the market for studies on labour: thus, the market is pitting two sets of disadvantaged groups against each other as if they are discrete entities with no relationship, a typical ploy of the market maniacs now dominating the publishing world.

Among the first major moves made by feminist scholars was that of dismantling the dominant nationalist narrative of the glory of Hindu womanhood during the ancient past, specifically during the Vedic period. By breaking up the Hindu/Vedic woman into the 'Aryan' and the *dasi* woman attention was drawn to the differing histories of women according to respective social locations.[8] This corrective was important because while it was necessary to insert gender as an axis of stratification, it was equally necessary, perhaps more so, of also outlining the stratification that existed *within* women. The suppressions entailed in the homogenised product of the nationalists, the Hindu/Vedic or Aryan woman, became evident. At the same time the need to outline the distinctive social histories of women was highlighted. Thus, while the major tendency during these early years was to write a complementary, or supplementary, history of women to accompany the narratives of mainstream history by plotting the history of women in different arenas and in different types of struggles, the distinctive experiences of women in the context of class was built into the analysis of gender.

A second feature of the thrust in writing women's history was the painstaking uncovering and compiling of an archive of women's writing (Tharu and Lalitha 1991, 1993). Given the male biases of the sources normally relied upon by mainstream history, and the difficulties experienced by feminist historians in finding alternative sources, the putting together of this archive has been very significant. It has helped break down the canonisation of certain sources that are no longer invariably regarded as more reliable, but, more correctly, as having achieved authoritative status through their closeness to power. A parallel and no less significant development has been the appearance of some extremely rich and sensitive readings of women's writing, which I shall deal with more extensively below.

Ancient India

An overview of women's history and the insights derived from the new writing lead directly to the recognition that gender as a tool of analysis has been very unevenly used to explore the three conventional chronological phases of ancient, medieval and modern India. The bulk of the new writing is being done for colonial and post-colonial India, and there is very little of such writing for ancient and even less for medieval India. This is in part due to the need for a knowledge of the classical languages in which the sources are available for these phases, but it is also partly attributable to the dominant contemporary theoretical concerns which are focused *solely* on colonial and post-colonial Indian society. In practice this has also meant the abandonment of these phases to the continuing domination of the Indological framework that is locked into a high classical and consensus approach, unwilling to recognise that there could be other histories.

However, there have been pioneering works heralding a breakthrough in more ways than one. A recent study by Kumkum Roy (1995) on the emergence of monarchy in early India is significant because it uses precisely those sources that the Indologists have always relied upon, the brahmanical texts relevant for the period, but opened them up to a totally different line of inquiry. The study also links the interrelatedness of the different axes of stratification to outline the processes by which hierarchies were established and legitimised through the use of brahmanical rituals. Once the structure was in place, the king was regarded as the legitimate controller of the productive and reproductive resources of the kingdom. At the same time the *yajamana*, on whose behalf rituals were performed, came to be regarded as the controller of the productive and reproductive resources of the household. The most significant aspect of Roy's work is that it breaks down the false, but perhaps for the moment operationally necessary, divide between gender history and mainstream history. It demonstrates how our understanding of the past is expanded and enriched when gender is included as a category of analysis.

Other issues that have been probed at the conceptual level include the relationship between caste, class, patriarchy and the state (Chakravarti 1993a) and the dynamics of the household in early India (Roy 1992). Apart from these studies, which are attempts at exploring women's histories at the level of the relationship of gender to other institutions, there are studies of the changing versions of myths and other narratives, prostitution, motherhood, labouring women, property relations, women as gift-givers and women as rulers (see, for example, Bhattacharji 1994). These accounts have helped gradually build up a base for further conceptualisations and to break the hold of the Altekarian paradigm, which has dominated the field of women's history in the case of 'ancient' India.[9] A major lacuna that continues to restrict our understanding is the way in which gender shapes, and is in turn shaped by, other structures within a given social formation.

Medieval India

While a beginning has been made from the point of view of using a gender-based framework in the case of early Indian history, there is a singular paucity of works using gender as a category of analysis in medieval Indian history. Even a women's history that complements or supplements mainstream history is far from being systematically written. Perhaps this is because there has been a slow response to engage with gender as a category of analysis from scholars with a mastery over Persian in a situation where Persian sources continue to dominate the field of medieval Indian history. A slow beginning has been made recently.[10] The most sustained output comes from South Asia specialists from American academies, but these are usually narrowly empirical and steer clear of making broader analytical points (see, for instance, Taft 1990). The lack of a strong gender-based standpoint is unfortunate because it is not as if the sources for medieval India are peculiarly disadvantaged; in fact, the situation is quite the reverse. It is just that the sources have never been systematically explored from the point of view of gender. Kumkum Sangari's (1990) finely nuanced and elaborately analysed study of *bhakti* poetry and within that of Mira's location is an example of historicising literature and individuals during the medieval period. Sangari's analysis of the family, kinship and the state is a pointer to the direction that a gender-sensitive history could fruitfully take. Happily, studies are now under way on a range of themes on medieval India.[11] Perhaps these studies and others can be linked together, and others can be undertaken, leading to broader understanding of gender relations in medieval India.

An important gap in the gender history of both ancient and medieval India is the absence of region-based studies. With the exception of a few explorations of Tamil literature and inscriptions of early and medieval south India (see, for example, Mahanta 1999; Mukund 1992; Nandy and Raman 1997; Parasher and Naik 1986; Ramaswamy 1989, 1994, 1997; Talbot 1995), we have very little by which we can make connections between the social formations of different regions and the ways in which these would have shaped gender relations in their respective regions.[12]

Colonial and Post-colonial India

More wide-ranging explorations have been possible in the field of women's history during the colonial and post-colonial period. More accessible from the point of view of the languages in which the sources are available, these sources are also better preserved. Consequently, feminist scholars have been able to not only insert women into history, but also examine the relationship between various social and economic processes and gender. They have also been able to explore certain themes in some depth and have made a dent in historical debates about nationalism, class formation and the operations of caste.

Among the more rigorous areas of research in women's history during this period has been the analysis of the way in which new colonial structures, especially in the field of law, shaped the lives of women. An impressive body of writing has examined the working of specific laws such as the Widow Remarriage Act, the impetus and the forces behind the creation and codification of laws, the contradictions between the applications of different sets of legal systems such as customary law and statutory law, statutory law and 'personal' law, and the general move towards homogenising the diversity of social customs and cultural practices (Caroll 1989; Chakravarti 1998: chapter 3; Nair 1996; Singha 1988). One of the most exhaustive and significant studies by Bina Agrawal (1994) has focused on the way law shapes gender relations by denying women access to productive resources in the form of land. She has thus provided us with an understanding of the political economy of the vulnerability of women. While some of these studies have been empirical, others have examined the historical context, class dynamics and the relationship of law to colonialist and nationalist ideologies at given moments. These studies have also been able to reveal the possibilities and limitations of colonialist (and nationalist) hegemonic agendas.

The issue of women's education has been the subject of numerous writings. Initially, scholars tended to plot the different stages by which opportunities for women's education were created and expanded in the context of the movement for social reform, taking for granted its 'positive', liberatory and transformative potential (Basu [1989–90], Devji [1994], Karlekar [1991]; Metcalfe [1982]; Minault [1998]). Men's spearheading of the campaign for women's education then appeared to be genuinely 'liberal'; perhaps it was paternalistic (Lateef 1990), but it was presumed that it was a means by which women would be emancipated from an earlier deprivation. These studies have now been taken much further to examine the crucial role of education, or rather 'schooling', in the agendas of new patriarchies and the relationship of schooling for women to processes of class formation. Men's stake in women's education and power over them, women's agency and resistance in a conflict-ridden household in the process of many kinds of transition have also been outlined Bandhopadhyay 1994; Banerji 192; Chakravarti 1998; Sangari 1991.

Some of these analyses have been made possible through a close examination of women's writing. As women were drawn into literacy and education, mostly at the instance of their menfolk (to make them companionate wives and fitting mothers), but sometimes against their approval, they took to writing. Letters, memoirs, essays, autobiographies, biographies, poetry, stories, travelogues and, on occasion, social critiques of patriarchy appeared by the end of the 19th century and continued into the 20th century (see, for example, Bhattacharya 1998; Ghosh 1986; Kosambi 1988; Mukherji 1988;

O'Hanlon 1994; Sarkar 1999a and b). Feminist scholarship on this alternative archive has been significant in fine-tuning our understanding of social reform, but also in revealing to us what was suppressed in the accounts of mainstream history. It is to be expected that the social critiques written by 19th century women would be regarded as significant markers in the history of women's resistance to the ideologies and practices of male domination; women like Pandita Ramabai and Tarabai Shinde have thus become known in the world of feminist scholarship through the writings of Chakravarti, O'Hanlon and Kosambi. What is important is that through Sarkar's sensitive reading of a seemingly conformist piece of writing, by Rashsundari Devi, one can uncover an oblique but moving critique of upper-caste cultural practices.

The history of labouring women, too, has been sought to be included in the rewriting of history. Accounts of their participation in agrarian struggles, issues that were raised and others that were suppressed, and the perception of the women of those 'magic' days, as some of them put it, as for instance the work of Kannabiran and Lalitha (1989), Stree Shakti Sangatana (1989) and Custers (1987), have been important not only to balance out the accounts of 'peasant' struggles, but also in exploring the complicated relationship between issues of class and gender, and the strategies of left-wing groups in highlighting class oppression and suppressing gender oppression. Feminist scholars discovered that:

In their recuperation of earlier histories of women's political activism, questions of sexual politics and its complicated relations with broader struggles were of central, absorbing importance: struggles that needed women, mobilised them, conferred a political and public identity upon them, and yet subtly contained them and displaced their work for their own rights (Sarkar 1996: 5–6).

Women's place in the organised labour force, especially in the textile and jute industries, have been the subject of monographs (Banerjee 1989; Kumar 1989; Sen 1992) and currently there are a number of studies under way on women in the unorganised sector, especially in the context of globalisation and the structural adjustment programme (see Chhachhi et al. 1994). These studies, being the first of their kind, have, however, retained a largely empirical approach. Perhaps with more studies documenting the daily lives of labouring women, we might be able to write an account of the making of the working class from a woman-centred point of view. However, history is changing so rapidly in the new era of globalisation that the working class may be transformed beyond recognition even before we can write their history!

Among the more significant researches in writing an account of women's labour within an historical frame is the issue of domestic labour. This has been a central issue in feminism resulting in a considerable body of scholarship, in the West as well as the third world, the work of Delphi (1984) being a good example. Its relationship to capitalism has been repeatedly stressed in western feminist scholarship. In India studies have analysed domestic labour in its relationship to caste, class, widowhood, hierarchies within the household and the capacity of households to buy domestic services.[13] At the conceptual level, the relationship of domestic labour to the labour market and the proliferation of the sexual division of labour in wage work, even as it might appear to be outside the realm of market, has also been highlighted. The fact that domestic labour exists within a system of non-dissoluble, non-contractual marriage permeated by ideologies of service and nurture has meant that domestic labour and domestic ideologies not only co-exist but are also jointly reproduced even in a rapidly changing economic and social system has also been pointed out by Sangari (1993: 5–46).

Earlier on in this paper it has been suggested that feminist scholarship has had to be innovative in its use of sources as well as in their reading of them. One of the recent works that has been extremely successful in such an approach has used a range of sources, including conventional sources such as statistics and government reports, but has balanced these by folk literature, proverbs and fieldwork to locate women's perception of their own lives. The framework of the political economy of gender used by Prem Chowdhry (1994) has yielded an important study of the everyday experiences of labouring women of a peasant caste over a 100-year period.

The use of oral history by feminist historians to explicitly critique the inadequacies and biases of official and mainstream/malestream and elitist histories has been extremely significant in the field of partition history. Here, women have been the pioneers in writing an alternative history written from the point of view of the marginalised: women, children and *dalit*s. They have raised crucial questions

about the ideologies of the state in the context of notions of community, and honour in the recovery and rehabilitation of 'abducted'
women and the doubled dimensions of violence experienced by
women first at the hands of men, and then at the hands of a
patriarchal state that denied women agency as it sought to align
boundaries with communities (see, for instance, Butalia 1998;
Menon and Bhasin 1998). It is significant that feminist scholarship
has provided a systematic critique of nationalism at the very moment
of the birth of a new nation. Far from a recognition of their pioneering
work, even their critique of nationalism and of the post-colonial
Indian state is yet to be taken seriously by mainstream historians.
This is perhaps an outcome of the territoriality of mainstream/
malestream historians entrenched in the academy, with personal
stakes in retaining their hold on historical writing. Further, in
my view, these are part of an agenda of once more marginalising,
or even erasing, women's pioneering of a new field, thereby claiming
both originality and monopoly over theory. Given the backlash
against feminist scholars in terms of appointments to universities
at the highest level, currently under way, the political dimensions
of such marginalisations need to be seriously noted.

The issue of women's agency is part of a larger set of issues in
feminist scholarship and it is at the moment often being simplified.
The desire to write a different kind of history has led feminist
scholars to explore the histories of resistance by women, individually
and collectively, and also their use of strategies such as subversion
and manipulation of men's power over women. While it is important
to document acts of resistance, subversion and manipulation, it
is somewhat simplistic to celebrate all instances of 'subversion'
and 'manipulation'; these may certainly be examples of women's
agency, but particular instances of subversion such as the strategies
used by the tawaifs of Lucknow as described by Oldenberg (1991)
cannot be regarded as subversive as they work within, and therefore
reinforce, patriarchal ideologies. It is useful to bear in mind the
political consequences of actions as well as of theoretical formulations, especially in the context of feminist writing in India,
which owes its original impulse to a political agenda, as pointed
out earlier. Recent writings by Sangari (1993), and Sarkar and
Butalia (1995) have tried to provide a perspective for exploring
women's agency. The dialectical relationship between structure
and agency requires examining, and it may be useful to look at

structure and agency as processes that presuppose each other. There is also a need to bear in mind that social systems set limits and put pressures upon human action (Chakravarti 1998: chapter 6). Agency does not exist within a vacuum as women have come to understand.

Where Do We Go from Here?

The preceding sections of this paper have tried to outline some of the issues in writing history from a gender-sensitive standpoint and mark some of the major conceptual advances within the field of women's history. There are huge areas that still need to be explored, such as the histories of *dalit* women[14] and many issues are under-theorised, an example being the relationship between caste and gender (Chakravarti 2003; Omvedt 1995). There is an urgent need for a rigorous outlining of the structures in which women's oppression are located. In this context, I consider it important for feminist scholars to be wide-ranging in their research and not restrict themselves to theoretical approaches that may dominate academies in particular locations. I would even argue that it is neces-sary for feminist scholars to resist the tendency to take over their agendas by currently fashionable theories such as post-modernism. Its use in the Indian context has tended to valorise pre-colonial society, as well as the 'community' and the 'family' as pre-modern indigenous institutions that have remained outside the realm of colonial power and are therefore 'authentic'. It may be noted that we have a long tradition of examining the community and family in women's scholarship. The direction of these early works has been overtaken by works that are restricted to the modern/ pre-modern paradigm. The new focus is also almost entirely on culture. Scholars using the post-modernist framework appear to be antagonistic to any project that is engaged in locating the struc-tures that are the sources of the oppression of women. Perhaps the focus on 'women's culture' enables some of these scholars to highlight the happy spaces for women in the family and obliterate everything else. But for those who experience, or are sensitive to, the workings of multiple forms of patriarchies, it is crucial to understand social and economic processes and the hierarchical institutions that have put systems of oppression in place. For feminist scholars, an unqualified or non-contextualised concentration on culture as an autonomous realm, or discussions of agency without a look at its relationship to structure, will be disastrous. It will push us back, not take us forward in theorising patriarchies and the complex ways in which they work in India.

Notes

1. Scholars and students have for generations been bemoaning the absence of a 'historical' sense amongst ancient Indians, missing the point that this could actually have been an advantage in the context of working with a fuller notion of history.
2. See, for example, the numerous works of R.K. Mukherji, R.C. Majumdar and K.P. Jayaswal, among others. This trend in the writing of Indian history found its most systematic formulation in the *Indian History and Culture* volumes edited by R.C. Majumdar and published by the Bharatiya Vidya Bhavan, Bombay, between 1956 and 1963.
3. Tilak, the militant nationalist, for example, argued that the distinctions between labourers and masters was false; all Indians were labourers or rather Shudras and slaves, and the British were the only masters (Cashman 1975: 185).
4. The limitations of earlier works are evident in the sensitive and richly nuanced recent writings of Sarkar (1996) and Bandhopadhyaya (1995).
5. Thompson (1977: 251) has suggested that the neglect of women's history by historians is due to their preoccupation with 'becoming' a process in which women are rarely seen as prime agents in political, military or even in economic life.
6. See especially the first four volumes of *Subaltern Studies* edited by Ranajit Guha where women did not feature. Volume 5 contained the first piece on gender by Ranajit Guha, but this sensitive piece of writing has remained unique in the subaltern corpus. Acting almost as a counter, volume 6 contained an essay by Julie Stephens on feminist writings on India, but that can hardly be considered a contribution to *women's history*. Its inclusion may in fact be read as a statement on the subaltern school's cavalier attitude to women as a legitimate and necessary focus of subaltern concern. Finally, with volume 9, gender is featuring *as it should* with the inclusion of an essay by Indrani Chatterjee. All subaltern volumes cited here are published by Oxford University Press, Delhi.
7. This paper is an attempt to provide a review of the main ideas and themes in women's history and is not an exhaustive account of all the published work on the subject. A number of very fine works may therefore not find a mention here.
8. Chakravarti (1985, 1989). A beginning had already been made by I.B. Horner (1930) who was the first scholar to focus on the labouring woman. However, apart from suggesting the need to write the history of labouring women, no

really substantial work has been written on women of the lower castes, either in the case of ancient or medieval India. An unusual study published recently of a contemporary *dalit* woman, Viramma, is cited in Note 14.

9. Altekar's (1987) work has been critiqued in recent years. See Chakravarti (1988) and Parasher (1994).

10. But the works tend to be episodic rather than conceptual. See, for example, Bilgrami (1986, 1987), Kozlowski (1989), O'Hanlon (1997) and Siddiqui (1996).

11. Themes include the genderedness of language, landownership, inheritance, the politics of the royal household, women against women in polygamous households, and the changing narratives that produced the model of the virtuous and chaste *virangana* (see, for example, Joshi 1995; Petevich 1990a, 1990b; Rangachari 1997; Sreenivasan 1998).

12. The importance of this kind of work is suggested in Mahanta's (1999) and Nandy and Raman's (1997) papers on Assam.

13. See, for example, the essays in the special issues of the *Social Scientist* (1993, 1994).

14. A rich contemporary account of a *dalit* woman by Racine and Racine (1997) is the only piece of writing that tells us something about the multiple dimensions of the life of a labouring woman. We have, as I have pointed out earlier, nothing like this work for the past.

References

Agrawal, Bina (1994). *A Field of One's Own: Gender and Land Rights in South Asia.* Cambridge: Cambridge University Press.

Altekar, A.S. (1987). *The Position of Women in Hindu Civilisation.* Delhi: Motilal Banarsidass.

Bandhopadhyaya, Sekhar (1995). 'Caste, Widow Remarriage, and the Reform of Popular-Culture', in Bharati Ray (ed.), *From the Seams of History: Essays on Indian Women,* 8–36. New Delhi: Oxford University Press.

Bandhopadhyay, Sibaji (1994). 'Producing and Re-producing the New Women: A Note on the Prefix "Re"', *Social Scientist* (22: 1–2).

Banerji, Himani (1992). 'Mothers and Teachers: Gender and Class in Educational Proposals for and by Women in Colonial Bengal', *Journal of Historical Sociology* (5: 1).

Banerjee, Nirmala (1989). 'Working Women in Colonial Bengal: Modernisation and Marginalisation' in *Recasting Women* (ed.), Sangari and Vaid. New Delhi: Kali and Women, 269–301.

Basu, A. (1989–90). 'The Reformed Family, Women Reformers: A Case Study of Vidyagauri Nilkanth', *Samya Shakti,* 4–5: 62–82.

Bhattacharji, Sukumari (1994). *Women and Society in Ancient India.* Basumati Corporation.

Bhattacharya, Rimli (1998) (tr. and ed.). *Binodini Dasi: My Life, My Story.* New Delhi: Kali for Women.

Bilgrami, Rafat (1986). 'Women Grantees of the Mughal Empire', in *Proceedings of the Indian History Congress*.

——— (1987). 'Property Rights of Muslim Women in Mughal India', in *Proceedings of the Indian History Congress*.

Butalia, Urvashi (1998). *The Other Side of Silence*. New Delhi: Penguin Books.

Caroll, Lucy (1989). 'Law, Custom, and Statutory Social Reform: The Hindu Widow's Remarriage Act of 1856', in J. Krishnamurty (ed.), *Women in Colonial India*, pp. 1–26. New Delhi: Oxford University Press.

Cashman, Richard (1975). *The Myth of the Lokamanya: Tilak and Mass Politics in Maharashtra*. Berkeley: University of California Press.

Chakravarty, Dipesh (1994). The 'Difference-Deferral' of a Colonial Modernity: Public Debates on Domesticity in British Bengal', in David Arnold (ed.), *Subaltern Studies*, Vol. VIII, pp. 50–80. New Delhi: Oxford University Press.

Chakravarti, Uma (1983). 'The Development of the Sita Myth: A Case Study of Women in Myth and Literature', *Samya Shakti*, (1:1) July 1983.

——— (1985). 'Women in Servitude and Bondage: The 'A'grihinis of Ancient India'. *Teaching Politics*, 10(1): 2.

——— (1988). 'Beyond the Altekarian Paradigm: Towards a New Understanding of Gender Relations in Early India', *Social Scientist*, 16(8): 44–52.

——— (1989). 'Whatever Happened to the Vedic Dasi: Orientalism, Nationalism and a Script for the Past', in Kumkum Sangari and Sudesh Vaid (eds.), *Recasting Women: Essays in Indian Colonial History*, pp. 27–87. New Delhi: Kali for Women.

——— (1993a). 'Conceptualising Brahmanical Patriarchy in Early India: Gender, Class, Caste and State', *Economic and Political Weekly*, 28(3): 579–85.

——— (1993b). 'Women, Men and Beasts: Popular Culture in the Jatakas', *Studies in History*, 9(1): 43–70.

——— (1994). *Rewriting History: Life and Times of Pandita Ramabai*. New Delhi: Kali for Women.

Chanana, D.R. (1960). *Slavery in Ancient India*. Delhi: People's Publishing House.

Chatterjee, Indrani (1999). 'Colouring Subalternity: Slaves, Concubines and Social Orphans in Early Colonial India', in Gautam Bhadra, Gyan Prakash and Susie Tharu (eds.), *Subaltern Studies*, Vol. X, 49–97. New Delhi: Oxford University Press.

Chhachhi, Amrita, Nandita Shah, Nandita Gandhi and Sujata Gothoskar (1994). 'Structural Adjustment, Feminisation of Labour Force and Organisational Strategies', *Economic and Political Weekly*, 29(18): 39–48.

Chowdhry, Prem (1994). *The Veiled Women: Shifting Gender Equations, Haryana 1880–1980*. New Delhi: Oxford University Press.

Custers, Peter (1987). *Women in the Tebhaga Struggle: Rural Poor Women and Revolutionary Leadership 1946–47*. Calcutta: Naya Prakash.

Delphi, Christine (1984). *Close to Home: A Materialist Analysis of Women's Oppression*. Amherst: University of Massachusetts Press.

Devahuti, D. (1979). 'Notes on Approaches to Indian History', in D. Devahuti, (ed.), *Problems of Indian Historiography*, pp. 89–96. Delhi: D.K. Publications.

Devji, Feisal (1994). 'Gender and the Politics of Space: The Movement for Women's Reform', in Zoya Hasan (ed.), *Forging Identities: Gender, Communities and the State*, 22–37. New Delhi: Kali for Women.

Ghosh, Srabashi (1986). 'Birds in a Cage: Changes in Bengali Social Life as Recorded in Autobiographies by Women', *Economic and Political Weekly*, 21(43): 88–96.

Joshi, Varsha (1995). *Polygamy and Purdah: Women and Society Among the Rajputs*. Jaipur: Rawat Publishers.

Horner, I.B. (1930). *Women Under Primitive Buddhism*. London: Routledge and Kegan Paul.

Jha, V.V. (1987). 'Chandalas and the Origins of Untouchability', *Indian Historical Review*, 13(1–2): 1–36.

Kannabhiran, Vasanth and K. Lalitha (1989). 'That Magic Time', in Kumkum Sangari and Sudesh Vaid (eds.), *Recasting Women: Essays in Indian Colonial History*, 180–203. New Delhi: Kali for Women.

Karlekar, Malavika (1991). *Voice From Within: Early Personal Narratives of Bengali Women*. New Delhi: Oxford University Press.

Kosambi, D.D. (1956). *An Introduction to the Study of Indian History*. Bombay: Popular Prakashan.

——— (1962). *Myth and Reality: Studies in the Formation of Indian Culture*. Bombay: Popular Prakashan.

——— (1970). *The Culture and Civilisation of Ancient India in Historical Outline*. Delhi: Vikas Publishing House.

Kosambi, Meera (1988). 'Women, Emancipation and Equality: Pandita Ramabai's Contribution to Women's Cause', *Economic and Political Weekly*, 29 October, WS 38–49.

Kozlowski, Gregory C. (1989). 'Muslim Women and the Control of Property in North India', in J. Krishnamurty (ed.), *Women in Colonial India: Essays on Survival, Work and the State*, 114–32. New Delhi: Oxford University Press.

Kumar, Radha (1989). 'Family and Factory: Women in the Bombay Cotton Textile Industry', 1919–39 in J. Krishnamurty (ed.), *Women in Colonial India: Essays on Survival, Work and the State*, 133–62.

Lateef, Shahida (1990). *Muslim Women in India: Political and Private Realities*. New Delhi: Kali for women.

Mahanta, Aparna (1999). 'Patrarchy and State Systems in the North-east', in Kumkum Sangari and Uma Chakravarti (ed.), *From Myths to Markets: Essays on Gender*, 341–67. Shimla: Indian Institute of Advanced Study.

Majumdar, R.C. (ed.) (1956–63). *Indian History and Culture* (Vols. 1–11). Bombay: Bharatiya Vidya Bhavan.

Menon, Ritu and Kamla Bhasin (1998). *Borders and Boundaries*. New Delhi: Kali for Women.

Metcalfe, Barbara (tr. and ed.) (1982). *Perfecting Women: Maulana Ashraf Ali Thanawi's Bihishti Zewar*. Berkeley: University of California Press.

Minault, Gail (1998). *Secluded Scholars: Women's Education and Muslim Social Reform in Colonial India*. New Delhi: Oxford University Press.

Mukherjee, Meenakshi (1988). 'The Unperceived Self: A Study of Nineteenth Century Biographies', in Karuna Chanana (ed.), *Socialisation, Education and Women*, pp. 249–72. Delhi: Orient Longman.

Mukhia, Harbans and Terry Byres (eds.) (1985). *Feudalism in Non-European Societies*. London: Frank Cass.

Mukund, Kanakalatha (1992). 'Turmeric Land: Women's Property Rights in Tamil Society Since Early Medieval Times', *Economic and Political Weekly*, 27(17): 2–6.

Nair, Janaki (1996). *Women and Law in Colonial India*. New Delhi: Kali for Women.

Nandy, Vaskar and Vasanti Raman (1997). 'The Long Transition: The Koch-Rajbangshis of North-eastern India' in Dev Nathan (ed). *From Tribe to Caste*, pp. 446–60. Shimla: Indian Institute of Advanced Study.

O'Hanlon, Rosalind (1994). *A Comparison Between Men and Women: Tarabai Shinde and the Critique of Gender Relations in Colonial India*. New Delhi: Oxford University Press.

——— (1997). 'Issues of Masculinity in North Indian History: The Bangash Nawabs of Farrukhabad', *Indian Journal of Gender Studies*, 4(1): 1–19.

Oldenberg, Veena Talwar (1991). 'Lifestyle as Resistance: The Case of the Court-esans of Lucknow', in Douglas Haynes and Gyan Prakash (eds.), *Resistance and Everyday Social Relations in South Asia*, pp. 23–61. New Delhi: Oxford University Press.

Omvedt, Gail (1995). *Dalit Visions*. Delhi: Orient Longman.

Parasher, Aloka (1994). 'Women in Nationalist Historiography: The Case of Altekar', in Leela Kasturi and Vina Majumdar (eds.), *Women in Indian Nationalism*, pp. 16–27. New Delhi: Vikas Publishing House.

Parasher, Aloka and Usha Naik (1986). 'Temple Girls of Medieval Karnataka', *Indian Economic and Social History Review*, 23(1), 64–92.

Petievich, Carla (1990a). 'The Feminine Voice in the Urdu Ghazal', *Indian Horizons*, 39(1–2).

——— (1990b). 'Making Manly Poetry: The Construction of a Golden Age in Urdu', in Richard Barnet (ed.), *Rethinking Early Modern India*. Delhi: Manmohan Press.

Racine, Josiane and Jean Luc Racine (1997). *Viramma: The Life of an Untouchable Woman*. London: Verso.

Ramaswamy, Vijaya (1989). 'Aspects of Women and Work in Early South India', *Indian Economic and Social History Review*, 26(1): 81–99.

——— (1994). *Divinity and Deviance*. New Delhi: Oxford University Press.

——— (1997). *Walking Naked: Women, Society, Spirituality in South India*. Shimla: Indian Institute of Advanced Study.

Rangachari, Devika (1997). 'Gender and the Historical Chronicle: A Study of Kalhana's "Rajtarangini"'. Delhi: M. Phil. dissertation, University of Delhi, Delhi.

Roy, Kumkum (1992). 'The King's Household: Structure and Space in Sastric Tradition', *Economic and Political Weekly*, 27: 43–44.

——— (1995). *The Emergence of Monarchy in Early India*. New Delhi: Oxford University Press.

Sangari, Kumkum (1990). 'Mirabai and the Spirtual Economy of Bhakti', *Economic and Political Weekly*, 15(27): 1464–75.

——— (1991). 'Relating Histories: Definitions of Literacy, Literature, Gender in Nineteenth Century Calcutta and England', in Svati Joshi (ed.), *Rethinking English: Essays in Literature, Language, History*. New Delhi: Trianka.

——— (1993). 'Consent, Agency and the Rhetorics of Incitement', *Economic and Political Weekly*, 28(18): 867–82.

Sangari, Kumkum (1994). 'The Amenities of Domestc Life: Questions on Labour', *Social Scientist*, 21(5): 5–46.

Sangari, Kumkum and Uma Chakravarti (eds.) (1999). *From Myths to Markets: Essays on Gender*, Shimla: Indian Institute of Advanced Study.

Sangari, Kumkum and Sudesh Vaid (eds.) (1989). *Recasting Women: Essays in Indian Colonial History*. New Delhi: Kali for Women.

Sarkar, Sumit (1996). *Writing Social History*. New Delhi: Oxford University Press.

Sarkar, Tanika (1996). 'Women's Histories' and 'Feminist Writings in India: A Review and a Caution'. Papers presented at the Berkshrire Women's Conference, Channel Hill, North Carolina.

——— (1999a). 'A Book of Her Own: A Life of Her Own', in Kumkum Sangari and Uma Chakravarti (eds.), *From Myths to Markets: Essay on Gender*, pp. 85–124. Shimla: Indian Institute of Advanced Study.

——— (tr. and ed.) (1999b). *Words to Win: Rashsundari Devi's Amar Jiban*. New Delhi: Kali for Women.

Sarkar, Tanika and Urvashi Butalia (1995). *Women in the Hindu Right: A Collection of Essays*. New Delhi: Kali for Women.

Sen, Samita (1992). *Women in the Bengal Jute Industry 1890–1940: Migration, Motherhood, and Militancy*, Ph.D dissertation University of Cambridge.

Sharma, R.S. (1958). *Sudras in Ancient India*. Delhi: Motilal Banarasidass.

——— (1985 [1965]). *Indian Feudalism*. Delhi: Macmillan.

Siddiqui, I.H. (1996). 'Socio-Political Role of Women in the Saltanat of Delhi', in Kiran Pawar (ed.), *Women in Indian History: Social, Economic, Political and Cultural Perspectives*. Patiala: Vision and Venture.

Singha, Radhika (1998). *A Despotism of Law: Crime and Justice in Early Colonial India*. New Delhi: Oxford University Press.

Social Scientist (1993). 21(9–11).

——— (1994). 22(1–2).

Sreenivasan, Ramya (1998). 'Padmini the Ideal Queen: Sufi and Rajput Codes in Malik Muhammad Jayasi's "Padmavat"'. Paper presented at a Seminar on 'Images and Self Images: Women in Myth and Literature', Indian Institute of Advanced Study, Shimla, November.

Stree Shakti Sangathana (1989). *We Were Making History*. New Delhi: Kali for Women.

Taft, Francis (1990). 'Honor and Alliance: Reconsidering Mughal-Rajput Marriages', in Karine Schoner et al. (eds.), *The Idea of Rajasthan*, pp. 217–41. New Delhi: Manohar.

Talbot, Cynthia (1995). 'Rudramma-devi, the Female King: Gender and Political Authority in Medieval India', in David Shulman (ed.), *Syllables of the Sky*. New Delhi: Oxford University Press.

Thapar, Romila (1997). 'Of Biographies and Kings', *The Book Review*, 21(8).

Tharu, Susie and K. Lalitha (1991, 1993). *Women Writing in India*, 2 Vols. New Delhi: Oxford University Press.

Thompson, E.P. (1977). 'Folklore, Anthropology, and Social History', *Indian Historical Review*, 3(2): 251.

14

The Humanist Perspective and the Civilising Role of History

Mariam Dossal

Good History Writing

The canvas on which the historian works today is vast, challenging and exciting. Whether it is the history of women, children, love, sex or death, the history of cities or the seas, of peasant revolts or tribal culture, all of them and many more have found a place in the writings of historians. To put it simply, there is no area of human endeavour, no issue, event or process that lies outside the purview of the historian's field of inquiry. In the process there is greater reliance on and reciprocity with other disciplines, prominent among them being sociology and economics. The variety of schools, the intensity of the debates, and the numbers of professional and lay historians trying to come to terms with their past and develop a vision for the future is greater today than ever before.

While drawing upon other disciplines does promise a more nuanced and finely textured analysis, not all efforts at undertaking historical research are equally successful or illuminating. What then distinguishes good history writing? This is a question that is frequently raised and one that every practitioner must address. It is our contention that good history writing requires exacting scholarship, readability and a responsible handling of its didactic role. For history, with its sister disciplines in the humanities, especially philosophy and literature, raises the consciousness of people, expands their intellectual horizons, empowers them with resources, and most important, with its humanist agenda of enlarging the sense of 'us' and reducing the sense of 'them', has a civilising, transforming effect. In other words, it enables the pluralising of our collective identity.[1]

It is in the effort to measure up to these standards, that some of the best history in India has been written. The works of Romila Thapar, Irfan Habib, Bipan Chandra, Sumit Sarkar, K.N. Panikkar, Mushir-ul-Hasan and many others come to mind. What unites them is their humanist concern.

This humanist tradition in Indian historiography can be traced back to the works of Vishwanath Kashinath Rajwade, Jadunath Sarkar, Mohammed Habib, Tarachand, Nilakanta Sastri, Hiren Mukherjee and Jawaharlal Nehru, professional and lay historians who wrote around the time of independence. They, in turn, were inspired by intellectual giants of the late 19th and early 20th centuries such as Mahadev Govind Ranade, Dadabhai Naoroji, Jyotiba Phule, Gopal Ganesh Agarkar, Dinshaw Erach Wacha, Phirozeshah Mehta, R.C. Dutt, Babasaheb Ambedkar and Mahatma Gandhi, leaders who combined social concern and political activism with historical awareness.

The rivers of historical inquiry, however, cannot be confined within national boundaries. The ideas that have inspired some of the best writing in Indian history have been fed by the melting snows of thought from both near and distant lands. One is only to think of the seminal works of E.P. Thompson, Fernand Braudel, Joseph Needham, Clifford Geertz, Charles Boxer, A.L. Basham and a galaxy of others to get a glimpse of the extent of our enrichment.

Thanks to the *Annales* school, historians have become increasingly conscious of the need to identify different time scales when studying the past. Environmental history as a distinct field of inquiry also owes a great deal to the *Annalists* with Ferdnand Braudel's *The Mediteranean and the Mediterranean World in the Age of Philip II* (1974) constituting a benchmark in historical research by highlighting the importance of climate and geography in affecting historical events.

And Many Flowers Bloom

Among the many sub-disciplines of history that have emerged in the last 50 years, social history occupies a special place. Be it the

Warli tribals of Thane district, agricultural workers in Burdwan or women in Haryana, social historians have sought to reconstruct in as great detail as possible the lives of the labouring poor in particular and that of common people in general, convinced that ordinary people lead extraordinary lives. No longer is it possible, acceptable or interesting to write the histories of only those in power and positions of authority.

The sources and methods used in reconstructing these histories range from oral interviews, commission reports, police records, family papers and diaries of individuals, as well as a wide spectrum of official documents. A good illustration of the researches in Indian social history is the work of the subaltern school. The many-volumed, multi-contributor works of the subaltern school have been edited in the main by Ranajit Guha. The debates generated by their writings are indicators of the impact of their work and the significance of the issues raised.

I have had the good fortune to have been part of a major international social history project that documented the lives of dock workers since the mid-18th century in more than 30 different port-cities of the world. These included Shanghai, Freemantle, Bombay, Tanga, Liverpool, London, Le Havre, Baltimore and San Francisco, to provide a comparative perspective. Emphasis was placed on recording specific skills, work experiences and cultural resources of dock workers. Special attention was paid to linguistic and cultural analyses to understand how dock workers saw themselves and how others saw them. Slang and the use of nicknames helped create a distinct dock identity and reinforced traditional working-class, masculine values of physical prowess and loyalty. Strategies of survival ranged from dance societies in Tanga, to socialising pubs in Liverpool, to gymnasia or *akhada*s in Mumbai. Apart from the detailed port reports that recorded the experiences of dock workers in a given port-city, the project also examined themes such as smuggling and crime on the waterfront, the growth of unions, the importance of support systems by way of families and neighbourhoods, as well as changes in living and working conditions brought about by modernisation of shipping and port technology (Davies et al., 2000).

Urban history is yet another important sub-discipline to develop in the last few decades. Cities everywhere but especially in the third world are challenged by unplanned growth and are a major cause for concern. Pollution, proliferation of slums and increase in urban crime are some of the important problems being studied. The politics of land use, the development or lack of civic infrastructure, the symbolic and cultural significance of buildings and public spaces have been extensively researched by historians such as R.S. Sharma, Champakalaxmi, Giles Tillotson, Narayani Gupta, Chris Bayly, Indu Banga, Rajat K. Ray, Veena Oldenberg and Samita Gupta.

Maritime history, too, has received a great deal of attention in recent times and rightly so, for India, with its long coastline and age-old traditions of seafaring and mercantile activity, has been part of one of the oldest and most important trading zones in the world. Investigations reveal the nature and extent of the economic networks that developed, the forms of credit facilities and commodities exchanged, as well as the business culture of mercantile communities. These fascinating studies have contributed greatly to our awareness of India's rich multicultural heritage.

An important research project directed by the Centre for Scientific and Industrial Research (CSIR) has done much to document India's maritime history by studying the specific histories of its four maritime regions, that of the Konkan, Malabar, Coromandel and Bay of Bengal. Indigenous navigation and shipbuilding techniques, the role of Indian merchant capital and its financing of both long-distance and coastal trade, seafaring communities and their contacts with their Arab, Chinese and Malay counterparts have been documented. With the coming of the Portugese, Dutch, Danish, French and English trading companies, a great deal changed in the world of the Indian Ocean from the late 15th century. This has been documented in the writings of K.N. Chaudhuri, S. Arasaratnam, Sanjay Subrahmanyam, Lotika Varadarajan, Asiya Siddiqui and many others.

The search for indigenous systems of knowledge documenting the skills and implements of Indian craftsmen, of Indian systems of medicine, of environmental practices ranging from water harvesting to forest management, locating customary laws have all added significantly to our understanding of pre-colonial India. In part, this addresses our need to recover the Indian self from the shackles of cultural colonialism, shackles recognised to be even more deep-rooted than their political manifestations. The danger is, of course, of going overboard, in the need to retrieve the pre-colonial self and find resources to uphold the dignity and self-respect of the nation, to resurrect all that was there in the past, including all that was oppressive and retrograde, and justify it in the name of it being authentically Indian and therefore of value.

Even more dangerous is the trend to communalise the past, to see events such as the Partition of India and communal riots in the light of irreconcilable religious differences between Hindus and Muslims, differences that some writers contend existed since their first encounters in medieval times. The two communities are depicted as homogenous and unchanging, with a fine disregard for region, language, local cultures, in short, their specific histories. It is done with the intention of fomenting division. This exercise is not history writing, but one undertaken with a clear political agenda—to feed the public on insecurity, discount severe political and economic problems confronting the country, and advocate instead the politics of hate by catering to the basest of human emotions and thereby reap a terrible harvest. Just as political opportunism poses in the garb of protecting religion, so too do political pamphleteers pose·in the garb of historians, rearranging India's past to make it read as a record of unresolvable differences between caste groups and religious communities. This is not to suggest that there are not barbaric features in India's past or that the unpleasant features of its history ought to be hidden. Rather, the reverse is true. When brought into the full light of scrutiny by responsible historians, the judicious humanist vision promotes that which is shared between people, regardless of caste, community and creed. The writings of Mushir-ul-Hasan, Gyan Pandey, Veena Das and others have sought to do just this and made significant contributions in this field. Their work both informs and educates and teaches the futility of violence.

Thus, whether it be the study of maritime history, the history of science, of ideas, of childhood, or social or urban history, or histories of riots, protest and violence, all areas of human and natural activity have a specific history, and are legitimate subjects of research. The important thing is that the writing about them is informed by a humanist vision. Some of these issues were discussed in interviews conducted by the Radical Historians' Organisation, MARHO, with leading historians and published in an important volume entitled *Visions of History* (Abelove et al. 1976).

Historians, Their Craft and Their Vision

Historians such as E.P. Thompson, E.J. Hobsbawm, Natalie Zemon Davis, Herbert Gutmaan and Sheila Rowbotham were among those interviewed by MARHO regarding their craft and their political commitments.

When interviewed, E.P. Thompson, author of the now classic historical work *The Making of the English Working Class*, was asked whether his book had been 'written with immediate political goals or intentions in mind, as an intervention, somewhat veiled, in the current political scene', or whether it was motivated by other factors? Thompson replied that every historian had a political and ideological agenda, no matter how hidden. Unfortunately, it was historians who admitted their commitment to a particular cause or ideology, who were often dismissed as propagandists, not considered to be 'true historians', and their writing not taken seriously. In his view, it was important for the reader to be aware of this to better understand both the historian and the writing. Those who were supposedly 'free from bias' often served as apologists of the ruling class, often without being conscious that they were so. It was important that historians shift their attention from documenting the histories of the elite to retrieving the histories of the people and simultaneously engaging in a polemic against an established ideology (Abelove et al. 1976: 6). This did not reduce history writing to a mere statement of ideological positions of either left or right political parties. Each subject of research possessed its own character and contradictions. By documenting these specific configurations and identifying what was new, one added to learning and knowledge. Once the analysis was undertaken, it was then possible for the historian to offer his/her opinion on the subject, to 'make a judge-ment', but that was clearly only a secondary activity.

Thompson provided an illustration of how he handled his material:

When I am looking at a question like work discipline, or popular ritual in the eighteenth century, I am not bringing into it a whole set of readymade attitudes. I am holding it at a distance and attempting to examine it in its own terms and within its own set of relations. But having done that, then, if one wishes, one may make a comment. Because one may wish to evaluate the meaning to us of that process. *The meaning isn't there in the process; the meaning is in what we make of the process.* (Abelove et al. 1976: 8)

Historians had also to distinguish methodology from theory, for often the two were confused, and methodology acquired the status of theory. Methodology, pointed out E.P. Thompson, must be seen as that intermediate level at which a theory was broken down into the application of methods to be used—quantitative or literary or other—to test a theory. These methods brought to light empirical findings that, in turn, could modify the theory. Thompson was particularly critical of the ideological right who put forward the 'modernisation theory', which saw all societies following the same path of development, that is, from so-called 'primitive' to 'modern' conditions, the same social trajectory as Western Europe and North America. This was a great obfuscation, for what was hidden was the theory, 'locked in the drawer', so to speak, which was 'pure positivistic, capitalist ideology'. But modernisation theorists 'refuse to admit to this' (Abelove et al. 1976: 15).

Eric Hobsbawm in his interview stressed the importance of the historian's audience. It was necessary not to write just for other academics but to address and educate a much wider audience. Unless this was done, universities would become rarified institutions removed from the concerns of ordinary citizens who in their turn would not be intellectually equipped to cope with the growing complexities of everyday life. Scholars in the past such as Adam Smith, Karl Marx and John Maynard Keynes did not write only for their tribe but saw their work as intervention of an important kind in the key issues of the day (Abelove et al. 1976: 31–32).

One of the most important tasks before the historian, said Hobsbawm, was for them to help their audience locate what was new and different from what had gone before, and make it possible for them to cope with new situations. For instance, Marxists in the early 20th century had read the past believing that the logic of capitalism would alter the class composition of industrialising societies, turn the majority of producers into an industrial proletariat, which would lead the movement for revolutionary change and bring about a socialist society. However, this was not what happened. It was, therefore, important to understand why this had not happened to understand the new class configurations that had emerged and develop a better understanding of the workings of capitalism and the global economy. To hold on to the paradigms of the past was to have a poor sense of history, which would be of little value as a resource for action in the present (Abelove et al. 1976: 43).

Feminist historians such as Sheila Rowbotham highlighted the importance of gender as one of the crucial determinants in history. Taking into account the numerous debates over patriarchy, it was time, believed Rowbotham, that a more complex understanding of gender be developed, one which took account of the mutual needs and relations between the sexes and did not view their relations only in terms of conflict, but also examined the nature and extent of dependence (Abelove et al. 1976: 61).

Whatever the subject of historical inquiry, says Natalie Zemon Davis, well-known historian of early modern France, it requires both passion and commitment. It is an important part of the historians' responsibility to help people understand how they have made their own history and in the process recognise the possibilities of change. History, then, was a crucial bank of resources, cultural, political and social. As she explained:

> Even in a complex society with lots of prescriptions, there can be give in the way in which human beings manipulate the prescriptions. I'm interested in where the cracks, where the fault lines are in different societies that shake people up to change things. Sometimes the things they try are what you'd expect; other times they are really surprising. I want to be a historian of hope. That's really what I'm saying (Abelove et al. 1976: 115).

The historians interviewed by MARHO saw their discipline as a craft whose writing requires commitment, skill and attention to detail. It was not the good review they sought, but the use to which their writing was put. It was the enlightenment that came from reading history that made a difference in people's lives. It is this that raised history writing to the status of a 'calling or vocation'. (Abelove et al. 1976: 119). These concerns have been shared by many Indian historians who are also conscious of their public responsibility: to read the past judiciously, thereby making intellectual resources available for people to make enlightened choices for their future.

Note

1. Since the 1960s French structuralists such as Louis Althusser, Roland Barthes and Michel Foucalt critiqued scholarship that they termed 'agency-centred social theory' based on what they called 'humanism' propounded by philosophers such as Jean Paul Sartre and Maurice Merleau-Ponty whom they termed 'humanists' (Lash 1990: 62–63). This use of the term 'humanism' has little to do with the Renaissance and the 18th century search for classical and humanist values in Greek antiquity. My use of the term humanism in this essay derives from the Renaissance tradition.

References

Abelove, Henry, Betsy Blackmare, Peter Dimock and Jenathan Schneer (eds.), (1976). *Visions of History: Interviews with Historians* by MARHO, The Radical Historians' Organization. Manchester: Manchester University Press.

Braudel, Fernand (1974). *The Mediterranean and the Mediterranean World in the Age of Philip II*, London: Collins.

Davies, Sam, Colin J. Davis, David de Vries, Lex Heerma van Voss, Lidewij Hesselink and Klaus Weinhauer (eds.) (2000). *Dock Workers: International Explorations in Comparative Labour History, 1790–1970*, Vols 1 and 2. Aldershot: Ashgate.

Dossal, Mariam (2002). 'Managing Cities: Professional Expertise, Popular Participation and Political Will'. Sectional President's Address, Modern India Section, Indian History Congress Proceedings, Amritsar.

Guha, Ranajit (ed.) (1986–2000). *Subaltern Studies*, Vols. I–X. New Delhi: Oxford University Press.

Lash, Scott (1990). 'Postmodernism as Humanism? Urban Space and Social Theory', in Bryan S. Turner (ed.), *Theories of Modernity and Postmodernity*. London: Sage Publications.

Thompson, E.P. (1963). *The Making of the English Working Class*. Harmondsworth: Penguin.

Part 4

15

Indigenous Knowledges and the Hegemony of Science

Claude Alvares

For the purpose of this article I shall focus on only two aspects of modern science, which I, like several others, find particularly revolting and unacceptable. One is the mindless overt violence associated with the practice of modern science. This is not an unintended feature. The second is its capacity for causing large-scale ecosystem distress, which is mostly an unintended feature.

A few words about each in turn. Since its early beginnings in Europe in the 16th century, the modern science tradition has cultivated and deployed a rather specific attitude of violence towards nature. Such violence has been justified on the grounds of gaining knowledge that would accrue to the benefit and welfare of human beings. J.K. Bajaj (1985) has shown in a perceptive essay on Francis Bacon (one of the founders of the modern science tradition) how even the language Bacon used for his description of scientific method reflected such extreme violence. The assumptions under which modern science is willing to operate may not be acceptable to the practitioners of other science traditions under discussion. For instance, vivisection is standard procedure in modern science. But knowledge gained from experimentation requiring suffering of other living beings would be unacceptable to other science traditions. These, like the Jaina, for instance, would preclude scientific activity of this kind from the very start. It is not that the Jainas do not have a science tradition: they have one as well as anyone else, which is based on valid knowledge. Only, their science tradition is based on non-negotiable respect for all living beings, for other species, and on the scrupulous avoidance of suffering caused to other sentient beings. True and useful knowledge—particularly for the soul—cannot be gained by causing *hinsa* or violence. This manner of thinking is a commonplace assumption within such indigenous traditions, which can doubt whether knowledge won after torturing helpless creatures can be of any fundamental use to human beings. Hindu cultural traditions represented in Lord Ganesha, for example, exhort all to win prosperity, but require that it shall be obtained without harming others. Riches (wealth or knowledge) generated by such means are undesirable. In contrast, modern science has come up in life largely due to vaunted unconcern with any suffering caused by its actions. It is the symbiotic association of modern science with economic and political power that permits the generation of such knowledge at all. The powerful have always been known to torture the weak (or powerless) with impunity. The use of unprivileged people as guinea pigs for new drugs, particularly contraceptive drugs, is well documented. But the violence in western science is pervasive and unquestioned: from the mass killing of other species dubbed 'pests' in agriculture to the eradication of soil bacteria by synthetic fertilisers or the benign organisms in the gut by powerful antibiotics. About vivisection, the mass torture and infliction of pain on millions of animals in laboratories, the less said the better. But that is the river on which mainstream science flows. It can be carried on ruthlessly, mindlessly, monotonously, since that is one of the fundamental assumptions on which the modern science tradition is based, rooted in the ancient, biblically inspired view that man is the master of all creation or all creation was made for his pleasure. This is a theory created by a specific religious tradition, the Judea-Christian one. In this radical sense, modern science is a creature of western culture and cosmology. However, there are no indications that this theory is either warranted or that it has any rational basis. It is in fact profoundly anti-ecological and for that reason unsupported by other traditions.

Let me go, then, to the second feature: the ready ability of modern science to cause mass ecosystem distress. This is not often emphasised in the literature, which often exclusively focuses on the alleged positive contributions of the tradition to human welfare. This is largely because the literature on the greatness of modern science is actually generated by the practitioners of modern science: judges in their own cause.[1] For this reason, the distress caused by modern science is rarely given as much credence, or discussion of it is avoided altogether. In fact, the modern science lobby and its technological manifestations are liable to generate large-scale mass havoc without fearing any serious challenge rebounding to their prevailing orthodoxy. Earlier genocides and mass killings were associated with wars, conquests and other inter-human conflicts. But ever since the advent of modern science, they have closely been associated with the expansion of the influence of the scientific world-view—the thoughtless and nonchalant invention of toxic chemicals, including persistent organic pollutants, which are threatening the planet's various species (including the human) in profoundly disturbing ways, is part of the active legacy of modern chemistry. So are Bhopal, Minamata and Seveso. In physics, count the creation of plutonium and the deadly harvest of radiation from nuclear testing, nuclear warfare and nuclear accidents (including Hiroshima and Nagasaki, and Chernobyl). These were once considered the results of successful science, but today they are seen as the opposite. And what colossal failures! The destruction they have caused is enormous and the suffering inflicted is on a scale that could never be matched by all the butchers of world history acting in concert. Yet this does not function as a challenge to orthodoxy in any fundamental sense. (In contrast, even a small failing in other science traditions will often be used to damn the entire tradition.) Therefore, I would like to reiterate my profound sense of doubt and unease in the modern scientific enterprise. The alleged virtues on which modern science is based—to my mind and to the minds of several others—in fact has no earth-shaking basis except in a few people's heads. The enterprise is profoundly immoral and anti-nature. Best we were never associated with the circumstances of its birth, even if we are forced to associate with it for political reasons today.

How Scientists in India Have Viewed Modern Science

The modern science tradition has long mesmerised the people within the industrialised world. It was bound to impress the influential people in the former colonised countries as well. It is, therefore, not surprising that around 50 years ago, when India became an autonomous republic, the educated elite in charge of India's administration preferred to adopt western science lock, stock and barrel as they identified genuine scientific activity almost completely with it. While several features of western culture—including the religion of the colonisers—were found by the colonised to be alien and unattractive and therefore rejected (even technology was sometimes confronted or fought), the modern science tradition seems to have been exempted from this general hostility. So while they entertained no doubt about kicking out the English, they embraced the science tradition that had come along with the British with great determination, for they saw in it their only hopes (or opium) of collective salvation. The modern science tradition generally received positive reception among intellectuals and political leaders in all cultures everywhere, even when the more prescient of them acknowledged that it carried the fatal seeds of destruction of all perceptions and cosmologies except its own. This well-garnished image of science had not changed over a hundred years and it bore, in fact, very little relation to the barbaric conduct of modern science in the real world symbolised in the two World Wars and the testing of atomic bombs on the human populations of Hiroshima and Nagasaki. Today, the science tradition we fund, research and rule by continues to be imported, borrowed, second-hand tradition. By saying so, we are also categorically submitting it is not part of our tradition of acquiring knowledge. The common people of this country—in contrast to its ruling intellectual elite—at least appear to have a better control over their brains. They continue to organise their lives by firm allegiance to cosmologies that owe nothing to modern science.

The general ignorance of the contributions of the indigenous science traditions within our ruling intellectual class need not be condemned too severely since much prevailing wisdom was actually thrust down their throats by the existing colonial system of education, which was designed to extend the range of one knowledge system and to eradicate the others. The colonial system of education impregnated large numbers of minds with a thoroughly useless arts education so that generations of historians who passed out of it had little or no competence or mental equipment, and thereby inkling or inclination, to understand the history of either Indian science, technology or even mathematics. Here we are at the heart of the matter. Why did the modern science tradition in the West ignore or marginalise knowledge that human beings in other cultures accumulated in a diverse variety of fields when it claimed that it respected all useful and valid knowledge? Modern science itself did not spring into existence one fine morning in Galileo's head. It bears emphasis that it emerged from existing bodies of knowledge (including the Islamic) one calls traditional science. For thousands of years human beings survived well enough with traditional science. It is not that any of the practitioners of modern science would even today deny that a good deal of the modern science tradition came from science and technology traditions outside Europe. So it could never be denied that there was also valid knowledge gained by scientific methods outside Europe.

Scientific Temper

This brings us nicely to the issue of scientific temper. The discussion of scientific temper in this country in the recent past has manifested a great deal of patronising. Scientific temper is associated or identified exclusively with modern science to show that scientists themselves are often rarely devoted to the practice of scientific temper in their own dealings, laboratories, personal affairs or community, since no man really lives by science alone. The argument assumes that scientific temper is an exclusive quality of the modern mind. The scientific temper debate is often ludicrously reduced to a proselytising programme in which those steeped (or indoctrinated) in modern science information feel it is their bounden duty to see that others who do not have it also have it even if it is of doubtful value or relevance. In exchange for this gilded gift of modernity, the latter are persuaded to give up their allegiance to 'non-scientific', 'superstitious' beliefs, like astrology, the use of *mantras* or even religion. In this sense, the conduct of those who propagate scientific temper is not much different from that of Christian missionaries who are also motivated by similar assumptions. One can only assume that the reason for this appalling irrational attitude of modern science practitioners or devotees to other intellectual traditions was the real fear of competition and the possibilities of rival theories of knowledge reducing their own sphere of influence. There was also the emerging new papacy of science (the Royal Society was formed in 1662), which was keen on establishing its own dogmas and myths, and enforcing its own paradigms and theories, certifying knowledge and decertifying what it would not accept as knowledge.

The colonial conquests gave practitioners of modern science unremitting faith in their own science tradition and they were able to rule that this would be applicable elsewhere, without challenge, because of the circumstances of the colonial period, which we all well know. I am not stating here that modern science has not in its 400-year-old history produced valid knowledge of a special category, but that other systems too have produced valid knowledge and is interested in the pursuit of objective knowledge that is of benefit to the human species or enhances our understanding of the world, and there is no reason why one method of knowledge should be rejected wholly in favour of another, why others should be suppressed or merely used as hunting or foraging ground. Till today, the practitioners of modern science have no plausible explanation as to why they ignored valid knowledge from other science traditions or abused such knowledge as outdated or invalid without investigation, especially when they claim the patrimony over scientific temper.

We have to concede the influence of the 'power is knowledge' principle—that those who exercise clout also decide what is to be known, and when violence resulting from modern science can be ignored. I would like to suggest that if the world does modern science today, it is largely due to the power play of modern science practitioners and not to any inherently compelling attraction of its method. When we in fact see the close association between modern science practitioners and political power in our times, the argument becomes all the more irresistible. Scientists today revel in political power. They are often closely consulted on major political decisions and often are not accountable after the decision has been taken. The close association of scientists with the war goals of the United States led to enhanced funding for nuclear research and the invention of atomic bombs (which has now been repeated in India). Eventually, however, it can be seen that their contributions are not as impartial as they would seem, but can often be seen as contributing to their culture and economies having greater influence in the way the globe is organised or manipulated. In addition, they are often personally cash-enriched as well. Critics will say that even in traditional societies, knowledge and power have been closely associated. Knowledge is and always has been power. This is today's dictum, too: those who have knowledge also will have power. Guilds maintained their power by refusing to divulge secrets for that would mean the elimination of their trades.

Brahmans disallowed knowledge of the scriptures to those outside the pale of caste rights. Even so, in all these cases, enlightenment arrived first, followed by the exercise of power. However, the inversion, 'power is knowledge' is relatively new. By it, politics defines knowledge, science, the manner in which nature must be perceived and organised. The inverted principle actually differentiates modern science squarely from traditional science. For us, such attitudes ought to be difficult to accept or allow. In ancient India such were the canons of fairplay (or scientific temper) among intellectuals that we know of arguments of learned scholars of some of the schools of thought if at all largely from their opponents. For example, we know of the philosophical positions of the Charvakas largely from their opponents who first laid them out fairly and then sought to refute them. If one were to use the same method to reconstruct indigenous science history from the observations or representations about it associated with the modern science tradition and its ideologies, it would appear as if indigenous sciences either never existed or had produced no valid knowledge in their entire histories or merely deal with mysticism or myth. Or if they did, they existed merely as 'proto-sciences'. If indigenous science is 'proto-science', how do we explain recent attempts to wholly colonise and pirate indigenous medical knowledge relating to turmeric and neem by powerful American corporations? Would one call the breeding or conservation of 300,000 documented varieties of rice by farmers— who never went to modern agricultural universities—also 'proto-science'? On what basis? Today votaries of Ayurveda like Deepak Chopra are best-selling authors. And the corporate world is agog with the millions it can make by patenting indigenous knowledge.

This profoundly antagonistic attitude towards other indigenous science traditions has had undoubtedly profound implications for the perception of what these sciences really stood for, their methodologies, goals and the achievement of valid knowledge. First, they were neither well studied nor well represented. Worse, such phenomenal ignorance led to seriously deficient policies. In the case of public health, for example, due to the dominance of the western science of allopathy, health policies abandoned Ayurveda and other Indian medical systems despite the latter's enormous store of knowledge and expertise. It is generally conceded that most of the material that would constitute a proper history of scientific ideas and practice is still to be brought into the public domain, for it is not yet translated. Despite this enormous gap in exposure, efforts to dismiss it were routinely and successfully made.

Revaluation of Indigenous Science Traditions

Despite the suppression discussed above, there are several reasons why interest has resumed today in indigenous science traditions. As dissatisfaction with modern science (agriculture, medicine) has spread, the ready availability of their obvious utility to the common folk has resurrected options that had been blanked out before. There is added awareness that such wholly indigeneous traditions work, often in areas where the modern science tradition is wholly incompetent or has failed. So the conviction has gained ground that valid knowledge is not the exclusive prerogative of one science tradition alone and others, too, are associated with valid and useful knowledge. In India, with more than five decades having passed by since independence, there is scope for a more balanced view. In other cultures, too, the debate on indigenous science traditions is resuming with increasing vigour and intensity. Even in the United States, for example, and also in South America, there is a great deal of study of indigenous philosophies, languages, arts and science of the native American Indians. Such recoveries are well nigh impossible in the original European culture area, where it is a case of absolute hegemony of the modern science tradition and where alternatives—and competing knowledge systems—have long since been suppressed to the point of extinction.

This is as much true of their minds as it is of nature, where biodiversity has long been extinguished and replaced with monocultures. Even today, as the patenting by multinational corporations of indigenous knowledge from Asia referred to earlier generates controversies, and as the West forages within indigenous science traditions, it is clear that modern science practitioners acknowledge that valid knowledge is still available in other culture areas and can be used with profit in their own system. They do not even claim that they have generated this knowledge on their own. Their own claim is that this valid knowledge has not been patented for exploitation in the market and hence the general rush to do so. So we must conclude that it was actually modern scientific temper that prevented our own scientists from approaching these knowledge resources with an open mind.

An equally important aspect of this discussion, which could bear with some repeating because it is so easily forgotten, is that traditional science is also valid scientific method. It is only a bigot who will hold that scientific knowledge can only be achieved with modern science methods or only the knowledge won or vindicated through modern science methods (dependent on violence) is valid knowledge. This is easily demonstrated by parading numerous examples from history itself: till the time of the Galilean revolution and the inauguration of the modern science tradition, arts and technique were based on profound and competent knowledge of materials and living systems. Steel was made in India that was of a finer quality than any steel produced in England without Indian artisans having learnt the secret of modern metallurgy. Plastic surgery originated in India and the context within which it evolved was completely alien to the Galilean framework of understanding of nature. These are but two examples and one can literally give hundreds. The reader who wishes to have a good sampling should consult the recent Kluwer publication edited by Helaine Selin, *Encyclopaedia of the History of Science, Technology and Medicine in non-Western Cultures*.

Only those with minds profoundly damaged by colonial education will refuse to see the obvious. Indigenous science traditions—especially those that have existed in various parts of the globe outside the jurisdiction of the western/European world, what is generally identified as the modern science tradition—is characterised by quite distinct and mutually irreducible ways of perceiving nature and the self. For these reasons, despite 400 years of it existence, and despite its obvious clout and power, modern science has remained largely extraneous to societies, cultures and indigenous science traditions in the rest of the world—a foreign implant, not rejected for who can reject the powerful, but not wholly accepted either. Its claims of providing a substitute for other world-views (religious or metaphysical) have long since evaporated like some modern politician's electoral promises. Even in societies like ours where it continues to operate like an inconvenient lump in the throat, it remains happily restricted to mental compartments, at the cerebral level, sometimes not even at that level, merely as a humdrum and rather pointless activity whose principal justification is it can get you a livelihood. It is not associated with creativity in any fundamental way. Even the successes—like the generation of nuclear weapons—are based on close imitation and not originality. We can also kill as ruthlessly, blindly, heartlessly as anyone else! In fact, without the support of the state, modern science in India would be gladly dead.

Conclusion

Often a set of ideas may continue to hold sway over people's minds and beliefs long after their truth value has been seriously eroded. This seems to be the case with many aspects of the modern science tradition. Its failures are now conceded more matter-of-factly than earlier. Its successes are being increasingly qualified. The problems its tunnel vision has engendered are proving to be more numerous and intractable than the problems it helped solve. Only the absence of any alternative in the centres in which it has held power—like a papacy—for centuries and its association with economic power prevents large-scale desertion from its ranks. That, fortunately, is not a limitation set on us, with considerable access still available to a different way of thinking and doing science. We would be foolish to let the opportunity go by. Let us by all means be open to everything, including modern science, but let us also build a sustainable fire fully under our control, which we can use to temper the new myths we desperately need.

Note

1. Bronowski's (1973) work is a fine example.

References

Bajaj, J.K. (1985). 'The Roots of Modern Science: An Appraisal of the Philosophy of Francis Bacon', *PPST Bulletin*, 4(2): 155–74.

Bronowski, Jacob (1973). *The Ascent of Man*. Boston: Little, Brown.

Selin, Helaine (ed.) (1997). *Encyclopaedia of the History of Science, Technology and Medicine in Non-Western Cultures*. Dordrecht: Khuver.

16

Towards an Informed Science Criticism: The Debate on Science in Post Independence India

Gita Chadha

The Problem of Scientism

The theme of cultural transformations in post-colonial India and its organisation around areas where the effort is to integrate indigenous traditions into a contemporary perspective are interesting in themselves. Additionally, the significance of the theme gets enhanced by the measured overarching perspective that frames it. Reflecting the contemporary dilemma of post-colonial scholarship, this perspective neither stretches the nativist/traditionalist position to the extent of collapsing it into the play of identity politics nor allows a simplistic espousal of an undeflected modernism. It is precisely this critical space between the two extreme positions that needs to be developed and occupied in discussions on the transformations in various cultural disciplines, including science.

The range of areas covered in the volume—including theatre, art, music and literature—provides the opportunity to juxtapose the similarities and the differences that characterise specific contemporary post-colonial debates. These in turn could offer general insights for the development of interdisciplinary perspectives. It is significant that this theme includes science within the rubric of culture. Despite recent trends in the social sciences and in critical social movements challenging the autonomy and value of science, the public discourse continues to view science as an autonomous and intrinsically unique mode of knowing, superior to all others. Let me briefly elucidate some of the problems with this public discourse.

Within this discourse, science is given a paradigmatic status for the cultural and civilisational aspirations of people. It is also important to note here that in this discourse 'science' is defined in multiple ways and generally comes as a package deal. This discourse is about science as scientific method and its supremely rational character. It is about science as scientific knowledge, which is perceived as the 'truest'. It is also about science as scientific temper, which is equated to all critical thinking and progress. Due to its claim over rationality, its hegemony over truth and its control over all critical thinking, such a discourse leads to what is called 'scientism'. Besides dubbing other modes of knowing as non-rational, false and regressive, such a scientism leads to a gradual weakening of the impact of other knowledge systems, resulting in their marginalisation.

While posing a threat to other modes of knowing, such an account also does injustice to the dynamics within science. The actual process of doing science lies out of the domain of logical structures and rational explanations. But scientism constructs the functioning of science with a deceptive neatness to suit the canonical scientistic narrative of science. Taking the example of scientific creativity, it is evident that it is a fluid phenomenon that contains aesthetic and emotive components in its cognitive aspects. And yet the mainstream, textual discourse of science pushes this entire process of creativity into the realm of subjectivity. The actual process of scientific research bears little resemblance to the linear and rigid conceptions of scientific methodology endorsed by the mainstream discourse of science. Though in recent years there have been persistent efforts to accord space to 'other' modes of knowing and to bring forth aspects in science that do not conform to its canon, the scientific community in general and the scientific intellectual in particular willy-nilly become strong proponents of the scientistic account of science. Socialised to believe that science is the mode of knowing that civilisations must aspire to, the practitioner of science is inducted into a particular form of modernism that is synonymous with scientism. It leads to the formation of an exclusionist subculture in science, which trains the practitioner of science to view all reality through the lens of science.

As an experiment, try engaging a practising scientist in an intellectual debate on the role of science in the making of human disasters. One is bound to come across the following responses. First, that after all science is a part of society and, therefore, as blemished as society and, consequently, absolved of specific responsibility. Second, that the fault lies with 'society' or 'politics' or the 'public' or some external factor; thus, clearly making a user/abuser dichotomy, and reiterating the canonical image of science as pure and autonomous. It gets alarming when such a scientist asks for more control, more power and more funding for projects that might do nothing more than strengthen the existing canons of science, well-cushioned by the rhetoric of the 'benefits' such a project will provide to both science and to society. The exclusionist scientistic subculture of science becomes further evident when the same scientist is asked to make an intellectual assessment about the validity of the arts, religion and ideology as different modes of knowing—with their own methods, their own truths and their own critical tempers. It is likely that in this exercise one would come across great condescension towards these other modes of knowing. While religion, in all likelihood, will be perceived to be in direct opposition to science, politics will be perceived as contaminating the pure pursuit of science or as a distraction from it. Though art and literature would enjoy great respect among the scientists (since they are viewed as being part of 'high culture'), typically the approach to these is either to patronise or to recast them by explaining, analysing and dealing with them through as much of a scientific method as possible.

It is this culture of science that exerts a great deal of influence in the making of the canonical image of science as being pure, rational and special, which the larger public receives and uses to evaluate all other historical and cultural modes of knowing. The culture of science exerts, of course, a great deal of influence on the practitioners of science and in the making of the scientific intellectual, but importantly it also exerts a great deal of influence on the general intellectual life of a culture. The need of the hour is to develop a culture of science that takes cognisance of the relation between science and culture—a subculture that allows for an integrationist approach to knowledge, cemented by a broad-based, reflexive and self-critical attitude. And to develop this, one cannot underestimate the agency of the scientific community, the individual practitioners of science and the scientific intellectual.

Science Criticism: Externalist and Internalist Critiques

Within this general scenario, I see the present volume's perspective to science as necessarily externalist, non-scientistic, inclusionary and critical. For the purposes of this article, I use the term 'externalist' to subsume all these aspects. Setting an agenda for such a perspective on science has engaged many post-colonial and post-modernist scholars in the last four decades. Generally, an externalist account of science seeks to locate science as a mode of knowing within the larger context of culture. It views science as enmeshed in and produced by history and culture as much as art, religion or any other system of knowledge or belief are. In this sense, it democratises the arena, levels the playing field of knowledge production. The development of a comprehensive science criticism as a field of inquiry should be on the agenda of such an account. Ideally, it neither seeks to privilege nor debunk science. But, in practice, at times by default and at other times as a strategy to contest and counter the hegemony of science, it, that is, science criticism such as exists at present, appears to challenge the very foundations of science, categorising it as contaminated not pure, as determined not autonomous. At its extreme, such an account can lead to the dismissal of science as a gross error and its privileging in culture as a grave mistake and, in doing so, can appear to be anti-science.

In this article, I attempt to sketch the major positions in the science debate as they have been articulated in the decades after independence in India. These positions have either emerged as a critique of modernity and its paradigm of development based on science or as a defence of the modern scientific paradigm of development. Having critiqued the scientistic and internalist account of science and having made a case for the externalist approach, I would also like to submit, from a pedagogical perspective and also after having been involved in polemical discussions on approaches to science, that: (a) science studies and science criticism as a field needs to be developed in India in a systematic manner; and (b) such a development needs to include the 'sotto voce' that exists within science and, furthermore, not exclude the scientific community and scientific institutions at large. In other words, the internalist and externalist approaches should not be mutually exclusive, but find areas of dialogue and convergence.

Emergence of a Polemic:
The Debate on 'Scientific Temper'

In 1981, five years after the emergency and 34 years after independence, as the disenchantment with the Nehruvian paradigm of development was growing, a document on 'scientific temper' was issued by a group of intellectuals and thinkers drawn from a variety of disciplines. The statement—oblivious to its own scientistic assumptions—generated a polemical exchange of views on the role of science in cultural and social transformations in India. By this time the critique of science in the West had gained momentum not only through critical movements but also within the academic discourses. Strains of these trends were being heard in India, too. It is a significant fact that many of the signatories to the published draft on the 'scientific temper' were people who have had a very important role in matters of science policy in India. It is precisely for this reason that such a document should have reflected different viewpoints, including, importantly, those of the critics. Instead, it became what is essentially a monolithic, self-congratulatory document that provoked strong reactions from some circles in the academia. The debate, carried out in the issues of *Mainstream* (1981), revealed an intensity of responses on the issue of the scientific temper. Ashis Nandy criticised the extreme scientism of the statement on both epistemological and ethical grounds, arguing for the need for a humanist temper as opposed to the need for a scientific temper. Others, approaching the entire debate from a hard left perspective, criticised both the scientific temper lobby for its lip service to science and Ashis Nandy for merely being a defense of the status quo.

Though there were a variety of critical reactions and positions in this debate, I would identify three major views as framing the Indian response to modern science and technology. These could be categorised broadly and for convenience as follows: leftist, radical-post colonial and liberal-progressivist. The first view, held by the People's Science Movements among others, perceives modern science and technology as appropriated, controlled and abused by the elite, leading to economic and intellectual exploitation of the masses. The only desirable alternative in this view is to make modern science and technology seen as inherently beneficial, accessible to the masses so that they may initiate a process of radical social transformation.

The second view, generally associated with the post-colonial critics of science, questions the rationality and the superiority of modern scientific knowledge. It not only views science as inherently evil in its project to objectify life, but also as a source of spiritual poverty. Besides deconstructing scientific rationality, this view aims to validate the rationality of other systems of knowledge. The third view emerged along with the emergence of the Indian nation state and is characterised by a sense of uncritical optimism on the role of science and technology in building modern India. Nehruvian in spirit, this is the view held by the liberal ruling elite, scientific and political. This view is not only held by science policy makers in India, but is also the dominant public view about the role of science in India.

One outcome of this debate was a book, *Science, Hegemony, and Violence: A Requiem for Modernity* edited by Ashis Nandy (1990), wherein the innocence and purity of the culture of science and its acclaimed role for cultures at large were powerfully demolished. Claude Alvares, one of the contributors to the present volume, exemplifies a radical post-colonial science criticism, which at its extreme worst appears to be anti-science, but at its moderate best provides the desirable antidote to scientism. This position is espoused by a variety of scholars and activists based on developmental, environmental and feminist concerns. They range from polemical opposition to highly elaborate and complex critiques of the alliance of modern science with capitalism.

While it is true that this position has radically challenged the foundations of modern science and its perceived role in post-colonial cultures, the problem with this attack is that it forecloses the space for developing a critique of science using some of the strengths of an internalist viewpoint. Such voices do exist in science even if only from its margins. Voices of dissent, however feeble, need to be tapped rather than crushed by an overarching radical critique of science. Despite the problems and limitations of the internalist account, criticism from within the paradigm of science could help in making the space of science more pluralistic. Further, the radical science critiques' approach to tradition has largely been non-reflexive and monolithic. Besides, at times, its simplistic appropriation of traditions makes the radical critique easily available for rightist political agendas, a fate not all radical critics would be able to be at peace with. In fact, it is this very possibility—the danger being all too close in recent years—that has discredited the contribution of the radical science critique towards the making of science criticism in India. The strongest criticism of the radical science critique has naturally come from those who wish to preserve science at all costs. One such undeflected ally of science has been the orthodox left.

While the left has been critical of the elitist agenda of modern science and its class character, its view of science has largely been scientistic and in this sense similar to the liberal position and hence broadly internalist. In the post-colonial context in India, the left has had to contend with the issue of a historical past where modern science did not develop. Leftist scholarship on indigenous science tradition has, at heart, been a search for a materialistic component that could be shown to be compatible with modern science. Right from the times of pre-independence India, the question at the core of leftist scholarship vis-à-vis Indian science has been whether there was a theoretical basis in Indian science and whether this theoretical basis was a material one. These questions contest and challenge orientalist constructions about Indian science. Hemu Adhikari (1997), a scientist and activist of the People's Science Movement and one of the panelists at the discussion at the Asiatic Society, assumes the leftist position in the science debate. Drawing upon Debi Prasad Chattopadhyay's analysis of Indian science traditions, Adhikari puts up the case of ayurveda as an example of a theoretical, materialistic system of knowledge comparable to modern medicine. Discussing two source books of Ayurveda that mention that diseases are caused by defects and can be cured by medicine, he argues that the idea of intervening in a disease process was governed by theoretical considerations. Ayurveda challenges the other-world view of disease as a product of *karma* by locating the causes of disease in the material rather than the non-material realm.

In this materialistic interpretation of Indian history, the conclusion is that Ayurveda was suppressed by the dominant ideology of other-worldliness. It is further argued that according to ayurvedic texts, the body is equated with nature. This perception of the unity of body and nature indicates a search to understand material nature. For example, the *Charaka Samhita* raises the question, 'What is it that exists in the world and in man?', after mentioning the *panchamahabuta*s or the five material elements of the world. Matter leads to life. Transformation is clearly implied in the grand idea of universalisation of matter. In this sense, everything is medicine, and nature is the source of knowledge for the physician. It is argued by Adhikari that the normal understanding is that science and its method are 'West-given'. One, therefore, needs to highlight the materialistic aspect of Indian tradition. Science and anti-science coexisted and conflicted, and that scientific temper therefore is not alien to the Indian tradition.

My purpose in setting out Adhikari's exposition in detail is not so much to look at the particular case of ayurveda, but to bring out the elements of the leftist position with respect to science. The primary emphasis in this position is on looking at tradition to bring out its materialist aspects and, having discovered these in some examples, to overlook other factors that may be significant. In fact, for all the lip-service that this position pays to tradition, it really amounts to being another form of scientism. It is also interesting to note that the term 'science' in leftist movements to popularise science is used in a rather loose fashion. In this rhetoric, science becomes a thing in itself and the *leitmotif* of all change, all progress and all knowledge. Soon science is conflated with scientific temper and with all critical thinking. Besides, in this framework, what is often talked of as scientific temper and scientific rationality is nothing more than an application of simple-minded logic to everyday situations—something that people would do very well even without the appeal to and from science. In fact, I would argue that for a transformation, it is an appeal to values that might prove to be far more effective than an appeal to science.

As a reaction to the question raised by a visiting European scientist as to 'why did India have no modern science?' B.M. Udgaonkar (1997), an eminent scientist and science educationist, recounted at the discussion at the Asiatic Society that he initially felt a sense of anger. But it made him engage with the field of history of science. In the quest for an answer to this question, he analyses various possible reasons and discards some of them. Drawing upon the works of historians of science, he begins by arguing that a proper answer to this question requires a demolition of certain myths about India's past. Citing the historian Montgomery Martin to argue that Indian history bears testimony to the fact that it was as much a manufacturing country as any in Europe, Udgaonkar questions the myth of India as a purely agricultural civilisation. Further, the view that no science of any kind existed in India in particular and in the Orient at large is countered by citing the work of Joseph Needham vis-à-vis China. Udgaonkar argues that though no work of depth has been attempted for the history of science in India, it is clear from well-documented evidence that India has several achievements in the areas of mathematics, astronomy, medicine, agriculture, architecture and metallurgy. Systematically attacking another myth that a mechanical penchant is as characteristic of western civilisation as the aesthetic penchant was of the Hellenic and a religious penchant was of the Indian, he suggests that the perception of the Indian civilisation as essentially spiritual or religious is something that has emerged over the past 200 years. To substantiate this, he quotes a number of authors who have detailed the engineering and technological achievements of the Indians before the 18th century and have shown how the Europeans had to systematically introduce trade restrictions in order to effectively compete with what they regarded a technologically superior competitor. Indian achievements in other areas like ship-building and modern warfare are also described to make a case for the existence of science and technology in India. Paraphrasing the views of historians Romila Thapar and A. Rahman, he argues that the mechanical penchant was not a prerogative of the Europeans and that the stereotyping of Indians as spiritual was and is politically motivated to inculcate a sense of inferiority amongst the Asian people to make them intellectually dependent and to exploit their natural and other resources for the Europeans' own development. Having thus rediscovered the scientific self in Indian traditions to counter orientalist constructions of India, Udgaonkar delves further to ask: if Indians did make contributions to science and, more importantly, seemed to have been endowed with the spirit of enquiry characteristic of science, then why did India lag behind the rest of the world in the last couple of centuries? He discusses some of the ideological and attitudinal factors that have been held responsible for India's inability to build on its early base, such as the supposed other-worldliness of Indian culture, the rigidity of caste structures, the supreme authority of the Vedas, ban on foreign travel, the lack of a written tradition, reluctance to accept new technologies, especially printing, a fragile political system, and the destruction of universities by invaders.

Udgaonkar's pedagogical exercise in the history of Indian science tradition, while contesting certain orientalist constructions about Indian science and reflecting a critical spirit towards tradition, does not address the issue of the intrinsic value, worth or necessity of modern science. Nor does it question the cultural aspirations of post-colonial India for modern science. What it forecloses, therefore, is the possibility of science criticism and that is typical of the liberal approach to science.

Reconsidering Old Questions

In conclusion, I would like to say that an interdisciplinary and integrationist methodology towards modes of knowing—science being only one such mode—will be ably aided by an informed science criticism. In the project of widening our knowledge base to include indigenous traditions of science and other knowledge systems, what is required in my view is a qualified traditionalism that interprets indigenous systems from the past not in isolation, but within their historical structures and meanings, and allows for a flexible reconstruction of these within particular locations in the present day. The critical and cultural edge in this approach has to be provided by those on the margins of mainstream science and their multiple standpoints. Voices from feminists, pacifists and environmentalists need to be strengthened and brought together. Looking into the past and into the future from within such a framework will help us reconsider some of the questions that arise in our post-colonial context.

For example, there are two questions that commentaries on science in India frequently gravitate towards: 'Why didn't modern science develop in India?'; and 'Why hasn't post-independence Indian science produced a single Nobel laureate?' Asked by academic, intellectual and lay people alike, these questions reveal more than the answers. Reflecting the aspirations of an upper-class, educated elite, these questions privilege a eurocentric modernity at large and more specifically crave for recognition, rewards and acceptance from the centres of power located in the West. Though the questions often contain an earnest attitude of self-critical honesty that aims at turning the gaze inwards at flaws that would account for these perceptible failures—past and present—of Indian civilisation, these questions actually negotiate the sense of shame experienced by most modern colonised societies. The first question, though posed originally by Needham in the Chinese context, engages every historian of science in the Indian subcontinent. While it is an absolutely valid question for the purpose of writing a comparative historiography of science, the question often carries within itself the project of universalising science, albeit defining 'universal' in terms of 'modern' and 'modern' in terms of western. Those arguing that modern science did develop in India often end up making absurd claims like the Vedic mathematics lobby with a rightist agenda or then conceding—as the leftist nationalist does—only the proto-scientific character of indigenous knowledge bases of the past. On the other hand, those who argue that what is called modern science did not exist at all in India often fall into the orientalist trap of underscoring the indigenous knowledge bases as idealist, spiritual and other-worldly, undermining the rational, plural and materialistic aspects of indigenous knowledge. A more radical course has been to dismiss the question as a non-question, asserting that the value of indigenous traditions of knowledge cannot be assessed in terms of modern science, tainted in its very conception by violence, and in its construction by eurocentrism. Perhaps it is a combination of the answers that will make this class, whose question it is, come out of the sense of shame. This will, in turn, make it recover a cultural self that is strengthened by the acceptance of its hybridity in the search for alternatives to the orthodoxies of both extremes.

While the first question constructs a historiography of systems of knowledge and modes of knowing, the second question is analogous to writing the story of kings and queens because of its emphasis on the clan of the scientific community and on the genius of the individual scientist. Some answer the second question of why there has not been an Indian scientist winning the Noble after independence by asserting that it was a particularly invigorating environment of the nationalist spirit (that provided the impetus for individual excellence) that petered out later. Others argue that it was the presence of an Indian national science, mediated through colonialism as a 'big' power, that bestowed the recognition on individual scientists in the international arena pre-independence. This position willy-nilly asserts that the cultural milieu is instrumental in the production of a genius. Yet others argue that it is a relatively higher degree of state control in and over science that has led to the decline of individual excellence (poor working conditions, lack of incentives, etc.). Ironically, while the nationalist sentiment is perceived as having provided an impetus to the individual scientist, the linking of science with a nation-state is seen as having led to a decline in individual performance. This position also underscores the notion of science as an activity that requires freedom from control and not as an activity that controls. Still others dismiss the entire question by asking why after all should Indian scientists strive towards the Nobel Prize since the Indian scientist's role should be to apply the available resources to the shaping of the Indian society.

A reconsideration of such questions and a reflexivity towards the aspirations within these questions would help in the decentralisation of power, which would, in turn, help in the growth of contemporary indigenous science. While the first question negotiates indigeneity from the past, the second needs to be deconstructed for a negotiation of indigeneity in the present.

References

Adhikari, Hemu (1997). Presentation in *'Modes of Knowing and Creation of Knowledge Systems: Indigenous Science Traditions, Modern Science and the Scientific Temper'*, panel discussion, Asiatic Society, Mumbai, September.

Chadha, Gita (1997). 'Sokal's Hoax and Tensions in the Scientific Left', *Economic and Political Weekly*, XXXII, 35: 2194–96.

——— (1998). 'Sokal's Hoax: A Backlash to Science Criticism' *Economic and Political Weekly*, XXXIII, 48: 2964–68.

——— (1999). 'Truth, Scientism and Post-Modernism: The Experience in India' Paper presented at the American Philosophical Association Meeting held in Boston, U.S.A., in December 1999.

Mainstream (1981). 'Statement on Scientific Temper', 19(47): 5–10.

Nandy, Ashis (ed.) (1990). *Science, Hegemony, and Violence: A Requiem for Modernity*. New Delhi: Oxford University Press.

Udgaonkar, B.M. (1997). Presentation in *'Modes of Knowing and Creation of Knowledge Systems: Indigenous Science Traditions, Modern Science and the Scientific Temper'*, panel discussion, Asiatic Society, Mumbai, September.

About the Editors and Contributors

The Editors

Kamala Ganesh is Professor, Department of Sociology, University of Bombay, Mumbai. Her areas of interest include gender studies, caste and kinship, and cultural studies. Professor Ganesh has earlier taught Sociology at St Xavier's College and SNDT Women's University, both in Mumbai. She was also Senior Fellow of the Indian Council for Social Science Research (ICSSR), 1992–94, and Secretary of the Commission on Women, International Union of Anthropological and Ethnological Sciences (1988–93). She has been involved in research work for the ICSSR and for UNESCO's Population and Human Settlements Division. A member of the managing committee of the Asiatic Society of Mumbai, Kamala Ganesh has contributed numerous papers to journals and edited volumes, besides being the author of *Boundary Walls: Caste and Women in a Tamil Community* (1993) and the co-editor of *Negotiation and Social Space: A Gendered Analysis of Marriage and Kinship Relations in Sub-Saharan Africa and South Asia* (Sage, 1998).

Usha Thakkar is Honorary Director, Institute of Research on Gandhian Thought and Rural Development, Mumbai. She retired as Professor and Head of Department, Political Science, SNDT Women's University, Mumbai. Her research work has focused mainly on Indian politics, women's studies and Gandhian studies. Widely published, Usha Thakkar is the co-author of *Kautilya's Arthashastra* (1980), *Women and Men Voters* (1981) and *Women in India* (2001);

co-editor of *Politics in Maharashtra* (1995) and *India in World Affairs* (1999); and the author of various books in Gujarati, including *Bharatini Videsh Niti* ('India's Foreign Policy') and *Strio ane Rajkaran* ('Women and Politics in India'), both published in 2000.

The Contributors

Claude Alvares is an environmental activist, and has written several books on the environment, organic farming and on the history of science and technology. He is also Director of the Goa Foundation and Editor at The Other India Press.

U.R. Ananthamurthy is a writer in Kannada and a renowned scholar. He won the Jnanpeeth Award for literature in 1994. He is also former President of Sahitya Akademi and Chairman, National Book Trust.

Vimla Bahuguna is a social activist and Sarvodaya worker who, along with husband Sunderlal Bahuguna, has initiated several people's movements in the Tehri region.

Vidyut Bhagwat is Director, Krantijyoti Savitribai Phule Women's Studies Centre, University of Pune. She is a committed writer and teacher on issues of gender, caste and culture in Maharashtra, and is closely associated with the women's movement.

Gita Chadha is a sociologist with research interests in science and feminist studies. Presently she is pursuing her doctoral thesis at the University of Mumbai.

Uma Chakravarti, a feminist historian who taught at Miranda House, Delhi University, for over 30 years, is now an independent researcher and writer based in Delhi.

Dilip Chitre is a poet, writer, editor and translator. He has translated the poetry of Shri Jnandev and Tukaram into English.

Mariam Dossal is Professor, Department of History, University of Mumbai, with research interests in urban history, history of colonial Bombay and maritime history.

Tapati Guha-Thakurta is Fellow at the Centre for Studies in Social Sciences, Kolkata. She is a historian specialising in the history of art.

Devaki Jain activist and scholar, has many publications in women's studies and a strong commitment to the women's movement. She is Trustee, Institute of Social Studies Trust, Delhi.

Anuradha Kapur is Professor at the National School of Drama, Delhi. She has written widely on theatre as well as directed plays that have travelled in India and abroad.

Vijaya Mehta is Executive Director of the National Centre for the Performing Arts. She is known for her path-breaking experiments in Indian and international theatre.

Meenakshi Mukherjee is former Professor of English, Jawaharlal Nehru University, Delhi. She worked as visiting faculty at the University of Chicago, University of California at Berkely and other universities, and is the author of several books on the Indian novel in English and Bangla.

Ashok Ranade, a musicologist and Hindustani vocalist, has composed and compered musical presentations for stage and television.

Kapila Vatsyayan is former Secretary, Department of Culture, Government of India, former Academic Director, Indira Gandhi National Centre for the Arts, and former President, India International Centre.

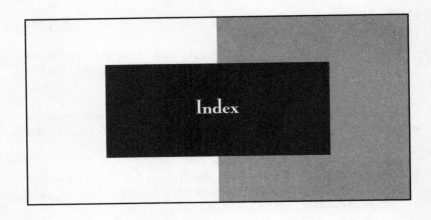

Index